The Anxiety Sisters' Survival Guide

"Anxiety ⸱⸱ ⸱⸱ake us feel hopeless and alone. This engaging guide offers support, ⸱⸱⸱⸱⸱⸱⸱ d practical techniques for breaking out of the cycle and coping b⸱⸱ ⸱⸱ ⸱ y day."

—Judson Brewer, MD, PhD, *New York Times* bestselling author of
Unwinding Anxiety

"If you're ⸱ ⸱ of feeling anxious and ready to make a change for a more peaceful life, this b⸱ ⸱ok c⸱n help you get there. *The Anxiety Sisters' Survival Guide* is truly that—a sr⸱⸱⸱ ⸱, funny, practical, and immensely helpful guide to getting a grip on your anx⸱⸱⸱⸱⸱ There isn't a better book to help us tackle our anxiety-provoking world. H⸱⸱⸱ ⸱⸱es within these pages."

—Claire Bidwell Smith, author of *Anxiety: The Missing Stage of Grief*

"Wheth⸱ ⸱ ⸱⸱⸱ have a phobia, or you've always been a bit of a worry wart, this book ca⸱ ⸱⸱⸱p you make sense of your anxiety."

—Amy Morin, LCSW, psychotherapist and bestselling author of
13 Things Mentally Strong People Don't Do

"*The Anx⸱⸱⸱ ⸱⸱⸱rs' Survival Guide* does for anxiety sufferers what *The Girlfriends' Guide to* ⸱⸱⸱⸱⸱⸱y did for moms-to-be. Mags and Abs tell it like it is as they demystif⸱ ⸱⸱ r⸱ offer evidence-based solutions, and make you laugh when you might ot⸱ hyperventilate. It's like having your nonjudgmental, BFF (who happens ⸱⸱ expert in anxiety) on speed dial."

⸱y Emling, Editor-in-Chief of AARP's *The Girlfriend* and author of
Marie Curie and Her Daughters

THE
anxiety
sisters'
SURVIVAL GUIDE

How You Can Become More
Hopeful, Connected, and Happy

ABBE GREENBERG &
MAGGIE SARACHEK

sheldon **PRESS**

First published in the US in 2021 by TarcherPerigee,
an imprint of Penguin Random House LLC.

First published in Great Britain by Sheldon Press in 2021
An imprint of John Murray Press
A division of Hodder & Stoughton Ltd,
An Hachette UK company

1

Illustrations by Simon Goodway

Book design by Laura K. Corless

A CIP catalogue record for this title is available from the British Library

Trade Paperback ISBN 978 1 529 38322 5
eBook ISBN 978 1 529 38324 9

Printed and bound in Great Britain by Clays Ltd, Elcograf S.p.A.

John Murray Press policy is to use papers that are natural, renewable and
recyclable products and made from wood grown in sustainable forests.
The logging and manufacturing processes are expected to conform
to the environmental regulations of the country of origin.

John Murray Press
Carmelite House
50 Victoria Embankment
London EC4Y 0DZ

www.sheldonpress.co.uk

We dedicate this book to the Anxiety Sisterhood:
Thank you for making us part of your lives,
for sharing your stories, and for taking care of each other.
We could not have written this book without you.

contents

introduction

You've come to the right place. Sit down. Grab a coffee (decaf, if you're anxious). Hang out with us for a while. We know what you're feeling because we've felt it too. We too have spent hours and hours looking through book titles, surfing the internet, combing through magazines, hoping to find answers or clues. We too have spent a small fortune (okay, not that small) seeing doctors, acupuncturists, therapists, hypnotists, nutritionists, and just about any other -ist. We've looked for something to grab on to, even though we weren't sure what it was we needed or where we could find it. We just knew we felt lousy and wanted to feel better.

Malcolm Gladwell, author of *Outliers* and, more recently, *Talking to Strangers*, wrote that to be an expert, one must practice for at least ten thousand hours. We've tripled that. We've practiced twenty thousand hours—the equivalent of twenty years—suffering from anxiety and another ten thousand learning how to manage it. We've not only walked the walk, but we've huddled, heaved, hurled, sweated, palpitated, and hyperventilated our way through our life journeys: on planes, on trains, in cars, at weddings, at funerals, in grocery stores, on playgrounds, at work, at home, and at family gatherings. Been there. Done that. Got the T-shirt.

We've spent at least a full year of our lives googling symptoms of diseases we didn't actually have (and some that don't actually exist). If there were a PhD in obsessive thinking, we'd both have one. And if there is a more adept catastrophizer than us, we have yet to meet her. There was no molehill too tiny for our mountain-building skills. Put it this way: no paper cut went unwatched for signs of flesh-eating bacteria.

Kidding aside, anxiety is a very real illness and we really suffered for a long time. So how did we start to feel better? Recovery is messy and healing is not linear, so there aren't four easy steps we can lay out for you (and don't trust anyone who claims he or she has such a plan). We approach anxiety not as a problem to be solved or a tumor to be excised, but rather as a part of who we are as human beings. Therefore, our goal is to live happily with our anxiety. This can only happen, however, if anxiety doesn't rule the roost. We began feeling better when we regained control over our own decisions and choices. This book is all about keeping *you* in charge, and every strategy and technique we present serves that function.

Our goal is to live happily with our anxiety

One of the hardest parts of having an anxiety disorder is the loneliness and sense of isolation that accompany it. The reality is that we couldn't be less alone. In fact, according to the National Institute of Mental Health, 31.1 percent of adults in the United States will experience an anxiety disorder at some point in their lives, and—here's the kicker—women are twice as likely to suffer from these disorders as men. We may be members of the world's largest sorority (with the toughest initiation)!

When your world is upside down, it helps to know that others understand what you are going through, especially because mental health issues are still so stigmatized in many places. So many of us deal with blame and shame—the antidote for which is realizing that you are not alone in your struggles.

As such, we believe an important part of the healing process is connecting with others experiencing similar challenges. In fact, we know that connection is a crucial component of happiness. Recognizing this, we've spent the better part of the past decade interviewing, coaching, and doing workshops for thousands of anxiety sufferers. In addition, we created an online community of more than two hundred thousand folks (at the time of writing) from two hundred–plus countries and territories around the world. In our professional lives as educators, researchers, counselors, and podcasters, we have had the opportunity to speak with countless other mental health experts as well. The result of all these interactions is a treasure chest filled with stories of the anxiety experience as well as real-world anxiety management techniques, both of which we will share with you in this book. It is our hope that you will see some of your own story in the stories we present and that you will feel comforted knowing you are not alone. You will hear what has helped, what hasn't helped, and what we wish we knew at the beginning of our struggles.

Because anxiety is an "invisible" illness, people don't treat it with the same gravitas as other physical disorders. If you break your leg, your cast guarantees that no one will expect you to climb a flight of stairs. In fact, people will offer to carry your things and help you to the elevator. No such luck for Anxiety Sisters. The help you will most likely be offered is the suggestion to simply "relax" or "calm down." And we all know that, in the entire history of calming down, no one has ever calmed down by being told to calm down.

For this reason, we refer to anxiety as a "brain" illness rather than a "mental" illness. (You'll find we like to rename lots of stuff.) Anxiety disorder is not a personality trait or a moral failing—it is a malfunction of parts of the brain, which can be seen on an MRI scan. Anxiety is a real thing. It is a disorder, not a decision.

When we started to learn about basic neuroscience, we understood that our disorders were just as physical as more visible illnesses—that having anxiety disorder was no more our fault than having a broken leg. This realization enabled us to stop blaming ourselves for our struggles. We weren't weak, lazy, unmotivated, or flaky. We had an *illness*.

Shame is a huge energy suck. Constantly berating yourself and internalizing external criticism only exacerbates anxiety symptoms and makes you feel exhausted and, even worse, powerless. All the time. Placing the blame where it belongs—on your brain—frees up energy so you can focus on healing. So—and don't get anxious—we are going to teach you some very basic neuroscience in this book. We promise it will be very easy to understand. And we want you to stop blaming yourself for your disorder.

Once we understood that we weren't alone or at fault in our struggles, we started to feel some relief. But we didn't learn to live happily until we overhauled our thinking completely because the way we had conceptualized anxiety and happiness was precisely what kept us anxious and unhappy. We know how this sounds, but—trust us—this is the Secret Sauce. We are going to dive right into it in chapter one, so hang on one more minute.

If you're wondering about strategies and techniques, including medication, there will be plenty for you in the upcoming chapters. (Plenty of techniques, not medication.) We use techniques every day, and we will teach you how to use them too. But the techniques are most helpful once you've dumped the blame and shame, understood the underlying science, and learned the recipe for the Secret Sauce.

The Anxiety Sisters' Survival Guide is meant to be a field guide to anxiety— everything you've ever wanted to know about anxiety but were too anxious to ask. Aside from anecdotes and strategies, you can also read about the current research in the mental health field, basic neuroscience, and our overarching philosophy of how to live happily with anxiety.

We used to feel that we would never be able to fully enjoy our lives. But here's some good news: *we don't feel that way anymore.* We once felt overwhelmed, lonely, hopeless, frightened, ashamed, and, at times, more than a little crazy. Sound familiar? More good news: you too can feel connected, hopeful, normal (mostly), and able to cope. This book will show you how.

authors' notes

First, every story you read in this book is from a real person. We have done our best to use the actual words, editing only for clarity. To honor confidentiality, we have changed all names, although we have kept the true ages at the time of the interview. We are deeply grateful to all of these strong, generous women.

Second, there are stories in this book that reflect traumatic experiences, which may be triggering for some readers. We included them because trauma is a part of so many Anxiety Sisters' lives; to leave those stories out would invalidate their experiences. We believe it's important in the healing process to talk about the hard stuff. Feel free to skip over anything that makes you uncomfortable.

One more note: you will see us using the term "Anxiety Sisters" throughout this book. For us, Anxiety Sisters include anyone of any gender who suffers from anxiety on any level. The concept of sisterhood in our minds refers to community in general, but "Anxiety Community" just isn't that catchy.

THE
anxiety
sisters'
SURVIVAL GUIDE

one

Anxious and Happy Are Friends

We know, we know. You wanna hear about the Secret Sauce. If you skipped the introduction (no judgment—we do it all the time), we talked about redefining both anxiety and happiness as the cornerstone of our healing process, a.k.a. the Secret Sauce. It's the magical ingredient that changes everything. Kind of like chocolate chips.

So let's begin with anxiety, which is why you're here.

What Is Anxiety?

Did reading that heading make your heart beat a little faster? (Writing it sure did.) We could talk to you right now about the medical definition of anxiety, but that makes us *really* anxious. So here you'll find our slightly less threatening take.

To us, anxiety is like bouillabaisse. You've tasted it. You'd recognize it if you saw it. But if asked to make it, you wouldn't be exactly sure of all the ingredients. In fact, we're arguing over them right now. We've agreed on the seafood, the tomato base, and that yummy bread on top, but what about all those spices, and how do you make that broth?

Similarly, we know the main component of anxiety is fear, but there are plenty of hidden ingredients—a little depression, obsession, catastrophizing, for example—and for each of us, the broth will be just a little different. Some of us are Panic Sisters. Some of us are Worry Sisters. Some of us grapple with phobias. (Some of us do all of the above!) Anxiety is the whole stew because those ingredients tend to mesh and merge.

Anxiety begins in your body and quickly takes over. For some of us, it stays like this—an uneasiness that hangs over us and keeps us from completely engaging in our lives. We may not be able to explain what is wrong, but something definitely is off. Doctors call this generalized anxiety disorder (GAD). We call it the Worry Cloud.

Many Anxiety Sisters have described this cloud as a sense of restlessness or irritability. Like you've had too much coffee. Other Anxiety Sisters report feelings of dread, doom, apocalypse, and so on. A common theme is the sense of being on high alert all the time. There's just no settling down. For others, this Worry Cloud can be far more severe. A fleeting thought (*My son sneezed before school this morning*) takes on epic proportions (*He's going to be so sick*) and becomes obsessive. Doctors call this "catastrophic thinking"—when the brain turns a sneeze into viral meningitis.

> *I worry about money all the time. I don't just watch what I spend; I really worry that one thing will lead to another . . . that we'll end up in trouble. Last year our daughter needed expensive therapy, and I couldn't sleep. I kept thinking we'd run out of money. What if one of our other kids needed the same treatment? My husband kept trying to assure me*

that we were gonna be okay, but I couldn't stop worrying. I was exhausted and short with everyone around me. (Andrea, age 45)

My body gets very stiff. It feels like it could break apart. Like I could just be snapped in half. No matter what I do, I can't seem to relax my body. I walk around feeling brittle. It's a hard feeling to describe, and it is really uncomfortable. (Paula, age 67)

When anxiety escalates from a general uneasiness to a more intense episode, normal functioning goes out the window. This is what many folks refer to as a panic "attack." We prefer the kinder, gentler term "spinning." (When our brains hear the word "panic," they think it's a command.)

The way panic expresses itself varies from person to person. For Mags (a.k.a. Maggie), it's all about the stomach: dry heaving, diarrhea, and extreme nausea with a healthy dose of dizziness. It feels like a bad case of food poisoning or a stomach flu. For Abs (a.k.a. Abbe), it's a more traditional blend: shortness of breath, rapid heartbeat, dizziness, burping, and a teaspoon of hand numbness.

Other sufferers experience different symptoms. Janice wakes up to her anxiety in the middle of the night—flushed and sweaty with her heart leaping from her chest. Kelly experiences profound itching, which she describes as ants crawling under her skin. She often wears ice packs on her arms to soothe them. For Evelyn, the anxiety comes as sharp chest pains with rapid heartbeat—the whole episode lasts only a minute or two, but often occurs several times a day. Geena's anxiety, however, is a whole-day affair: moderate dizziness that intensifies until she is afraid she's going to pass out.

Another one of anxiety's delightful forms is obsessive thinking. A distressing thought repeated over and over again becomes an insurmountable wall. No matter what you do, you cannot get away from that thought. It completely takes over.

It wasn't during every panic attack, but as I started getting more of them, I would get one obsessive uncomfortable thought such as "I'm so sick" or "I'm having a panic attack." The thought would keep running in my head and I couldn't interrupt it. It was a mantra that in itself became very scary because I couldn't stop it. (Terri, age 57)

You don't need to be having a panic attack to experience obsessive thinking, which can take the form of intrusive thoughts (for example, "Did I turn off the oven?") that get stuck in your head and repeat over and over and over. Ruminating—the clinical term—happens when you cannot let go of a thought and give it way more attention than it merits. Like ruminant animals (known for chewing their cud), from which the term was coined, ruminators keep chewing on partially digested thoughts. Gross, we know, but a really good metaphor for this exhausting behavior.

For some people, anxiety takes the form of a phobia, which is an irrational aversion to a situation or thing. To put it simply, you experience panic symptoms in response to a very specific prompt. Phobic reactions differ from panic attacks in that they have an easily identifiable cause such as boarding an airplane or riding an elevator. However, the physical sensations—rapid heartbeat, dizziness, nausea—are the same.

I feel like an idiot when I even think about it but when I see a cockroach, I get so scared I can't move. My heart starts racing and thudding, my mouth gets really dry, and my body shakes uncontrollably. (Abs, age 52)

The most insidious aspect of a phobia is its ability to metastasize. You can start out with one manageable phobia and end up riddled with them to the point of debilitation.

It began with a fear of flying. I got increasingly nervous before going on a plane and started to spend most of the flight dry-heaving in the bathroom. Taking a flight would involve a few days of general anxiety, the flight itself, and then a day to stabilize after the flight. Okay, I thought, I have this fear of flying. For the couple of times each year I fly, I can deal with it. But as my anxiety got worse in general, so did my phobias. Instead of just planes, I started to get phobic on the subway (which I had to ride daily), and then came elevators and then driving in the rain. At some point, I became afraid of all modes of transportation. Trains, planes, cars could all trigger a panic attack. (Mags, age 52)

Now seems like a good time to mention what is often called the Anxiety Loop, which happens when you become anxious about anxiety (which is not hard to do, considering how excruciating the experience of anxiety can be). It's a vicious cycle if we've ever heard of one. It starts with a symptom—let's say a racing heart. You notice this symptom and worry that something is wrong (*Am I having a heart attack?*), which results in the symptom intensifying. Which seems to confirm that something is indeed very wrong (*I'm feeling worse—this*

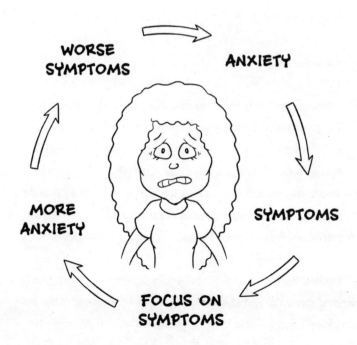

must *be a heart attack*). Which intensifies the fear and racing heart. And so on. We'll talk more about this later, but what you need to know is that anxiety escalates quickly because of the loop.

Similarly, the Panic Loop occurs when you panic about panic.

> *Lately, I started to have panic attacks about the idea of doing something that would bring on a panic attack. I would get a pre–panic attack, which feels just like a regular panic attack!* (Justine, age 40)

We can agree that anxiety is very physical—when you are in its grip, you can't think about anything else. As much as anxiety is about symptoms, however, it is also a necessary part of the human experience. We're going to spend a lot of time talking about this and about how reframing the experience of anxiety is a huge part of the healing process. This may surprise you, but we don't believe in eliminating anxiety. Instead, we believe in accepting it and limiting its power.

What Is Happiness?

If you look through magazines or watch television, happiness looks easy. Or at least very tidy. Families get along, houses are immaculate, skin is unblemished, and *everyone* is smiling (with really straight teeth). Nothing is out of order; nobody is struggling. The message is clear: In order for you to be happy, everything must be going right. The easier your life, the happier you'll be.

In this paradigm, if things do get a bit messy, there will always be a quick fix to help you clean it up. Consider the following book titles:

10 Minute Solution
Mandarin Chinese in 30 Days
Get Married This Year: 365 Days to "I Do"

Really? What all these books have in common is a quick and easy solution to some incredibly complex challenges. This illuminates Western culture's belief that everything can be resolved in a step-by-step manner and in a predetermined amount of time. Implicit in this message is the idea that if you can't solve your problems quickly and neatly, there is something wrong with you. If there's a mess in your life, it's your flaw. After all, if you could just get with the program, everything should work out fine.

To sum up, in our culture, happiness is living a problem-free life. If a problem should by chance arise, the goal is to eliminate it as quickly and neatly as possible. And if you can't get rid of the problem, well, that's your failing. To add to that, social media will have you believe that everyone else is sailing along on a problem-free sea.

Lately I notice that Facebook is making my anxiety worse. It seems that everyone I know and their friends are traveling the world, renovating

their houses, and having these perfect kids while I can barely leave my
house. I can't post anything interesting or exciting because my life is a
disaster. Does anyone else feel this way? (Deanna, age 43)

Clearly, there is no such thing as a life without challenge. And we refuse to believe that happy means struggle-free. Or that all problems have a tidy solution. In fact, anyone who's been alive for more than twenty minutes knows that life is full of complicated struggles. So why the quick-fix culture? Simply put, believing in the quick fix makes us buy stuff. Lots of it. You know what we're talking about (raise your hand if you own wrinkle-reducing cream, cellulite wraps, or a Thigh-Master). Basically, problems create the need for products to solve them, and since we all want to believe in the possibility of a painless fix, we buy into it. Even when our inner voices tell us, "There's no way this can work."

Aside from the financial consequences of this philosophy (and the need for a place to store all our "solutions"), there is, in our minds, a bigger problem with the tidy solution mentality: it leads us to believe

Anxiety does not make you broken—it makes you human

that if we struggle with anxiety, we are broken and need to be fixed. We do not buy into this sentiment at all, and neither should you. It only perpetuates the blame and shame so many anxiety sufferers report and accentuates the need to quickly and neatly "fix" ourselves. Anxiety does not make you broken—it makes you human, with all the complicated mess that humanity entails.

The worst part of having anxiety is how broken it makes you feel—like
you can't even do the simplest things in life. Everything is a challenge.
And I feel like I can't commit to anything or make any plans because I
don't know if I'll be able to follow through. (Melissa, age 34)

Our journey to recovery starts when we realize that the happiness we are programmed to chase is in itself anxiety-provoking. We need to recognize the daily pressure we feel to live up to a completely unrealistic ideal and how that contributes to our disorder. Here's what we've learned in our messy, complicated struggle with anxiety: to heal, you must embrace the mess. And this is no easy feat. It took us years to figure out how to do this; we are hoping we can save you some time.

Once you are able to see through the tidy solution mindset, you can outright reject its implications:

• MYTH 1: Healing is a linear, step-by-step process.

In quick-fix land, healing looks like this: You start at point A, continue on to point B, and cruise toward point C. In reality, healing more closely resembles the cha-cha—two steps forward, one step back, three steps forward, two steps back, and so on. Between the steps, there will be a few stumbles and some major falls. You will start over many times, although each time, you will have a greater understanding of where you're going and where you've been. As such, healing requires a lot of patience, which is usually an unrewarded virtue in quick-fix culture. Rejecting healing as a linear process means expecting the pitfalls, the setbacks, the stops and starts.

> *I was doing so much better for so long, and now I feel like I am back to square one. I already worked past so much of this [anxiety] and here it is again, just as bad as before.* (Monica, age 48)

> *My family doesn't understand why I can do something one day and not the next. . . . To tell you the truth, neither do I. But some days I can be out and about and other days I am scared to leave the house.* (Anne, age 61)

• MYTH 2: I am the only one struggling like this.

When we pretend problems are not complex, we deny what it means to be human. In doing so, we isolate ourselves because we have to act like every-

"Anxiety Sisters don't go it alone" thing is hunky-dory, when in fact it is not. "Fake it till you make it" tells us that we shouldn't share our true human experiences—that we can't be real with one another. We can't think of anything lonelier. Rejecting this notion means sharing authentic experiences, which is in itself very healing. This is why we say, "Anxiety Sisters don't go it alone."

• MYTH 3: I am to blame if I can't control my anxiety.

Quick-fix culture would have you believe that if you just follow [insert program of choice], you will get better. And if you aren't getting better, well, that's on *you*. Clearly, you have not been heeding instructions. Rejecting this belief means understanding in the depths of your soul that anxiety is a disorder, not a decision. Ergo, it's not your fault. Our brains are extraordinarily complicated—science hasn't even figured it all out yet. So give yourself a break.

> *I have really bad anxiety, usually in the mornings, so I get to work late a lot. I've tried to explain the situation to my boss, and I stay late on most days to make up for it. But my boss keeps giving me such a hard time—she just doesn't understand why my treatment isn't "working." She keeps asking me if I'm on the right meds or if I'm taking enough of them. The thing is, the meds are working. I wouldn't be able to get out of bed at all if I wasn't taking them. Honestly, I think I'm a lot better than I was. I hate feeling like I'm not trying hard enough to push through.*
> (Liz, age 33)

• MYTH 4: Strong people don't have anxiety disorders.

Mental disorders don't fit well into the quick-fix paradigm, and for this reason, mental illness is greatly stigmatized in our culture as a sign of weakness. This is why we are told to "get over it" or "chill out" or "stop worrying" in response to our anxiety. Rejecting this notion means equating brain disorders with any other physical disorder and giving mental illness the legitimacy it deserves. Having a brain disorder has nothing more to do with strength than having breast cancer or appendicitis; what does take tremendous strength is living with *any* kind of disorder. Some of the strongest people we know suffer from anxiety disorders.

> *In the Black community, mental illness is thought of as a personal failing or a lack of inner fortitude—especially with the older generations. My parents think my anxiety is really just an excuse for laziness. They think I use it to get out of doing things I don't want to do. And they keep telling me to stop talking about it.* (Cami, age 20)

• MYTH 5: Asking for help makes me weak.

Part of our American optimism is the idea that nothing can hold you back if you just *decide* not to let it. We tap into the essence of quick-fix culture when we say "mind over matter," "you just have to want it enough," "just do it," etc. These slogans, as cool as they sound (and as many products as they sell), suggest that if you are not overcoming your obstacle, it is a motivation problem. Rejecting this mentality and all its accompanying catchphrases means redefining strength as not just an individual effort. As social animals, our strength resides in our ability to connect with one another, which requires vulnerability and empathy. Asking for help is thus a sign of strength.

Asking for help is thus a sign of strength

• **MYTH 6: Anxiety management techniques will always work if I'm doing them right.**

Quick-fix culture promotes the belief that there is one right way to do things, and if you do it correctly and diligently, the "right" way will always work. Rejecting this belief means understanding that one size does *not* fit all and, beyond that, what fits one day may not fit the next. For this reason, we believe in having a huge anxiety management tool kit (which we will share with you in the coming pages).

• **MYTH 7: If I need to cancel or change plans due to my anxiety, I am irresponsible or flaky.**

Well then, we were the flakiest, most irresponsible people roaming the earth! We missed weddings, funerals, parties, work, playdates, doctors' appointments, and vacations. Twenty years later, Mags is still apologizing to her (former) friend Wendy for bailing on her black-tie affair. And "The Great Bake Sale Debacle" cost Abs an entire playgroup. (Don't ask!) Anxiety is an unpredictable illness. You are not flaky or irresponsible for having to alter your plans when your disorder flares up. Keep in mind that we don't punish or label people who cancel plans because of the flu. Quick-fix culture assigns a lot of blame and shame, which only deepens our isolation and anxiety. Rejecting this faulty notion means understanding that at some point in your anxiety struggles, plans may have to change. Although as you get further into your recovery, this will happen less and less.

People get really mad that I cancel plans a lot. I could not make it to my granddad's eighty-third birthday party. Everyone in my family was so pissed. Now I don't make any plans because I don't know if I can get there. But they give me grief about that too. (Lindsay, age 25)

• MYTH 8: I cannot have an anxiety disorder and be happy.

If we no longer define happiness as the absence of messy challenges that need to be solved quickly, then there is absolutely no reason why you can't have an anxiety disorder and still be happy. Anxious and happy are friends. They are both part of the human experience.

Now that we've done all that rejecting, let's do some accepting. We're starting with acceptance (Secret Sauce ingredient No. 1) because it is a prerequisite for happiness. For Anxiety Sisters, acceptance means acknowledging the brain disorder as part of our lives. It's expecting that anxiety is going to be around and that it probably won't magically disappear. Once we understand that anxiety is going to be our challenge and we accept that challenge, that's when the healing can begin. Accepting the anxiety lessens its power to surprise us, eliminates the need to be rid of it, and allows us to focus our energy on managing it. It is understanding that your brand of happy will be "anxiously happy."

> I used to think the goal was to get rid of my anxiety—that my life wouldn't be good until I was "cured." And I was so upset all the time because of course I couldn't get rid of the anxiety—the more I tried, the worse it got. Then I met this therapist who asked me what if I found out I could never get rid of it. That was a real aha moment! It's funny because I'm feeling so much better even though I still have anxiety. The difference is that I'm not trying so hard to be over it. *(Renee, age 37)*

In addition to acceptance, Anxiety Sisters also need agency (Secret Sauce ingredient No. 2) to be happy. This means that you—not your anxiety—are making your own decisions and choices. In an effort to avoid the discomfort that accompanies anxiety, we end up staying away from people, places, and activities that trigger it. Unwittingly, we put anxiety in the driver's seat; consequently, we take the backseat in our own lives. And each time we alter our plans because of our anxiety, it gets a little easier to justify. Pretty soon, it's the default.

> *I feel like I have lost my independence. I need someone to be with me to go to the grocery store, a routine doctor's visit, or just about anyplace outside my house. I feel like I'm such a burden. I want to be able to do things for myself and to go places when I want.* (Ashley, age 30)

> *I did not realize how much my anxiety had taken over my life. My friends all went on a trip together and I stayed home. I tried to tell my-self that I would be saving so much money. But the truth was that the thought of getting on a plane, going to a hotel, and doing a bunch of activities just felt like too much for me.* (Nellie, age 23)

We've all done our share of giving the reins over to anxiety. It's part of the disorder. The challenge for us is to figure out how to take back our freedom—at least, most of the time. As you'll soon read, there are real, concrete steps you can take to ease anxiety's grip on your life; once you reclaim your agency, happiness will be within reach.

In order to understand our third Secret Sauce ingredient, you're going to have to go with us on a bus ride. Don't worry—it's a nice bus with comfy seats and air-conditioning. And in this flashback, it doesn't smell. The year is 2010 and we are headed into Manhattan from New Jersey. We are chatting rather loudly about the side effects of our anxiety meds (we know—most people whisper about this kind of thing, but we are the Anxiety Sisters). Suddenly, the woman in the seat across from us says, "I'm sorry to interrupt you but I heard you mention dry mouth and Paxil. I have that too—what do you do about it?" Within a few minutes, her seatmate, who is on a similar medication, joins the discussion. By the time we reach Port Authority, more than half of the bus riders have shared their own experiences with these drugs and their anxiety. It astounds us how eager people are to talk about such a personal matter with complete strangers.

That bus ride was a pivotal experience for us. It showed us how desperately people want to connect and share their stories. And it was the day the Anxiety Sisterhood was born. Since that ride, we have communicated with thousands of anxiety sufferers and we have learned that the one thing we have in common is the need to know that we are not alone in our struggles.

When we researched this subject, we learned that our brains are actually hardwired for connection (Secret Sauce ingredient No. 3). Evolutionarily speaking, you couldn't survive for too long on your own. You needed your clan to keep you safe. Nowadays, it's quite easy to survive on your own, but our brains still search for connection. We are, after all, social animals.

Anxiety can be a very isolating disorder. Connection is difficult when anxiety is making your decisions. Most anxiety sufferers have seen their social circles shrink; it's hard to keep friends when you constantly cancel plans with them. For that matter, all relationships can become strained by anxiety.

> *My husband and kids don't get my anxiety at all and sometimes I feel like they just discount me altogether. It feels like I barely exist in my own family or like I am just someone to take care of . . . a nuisance, if anything. Even though I have a family, I am really alone.* (Helen, age 60)

> *When my OCD got really bad, none of my friends understood. There was just so much I was afraid of doing because I was so worried I would get sick. I had to leave school. But by then I really didn't have many friends left.* (Sophie, age 21)

And don't get us started on the mental health stigma, which causes so much shame. When we feel ashamed, we tend to stop talking and pull away from others. As such, anxiety can leave us feeling deeply alone and misunderstood. This then becomes a vicious cycle because lack of connection both causes and results from anxiety.

Scientific research has shown that loneliness or feelings of isolation affect more than just our mental health. A 2015 study conducted by Brigham Young University revealed that the lack of social connection results in the same health risks as smoking fifteen cigarettes daily or being an alcoholic.[1] Another study, done in 2016, revealed a 30 percent increased risk of heart disease and/or stroke in people suffering from loneliness.[2] Furthermore, in 2019, a public health researcher, Dr. Kassandra Alcaraz, examined data from more than 580,000 adults and discovered that regardless of race, social isolation more than doubled the possibility of premature death.[3] For all these reasons (and because we are writing this book during the coronavirus pandemic, so we are feeling particularly isolated), connection is crucial to happiness.

You may be thinking that acceptance, agency, and connection are impossible if you are suffering from anxiety. We get that. We felt it too. But here's the thing: acceptance, agency, and connection are both the tools you use to manage your anxiety and the result of doing so. Like coloring your own hair, the process isn't easy. And it won't be tidy. But we promise, it's possible.

two

Are You an Anxiety Sister?

> *Trigger warning!*
>
> *This chapter contains detailed information about symptoms that may make some of you anxious.*
>
> *Feel free to skip ahead to chapter three.*

I was losing weight so quickly that I thought there was something wrong with me. But no matter how hard I tried, I could not eat more than a couple of bites. When my therapist told me that she thought this was because of my anxiety, I thought she was totally off base. It took a lot of doctor visits to learn that she was right. (Nora, age 36)

I get all of the heart attack symptoms—even the numbness in my left arm. Then I can't breathe. It's like something huge is sitting on my chest. I have been to a few different cardiologists. I've done the stress test, the EKG, you name it. No sign of heart disease at all! Even though several people have told me it's anxiety, I just can't make myself believe it. (Betty, age 62)

Here is the most common question we get from our online community: "Can this *really* be anxiety?" We ask ourselves this too—often—and yet the answer is always *yes*! This is a major stumbling block for almost everyone who suffers from anxiety. In fact, this incredulity is one of the most frustrating aspects of an anxiety diagnosis. Even for veteran Anxiety Sisters, it's really hard to believe how much physical havoc anxiety can wreak.

> *For the last several months, I have been breaking out in hives all over my chest and arms. There's no real reason that I can pinpoint. At first I thought it was some kind of allergy, but it happens so randomly. So I've been going to the allergist and now I'm on my second dermatologist. Nobody can find anything wrong. My GP thinks it's anxiety. It doesn't seem likely to me—I mean, how can a mental thing cause hives? It makes no sense. (Eliza, age 41)*

When you accidentally staple your thumb to your son's science project (true story), you are not at all surprised to find that your thumb is throbbing. Similarly, after hours of dental work, a headache would not be unexpected. But shortness of breath and heart palpitations while standing in line at the grocery store point toward cardiac issues, not psychological ones. If you understand a teeny bit of science, however, it actually does make sense, which will go a long way toward getting you started on that acceptance thing we talked about in chapter one.

The Three F's

From an evolutionary perspective, anxiety was lifesaving. You've heard of fight-or-flight, right? Well, this is where the concept comes from. Back in the cave-people days, if you didn't want to be eaten by a saber-toothed tiger or trampled by a woolly mammoth, you needed to be able to haul ass at a moment's notice.

In order to do this, our glands secrete stress hormones (such as adrenaline and cortisol), which cause our bodies to rev up the engines and prepare for fight-or-flight. For example, the release of stress hormones raises blood sugar levels and blood fats, both of which give our bodies the fuel to outrun predators. In addition, these hormones cause our hearts to pump faster and harder so blood can quickly get to the larger muscles in our legs and butts—the very muscles we need to get us away from danger (or fight the enemy).

In addition to fight and flight, there is a third possibility, which gets much less attention both in scientific study and in popular culture: the freeze response, which occurs when your brain decides that you cannot overcome or outrun the threat you are facing. In this instance, your body goes completely still, or "freezes." Evolutionarily, freezing is the equivalent of playing dead so that a predator might lose interest.

Anxiety sufferers often report feeling paralyzed by anxiety—numb, unable to move, disabled. This is the freeze response that results from the brain's split-second assessment that neither standing your ground nor fleeing will protect you from the imminent danger it perceives.

> *I freeze when someone yells at me. Everything stops and I can't respond, think, or move. (Carol, age 73)*

> *When I'm really stressed out all I can do is watch Netflix and eat. I get even more stressed because I don't get anything done and feel worse. It's a vicious cycle and I can't figure out how to get out of it.*
> *(Jeanine, age 55)*

The freeze response provides two benefits for the anxiety sufferer: (1) it allows you to turn away from or block out a truly frightening experience that may be too traumatic to process, and (2) it causes the release of endorphins, which act as calming agents and pain relievers to enable you to more comfortably handle the ordeal.

Fight, flight, and freeze responses originated when humans were living in constant danger. Today we do not live in such moment-to-moment peril (usually); however, the three F's are still very much a part of our nervous system response. Thus, when we feel threatened, certain symptoms make more sense, such as heart palpitations, sweating, shaking, flushing, and shallow breathing. Of course you would feel these things if you were trying to outrun a grizzly bear.

These symptoms become less understandable, however, when they show up when we are not experiencing an actual threat. Like when we are in the carpool line or sitting in a movie theater. In these instances, sweating, shaking, pounding heart, and panting make no sense at all. The only explanation that fits is that something is *physically* wrong. This is how Abs ended up in the emergency room, convinced she'd had a heart attack. Twice. Okay, three times. Maybe four.

It turns out Abs's heart was just fine. All four times. And it still is today, even though she had some cardiac symptoms just last week when she was pumping gas. Those symptoms, despite all evidence to the contrary, are caused by anxiety, *not* heart disease. It's a brain problem—a misfiring that convinces her body that she is in mortal danger, even though the only real threat to her life is all those germs on the nozzle and the toxic fumes wafting in the air.

Anxiety is a condition in which the brain sends out erroneous commands to fight, flee, or freeze. Your brain is saying, "Run for your life!" at inappropriate moments. It's helpful to remind yourself that these anxiety symptoms are the result of a *false alarm.* Don't be afraid to say that out loud during an anxiety episode. We've done it many times, and it is really helpful for your brain to hear your voice tell it that it got it wrong.

For those of you wondering if your particular symptoms could result from anxiety, here's the answer: Anything your body does that's weird or uncomfortable can be caused by anxiety. No organ or body part is excluded!

*When I am anxious I have to pee all the time. I was just at the doctor
for a checkup—I had to stop him twice so I could go to the bathroom.*

And whenever I take a test at school, I have to hold it in for so long. I can't concentrate. There is nothing I can do about it. (Graciela, age 18)

Wanna hear something weird? When I'm anxious, I start to blink like crazy. I mean, really fast and I can't stop it until I calm down. I feel like a freak. (Nikki, age 28)

The Catalog

We bet you're wondering if your particular set of symptoms can really be caused by anxiety. The answer is probably yes, although any Anxiety Sister worth her salt will check with her doctor and a specialist or two—just to be sure. We've heard from so many people about their symptoms that we created a catalog—not as much fun to flip through as Ikea's, but then again, you don't need an Allen wrench to figure it out.

THE CLASSICS

Let's start with what we call the Classics, which are those symptoms most closely associated in popular culture, within the medical profession, and in literature with the experience of anxiety. These are the most talked-about, most easily recognized parts of the anxiety package. Cardiac symptoms take center stage in this group. They include fast or irregular heartbeat, sweating or feeling clammy; tight chest (the feeling that something heavy is sitting on you); shallow breathing or feeling like you cannot get enough air; dizziness and light-headedness; numbness or tingling in your hands, arms, or feet; sharp chest pains; and any other symptom found in a Bayer aspirin commercial. These are the 911ers—the ones most likely to send you to the ER (maybe more than once).

Stomach flu symptoms are also part of the Classics collection. These include stomach upset, nausea, diarrhea, chills, flushing, shaking or trembling, dizziness, dry heaving or vomiting, gas, excessive burping, acid reflux, fatigue, or that feeling you get when you've eaten sushi at a cafeteria buffet. This group is seriously nasty business.

Allergy symptoms are the third member of the Classics. They include hives, itching, redness, irritation, swelling, and rash. This group makes sufferers ask which cat has fleas or where's the poison ivy, which adds exasperation to the already overwhelming anxiety as they hunt for the culprit.

THE AVANT-GARDES

Members of the Avant-Garde collection are not often identified as anxiety presentations, but in our thousands of conversations with Anxiety Sisters, we found them to be a significant part of the experience. These include insomnia, lethargy, headaches, muscle pain or weakness, dry mouth, jaw grinding, twitching, difficulty swallowing or lump in the throat, coughing, sneezing, changes in appetite, constipation, frequent urination, tics, hair pulling, and decreased libido.

This list is by no means exhaustive. There are as many symptoms as there are sufferers. What's important to know is that anxiety can cause intense physical manifestations. In other words, *anything* your body can do—any sensation, sound, or fluid it can generate—can be an anxiety symptom.

As we said previously, when you experience anxiety, your nervous system goes into fight-or-flight mode. All the physical symptoms you feel can be explained by this protective mechanism. For example, because sweating is a bodily response to rising temperature, and anxiety causes body temperature to rise (as we prepare for fight-or-flight), it makes sense that sweating could occur as you begin to feel anxious. Thus the connection between anxiety and drenched pits.

Let's look at another common symptom: burping. The fight-or-flight anxiety response we are always talking about causes your respiration to become shallow—this is what makes some sisters feel like they aren't getting enough air when they panic. The body's response to this shortness of breath is, of course, to gulp air or hyperventilate. And because everything that enters the body must at some point exit—well, there you have it. Loud and frequent belching. We call this Drunk Pirate Syndrome.

Here's an interesting statistic: one out of every four people who show up at the hospital with chest pain are experiencing anxiety and not a heart issue.[1] So what causes the pain you feel? It's actually from your chest wall muscles contracting rapidly, which happens during fight-or-flight. For this reason, some people even experience chest soreness the day after an anxiety attack.

One more comment about physical symptoms (you may want to sit down): they can change and multiply. What we mean by this is that just when you have begun to accept and manage your anxiety-induced dizziness, you may notice, say, headaches that seem to come out of nowhere. We call this anxiety relocation.

> It started in my twenties with a terrible stomach. Doctors said I had IBS. Then, in my thirties, out of the blue, I started having severe chest pain, shortness of breath, and palpitations. I went to the cardiologist, who did an exam and said it may be anxiety, but I didn't believe it, so I ended up having an angiogram, which showed my arteries were clear. Shortly after, however, I developed really bad itching in my arms and legs with no apparent cause. I went to dermatologists and allergists and even a rheumatologist, but all the tests were negative. I finally gave in and started taking Zoloft. Within a few months, the itching disappeared. (Bobbie, age 48)

THE HEADBANGERS

Although when we think of anxiety symptoms, they tend to be physical, in fact there are some pretty intense psychological ones as well. We call this group the Headbangers because they play with your head until you want to bang it into a wall. Here are a few we and other anxiety sufferers have experienced:

(1) obsessive or repetitive thoughts, (2) catastrophizing, (3) depersonalization, (4) fear of death, and (5) the Anxiety Loop.

As we said in chapter one, when a distressing thought enters your mind and repeats itself endlessly, you are experiencing obsessive thinking. It feels like you are being held prisoner by a thought, which plays over and over in your mind and from which you cannot escape or be distracted.

One Anxiety Sister we interviewed describes the experience as follows:

> *It's like one thought is on auto-play. It's all I can hear. Usually, it's some-thing like "I can't handle this" or "I'm gonna die." This one thought takes over and I'm completely out of control. (Carly, age 34)*

Another Anxiety Sister can't fall asleep at night because of her obsessive thinking:

> *When I'm in bed, I start thinking about my to-do list for the next day. Although I've already written it down, I can't stop going through the list and worrying that I've forgotten something. I might go through the list thirty times. Obviously, that interferes with my sleep. But I just can't stop. (Ellen, age 51)*

For folks diagnosed with obsessive-compulsive disorder (OCD), ruminating or getting stuck on one thought is a primary symptom.

> *I can spend hours thinking about past mistakes I have made in my life and whether I am a bad person because of them. Sometimes I am going over every detail of a relationship or breakup for hours and hours. All of a sudden I look up and three or four hours have passed. (BJ, age 44)*

Closely related to obsessive thinking is catastrophizing or exaggerating a negative thought to the point of disaster. You create a catastrophe and then buy into it wholeheartedly. Like playing the what-if game with progressively worse outcomes. The thing is, being able to anticipate danger was key to our ancestors' survival, so evolution has set us up to be quite good at catastrophizing. Except we don't have quite the same need for it now that woolly mammoths are out of the picture.

> *Every time I feel a twinge in my chest area—or even in my back or neck—I think I'm having a heart attack. It drives my wife crazy because it happens a lot. But that's just where my head goes. (Randi, age 40)*

The next Headbanger symptom is something clinicians call depersonalization or dissociation. We prefer the kinder, gentler term "floating," which many people use to describe the sensation of watching or hearing yourself as if you are not in your own body—as if you are floating from above.

> *During my first panic episode, I distinctly remember hearing myself say, "Something's not right." But my voice was coming from a place below me, where my body was sitting. It was the most frightening thing I've ever experienced. (Ann-Marie, age 49)*

Basically, what's happening is that you are so freaked out that you've decided (without your knowledge) to leave the scene. The good news is eventually

you'll float right back to where you started. But while you're gone, it's pretty intense. The sensation is so discombobulating, the only plausible explanations are (1) you have died and are on your way elsewhere, (2) you are in the process of dying, or (3) you are having a complete nervous breakdown. In any case, for most of us, the experience is pretty unpleasant.

> *I remember telling my therapist that when I was having a panic attack, I didn't feel "in" myself. I wondered if I was going crazy. She assured me that I wasn't—that I was just depersonalizing, which is a perfectly normal part of anxiety disorder.* (Brittany, age 29)

> *I never knew this had a name or that anyone else felt this way. I remember first feeling it when I was a young child but I didn't tell anyone about it.* (Barbara, age 64)

The fourth Headbanger is fear of death (we call it FOD). We have found that, more than any other symptom, this is part of the anxiety experience, particularly if you suffer from panic. Because so many symptoms mimic lethal conditions (heart attack, stroke, tumors), it is hard not to imagine that death is around the corner. And death feels just as possible whether you are in your first or five-hundredth episode. Even for us panic pros, FOD is still very much part of the event.

> *Even though I can tell you now it's panic, especially after all this time,*
> *during an attack, I just feel like I'm dying, no matter how many doctors*
> *I've been to or how much reassurance they give me. (Leigh, age 32)*

Let's just clarify that when we refer to FOD, we are talking about a reaction to extreme physical distress caused by anxiety. We recognize that some people suffer from thanatophobia, which is an excessive and irrational fear of death not necessarily associated with physical symptoms. While all phobias are technically anxiety disorders, FOD refers specifically to the fear that one might die during an anxiety episode as a direct result of what one believes is causing the physical symptoms. The important thing to remember about FOD is this: fearing that you will die during your panic episode is (1) an appropriate response to a faulty brain signal, and (2) a symptom of panic disorder, not an immediate reality.

We mentioned the final Headbanger in chapter one: the Anxiety Loop, which happens when you panic about panic or become anxious about anxiety. It's a vicious cycle if we've ever heard of one: you become so worried about having another bout that you actually bring one on, which confirms your fear and leads you to worry about the next one. This loop creates a state of constant anticipatory anxiety. One sister put it eloquently: "You're either coming down from the last one or gearing up for the next one. It never ends."

THE ILLUSIONISTS

Our last group of anxiety symptoms, the Illusionists, are behaviors that on the surface don't seem attributable to anxiety but in fact are caused by the disorder: (1) anger/irritability, (2) hyper-control, (3) restlessness, (4) spacing out, and (5) sensory symptoms. As you know by now, how we react to the fight, flight, or freeze response will determine our anxiety behaviors. For example, the fight response, which gears us up for battle, can for some people look like angry outbursts, tantrums, impatience, rudeness, exasperation, short-temperedness, or even rage. If you are snapping at your colleagues, shouting (too much) at the kids, or experiencing weird rages at relative strangers, you could be expressing your anxiety as anger.

> *I yelled at people who worked for me, coworkers, and even my boss. Eventually this anger cost me my job. The more stressed and overwhelmed I get, the more angry I become. (Kerry, age 56)*

> *I know my anxiety is bad when I start flying off the handle at everyone, especially my kids. Sometimes they are just wanting a cuddle and I feel so guilty, but I don't want to be touched when I am anxious. I yell at them for no reason—they're just being kids. (Kate, age 39)*

In the same way that anxiety can come out as anger or irritability, it can also take the form of control-freakism. Because the sufferer feels so out of control, she hyper-manages her environment and the people in it.

> *My business partner can always tell when I'm feeling very anxious because I start trying to control everything she says and does. I get so bossy, I don't know how she puts up with it. Lucky for me, she understands anxiety! (Abs, age 52)*

Some Anxiety Sisters experience their anxiety as restlessness (what our grandmothers would call the *shpilkes*). You know what we're talking about—when you can't find a place for yourself and nothing feels right. It's akin to not being able to settle in.

> *I can't concentrate or get into anything, and I can't figure out where I would be comfortable. I keep moving from place to place but I just can't seem to relax. Sometimes getting out helps, sometimes it doesn't.*
> (Shirley, age 75)

Our next Illusionist is spacing or numbing out, which happens when your mind gets so overwhelmed you can't really function. Numbing is an expression of the freeze response in which you can't figure out what to do, so you don't do anything.

> *I can't think straight when I am anxious. I can't figure out what to do first or how to do it, so I end up doing nothing. I take a lot of naps. I watch a lot of stuff on TV and I drink a lot of wine.* (Talia, age 23)

Our final Illusionist is a doozy, as those of us who experience it will attest: sensory symptoms. We expect to feel our anxiety through physical sensations, such as rapid heartbeat or stomach upset, as well as through emotional states, such as fear and distress, but we often forget how much anxiety can affect our senses. What we may not anticipate is that our response to anxiety can make us highly sensitive to light, sounds, smells, and even being touched.

Many of us with anxiety already have sensitive sensory systems, which is understandable if you think about what it means to always be on alert. Because of our hypervigilance, our senses are always on the lookout for threats. Likewise, those of us with sensitive sensory systems may be more wired to be hypervigilant. It's hard to feel mellow when our overactive sense of smell is picking up odors other people don't notice or when our super-sensitive ears magnify sound to the point of discomfort. Or when certain lights give us headaches. Or when we are in a space that feels overcrowded. No wonder we are so exhausted after being out in the world for any length of time—our senses have been assaulted.

> *I have a very intense job and I experience a lot of anxiety at work. Lately, I've been getting frequent headaches—sometimes so bad I have to find a dark room to sit in for a while. And it's not just the lights. The sounds around me—the typical background noise in an office setting— can feel deafening when I'm anxious. I've started bringing noise- canceling headphones to work. (Dawn, age 43)*

> *Long before COVID-19, I wore a mask on planes to deal with my sense of smell, which gets heightened when I am anxious. When I fly, I can detect the most horrendous odors. To manage this, I wear a fabric mask, which I've sprayed with lavender. I have to say that I haven't minded wearing masks during the pandemic! (Abs, age 52)*

Why are we spending so much time discussing symptoms of anxiety? First of all, we want you to know that you are not alone. We don't want to just say, "You are not alone." We want to show you. Your symptoms, no matter what they are (and they may change), are shared by many other people we have interviewed. Second, the only way we've found to demystify the experience of anxiety is to talk about what it feels like. Not from the medical perspective. Not from the academic perspective. From the sufferer's perspective. Because here's the thing: the most insidious part of having an anxiety disorder is that no one really believes that anxiety can actually cause what the sufferer is experiencing. We didn't believe it either. We've seen hundreds of doctors (Mags even had the acid-alkaline balance of her tongue tested, and Abs attempted past-life regressions), so we'd be hypocritical to discourage anyone else from doing the same. Ruling out other problems is part of the process.

And that's the tricky thing about anxiety. There's no blood test or X-ray to confirm your diagnosis. That little seed of doubt will always gnaw at you. After forty years of suffering from anxiety in its myriad forms, ten years of interviewing fellow sufferers, countless hours of research, and thousands of dollars in psychiatry bills, we still occasionally call each other to ask, "Are you *sure* this is anxiety?"

If you are still reading, chances are you are an Anxiety Sister. However, in case you're still not certain, here's a little quiz. Wait, quizzes make us anxious— a little survey:

Which of the following situations makes you anxious?

a) a grizzly bear in your tent
b) being pulled over by a police officer
c) your pilot (not Sully) saying, "Brace for impact"
d) sitting in a dental chair
e) standing in line at the supermarket
f) all of the above

If your answer was either e or f, welcome to the sisterhood.

Still not sure? Let's be more direct. Has anxiety ever caused you to . . . Miss a wedding or funeral? (We've missed five.) Cancel a getaway? (We've canceled a dozen.) Call in sick to work? (Including personal days, nearly a hundred.) You are an Anxiety Sister if your life has been changed, interrupted, or taken over by anxiety. Congratulations! You've found your people!

three

Brain Matters

We are not neuroscientists. In fact, we barely passed high school chemistry. However, we would be remiss if we did not share what we have learned about the undeniable role of the brain in the development of anxiety. Plus, it's helpful to turn to science for confirmation that anxiety disorder is real and not our fault.

We are presenting a very rudimentary and reductive explanation of otherwise fairly complex concepts. But if you too had trouble in science class, feel free to skip to the recap at the end of the chapter. On the other hand, if you did pass high school chemistry, check out our resources for further reading on our website.

Our experience of anxiety is rooted in the brain. As a tummy ache is a sign of intestinal distress, so anxiety is a sign of an imbalance in the brain. In other words, anxiety is a "brain pain." Learning this changed everything for us. No longer were we to blame for our symptoms or weak for not being able to overcome them. Just like any other illness, anxiety is fundamentally a physical malfunction.

We often think of the brain as an organ in our bodies, but this is a bit of an understatement. The brain is the Organ—it controls everything from movement to emotion. Nothing in the body happens without interacting with the brain. Everyone talks about the "mind-body" connection, but this implies that each could be without the other—which is not the case. The brain is the body and directs every bodily function. Just think of this: when you break your ankle, you lose mobility in that foot, but we do not expect this fracture to compromise your ability to do a crossword puzzle. When a part of your brain malfunctions (as in the case of a stroke), the ability to move your foot may be affected. As will possibly be your speech, your emotions, and your intellectual abilities.

The Limbic System

This drawing is a representation of the brain's limbic system, which is its emotional center. Of particular importance is the amygdala, often referred to as the brain's "early warning system," which lets the hypothalamus (the brain's "command center") know when it perceives that danger is near. The hypothalamus then initiates the fight-or-flight

response we Anxiety Sisters are so familiar with: the rapid heartbeat, the shallow breathing, the nausea, the tight muscles, the sweatiness, the dizziness, and so on. This process is so fast that you may startle before you even know why. Your emotional brain has taken over—rational thought is not part of this equation.

Imagine a startling scenario: snakes on the patio, a car backfiring, or smoke coming from your kitchen. In any of these situations, your amygdala is alerted by your eyes, ears, or nose to the stimulus. The amygdala then sends a danger signal to your hypothalamus, which sets off the somatic fear response through the nervous system.

In an anxiety sufferer, the amygdala tends to overreact and send out the danger signal prematurely, too often, or too intensely, thereby sending the hypothalamus and the entire limbic system into overdrive. It is this process that leads to panic attacks and can also account for the constant heightened state of vigilance many anxiety sufferers report. Daniel Goleman named this phenomenon "amygdala hijack" because the limbic system completely overrides the analytical parts of the brain and seizes control of the body's response.[1]

The amygdala, like our mothers-in-law, forgets nothing. Which is bad news for Anxiety Sisters. As archivist for sensory memories, the amygdala associates various smells, sounds, tastes, and sights with emotions, which explains why a place where we experienced a panic attack can itself bring one on. What the amygdala perceives as threatening or dangerous becomes a cue for future reference. Thus, whenever one of those cues is present, a person will usually feel scared or anxious, even if that cue is not currently threatening.

The Prefrontal Cortex

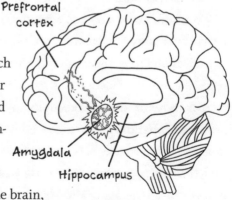

This drawing shows the limbic system in relation to the prefrontal cortex, which is the part of your brain (under your forehead) responsible for what's called executive function—planning, task completion, reasoning, inhibiting impulses (self-control), directing attention, and problem-solving. Without this part of the brain, you would be unable to think about the future or about the consequences of your actions. You'd just be a walking bundle of urges. (No judgment. Been there, done that.)

The amygdala is wired to the prefrontal cortex so that messages can easily be transmitted by neurons between the two regions. As the seat of executive function, the prefrontal cortex acts as a mediator between emotion from the limbic system and action. In other words, it assesses the emotion and determines a reaction based on that assessment. For *Star Trek* fans, the prefrontal cortex is your Mr. Spock.

When your limbic system is in overdrive, as is the case with anxiety, the path of those wires connecting the amygdala and the prefrontal cortex is disrupted, so the neurons have difficulty communicating with each other. If messages aren't getting through from your amygdala to your prefrontal cortex, there's no rational voice to control your emotions. This is why we cannot think clearly or problem-solve when we are experiencing anxiety.

> *I can't think straight when I am over-the-top anxious. It's like my brain completely shuts down and all I can feel is anxiety. I have learned to not make any big decisions about anything when I am really anxious because my thinking is so off. (Padma, age 55)*

As all this brainspeak shows, anxiety is absolutely a real thing that is located in your body. You can actually see parts of the anxious brain light up on an MRI. Anxiety is a disorder, not a decision—it is not your fault. Also, it's good to understand why you can't think logically when you are under the influence of anxiety.

For those of us with preadults in our lives (our brains are not fully developed and functional until around age twenty-five), there is some really important and illuminating neuroscience worthy of discussion. You know how we said that anxious adults have trigger-happy amygdalae? Well, in adolescent brains, the amygdala is already in overdrive—it is highly sensitized and more easily stimulated than the fully adult amygdala (thus all the high school drama). The preadult amygdala is akin to dry, brittle timber just waiting for anything to spark it into a wildfire. This is why it seems that teens and young adults are constantly in a state of amygdala hijack. Also, it explains why teen-agers have a reputation for impulsive, overemotional, risky behavior. Remember that time you decided to see if you could jump from the roof of the neighbor's house into your swimming pool? Now you know why.

Perhaps the most important takeaway from the research on the preadult brain is that it is more prone to anxiety and depression than the adult brain. This adds a whole new dimension to parenting, educating, and counseling our nation's youth and explains why anxiety and depression are at epidemic proportions in high schools and on college campuses. Did you know that today's average high schooler experiences the same amount of anxiety as the average psychiatric patient of the 1950s?[2] True (but really sad) story.

Neurotransmitters

Another important neurological topic we need to address concerns neurotransmitters, which are brain chemicals. These brain chemicals are messengers that transmit signals throughout the body, telling, for example, the heart to beat, the lungs to breathe, and the stomach to digest. Neurotransmitters are the mechanism by which nerve cells (neurons) communicate. When they have finished their job, they are reabsorbed by the nerve cells and put in the recycling bin.

What is most important to know about these neurotransmitters is that they need to be in balance. Much like our three-tiered system of government, these guys work together and keep each other in check. (Okay, maybe not like our government.) If the neurotransmitters become unbalanced, the whole system is thrown off kilter, resulting in mental disorders like anxiety and depression.

There are many different neurotransmitters, but we are going to talk about the two most well known: (1) serotonin, most of which is found in the gut (anxious stomach, anyone?), which regulates mood, appetite, impulse control, sleep, and libido, and (2) norepinephrine, which is located in the brain and is a stimulant responsible for physiological arousal, such as increased blood pressure. Clearly, these neurotransmitters have important jobs, and if unbalanced, they can cause a host of problems, including but not limited to anxiety and depression.

The reason it's important for you to know about neurotransmitters is that they are the targets of drug intervention in the treatment of anxiety and depression. Selective serotonin reuptake inhibitors, commonly referred to as SSRIs, are a class of medication that aims to increase the availability of serotonin by stopping its reabsorption. Examples of these meds include Prozac, Paxil, Zoloft, Celexa, and Lexapro. Serotonin-norepinephrine reuptake inhibitors (SNRIs) are designed to increase the availability of both serotonin and norepinephrine. Examples include Effexor, Cymbalta, and Pristiq. We'll talk much more about these medications in chapter eleven.

Neuroplasticity

Until the early part of the twenty-first century, neuroscience as a field subscribed to the notion that the brain, after childhood growth, was relatively unchanging (except for its decline through aging, illness, or physical trauma). Now, however, it is widely accepted that the brain can and does change in structure and function throughout one's lifetime—in fact, every time you learn a new skill or think in a new way, you alter your brain. Essentially, your brain is constantly being updated as you experience new things. This is called neuroplasticity.

Each day, our brains are bombarded by millions of stimuli—sights, sounds, smells, thoughts, feelings, and more. It would be too much for the brain to process each and every one of these stimuli, so it takes shortcuts—it goes on autopilot in order to manage the onslaught of information. You can see how this works when you find yourself automatically driving to work on a Sunday, even though it's your day off. When we do something over and over, our brains create a neural pathway, which becomes a default mechanism—what we do without having to think about it. And the more we practice or repeat a thought, feeling, or behavior, the more we strengthen the neural pathway. Frequently traveled neural pathways turn into habits.

Neuroplasticity tells us that our neural pathways can be rewired so we can change our default thoughts, feelings, and actions. Rewiring involves creating a new pathway and then repeatedly using it through practice in order to strengthen it. At the same time, the old neural pathway will weaken from lack of use until—voilà!—your new way of thinking, feeling, or doing is now the default.

Neuroplasticity is a double-edged sword for anxiety sufferers. The bad news is that if we repeat, say, a panicky response to a given situation, our brains will become wired to repeat that response in any similar situation. This is why if you've had a panic attack in the doctor's office, just thinking about going to the doc can make you feel panicky. And because how we think can itself become habitual, destructive thoughts can also become well-traveled neural pathways. (This is how the Anxiety Loop is formed.) Yes, you are reading this correctly: without our even knowing it, we actually train our brains to respond anxiously.

But there is good news here too. Just as we can train our brains to react anxiously to certain stimuli, we can retrain our brains to react calmly instead. Every technique and tool we show you in this book—from breathing and meditation to Tai Chi and walking in nature—is designed to help you carve new default responses to anxiety. We know these strategies work, because we've retrained our anxious brains. The process is not a quick one, and it can at times feel very difficult. But your persistence and effort will absolutely pay off.

We can retrain our brains to react calmly

> *I've been working with my psychiatrist to help reduce my handwashing. It had gotten so bad, my hands developed sores that were getting infected. I went up on my meds, but that didn't change things much. So he*

suggested we try to train my brain to think differently through relabeling. Instead of saying that I wash my hands all the time because I am worried they are constantly dirty, I am supposed to say out loud that I wash my hands because of my brain illness. When I talk about it with other people, I am supposed to say that my OCD causes me to think in a disordered way, to blame it on faulty assumptions caused by my disorder. I've only been doing it for a few weeks, but I'm already seeing a difference. I feel like I have more control over the OCD. (Blair, age 33)

My doctor encouraged me to learn something new as a way to deal with my excessive worry. I chose French. When I would become really agitated or when I found myself going into the what-ifs, I would do five minutes of work on my French lesson. It has helped me because I used to stay in worry for so long. Sure, the French distracts me, but it's more than that. It's like I'm relearning how to handle it when the worry shows up. (Tabitha, age 59)

The Second Brain

Your digestive system is home to some 200 million neurons (the nerve cells found in your central nervous system). That's right, your second "brain," also called your enteric nervous system (ENS), is located in your gut. In fact, 95 percent of your serotonin (your brain's feel-good neurotransmitter) is stored in your ENS.[3]

Digestion is not a simple process. Indeed, it is so complex that it requires a brain of its own to make it happen. Your gut, when uncoiled, is roughly the size of a badminton court.[4] This is why we have two brains: the one in our head is in charge of everything, and the one in our gut is in charge of digestion. It's true that the brain occupying the penthouse may have more authority, but the gut brain can operate independently and plays an important role as well. The two brains communicate continuously via the vagus nerve (see diagram). In this way, your gut influences your emotions and vice versa.

Anxiety Sisters have always known the connection between their gut and their brain—again, anxious stomach, anyone? Butterflies? Gut feeling? Gut-wrenching experience? So many of us have nervous tummies as a result of our mental state. What's not so obvious, however, is that your mental state may actually be a result of what's going on in your gut. Since your brain and gut each send signals to the other, your gastric distress can be both the cause and the product of your anxiety.

The idea of a second brain changes the way we understand irritable bowel syndrome (IBS), which is so often a co-diagnosis with anxiety disorders (up to 80 percent of folks with IBS experience anxiety and depression[5]). For those of us who suffer from IBS, we know how impossible it is to figure out what causes it. Now, with all the research on the gut-brain connection, we are learning that the problem may actually be a disruption in the communication between the two brains. Since serotonin is responsible for gut-brain messages, and 95 percent of your serotonin is stored in your gut, it makes sense that antidepressants that target serotonin have become a standard treatment for IBS. Also, doctors are turning more and more to meditation, hypnosis, and visualization techniques in order to calm disturbing gut-brain signals, thereby reducing abdominal pain.

VAGUS NERVE

Looking Ahead

The second brain will be the focus of future anxiety and depression treatments. A whole new field has recently emerged called neurogastroenterology, which is dedicated to the gut-brain connection. Of particular interest is the gut biome, the most concentrated ecosystem on the planet, with a hundred times more bacteria in the ENS than in your whole body.

The makeup of the bacteria, fungi, viruses, and other living organisms in our gut biome has implications for so many aspects of our health. In fact, it is the seat of our immune system. A study conducted by Dr. Stephen Collins at McMaster University in Canada illustrates the potential for using the biome to treat anxiety. In his experiment, Dr. Collins injected a group of anxious mice with the bacteria from the guts of calm mice and vice versa. The result was astounding: the calm mice became anxious and the anxious mice became calm.[6] This is only one of many studies exploring the ways we can use the bacteria in our guts to influence our mental health.

Recap

Just as other illnesses have physical locations in the body, anxiety is found in the brain. The trouble begins in your limbic or emotional system when your amygdala hijacks your ability to think rationally (using your prefrontal cortex). The hijacking leads to a full-body stress response, which results in anxiety and all its symptoms. The amygdala in preadults (those of us under twenty-five) is particularly sensitive and not yet fully wired to the prefrontal cortex, which makes impulse control and reasoned decision-making even more challenging. Because of neuroplasticity (the brain's ability to adapt and change), anxiety responses can become the default. Luckily, also because of neuroplasticity, you can create new neural pathways, which become the new default. (That's where this book comes in.)

four

Labels Are for Jeans, Not Anxiety

Unfortunately, we live in a label-happy culture: everything is categorized, including people. Especially people with mental illnesses. You may have an anxiety diagnosis; if so, you are labeled too. Here's what's problematic about that:

- Labels are arbitrary. For example, one of the criteria for many anxiety diagnoses is that the symptoms occur over a period of "at least six months." Why six months? Why not seven months? Or three? What is magical about the 180-day mark? And who can pinpoint the exact day their worry became excessive in order to track it? We understand the idea that sometimes symptoms are fleeting and therefore not indicative of a disorder. If you are avoiding social situations because of anxiety for ninety days, how is that not enough to be diagnosed with social anxiety disorder?

- Labels are polarizing, which means your behavior is designated as either "normal" or "pathological." You're put in one box or the other, even though most of us straddle both.

• Labels ignore nuance. Symptoms often change and morph and vary greatly in their intensity, which makes it difficult to place them in neat categories. Most anxiety sufferers we know experience a wide spectrum of symptoms—obsessive thinking coupled with some occasional panic and a dash of depression, for example. There's lots of crossover, which labels don't capture. To us, the symptoms of anxiety disorders are not discrete; therefore, we propose thinking about them as on the Anxiety Continuum. It makes more sense to consider the intensity and disruptiveness of symptoms, rather than how many of them there are.

• Labels are ascribed according to the dominant culture's model. This means that norms from nondominant cultures are classified as pathological. It matters who gets to determine what constitutes normal. In Western culture, that would be the white male of European descent. Normative behaviors for women are different from those of men, yet our society labels us based on the latter. This may be why women are twice as likely to receive an anxiety diagnosis as men.[1]

> I'm a therapist in a predominantly Haitian community. Some of the things I hear from my clients would be considered delusions in America. I had a client who believed his friend had a fatal heart attack because of a curse. He was experiencing a lot of anxiety around this. If you understood the voodoo religion, this would make complete sense to you. (Roseline, age 50)

• Labels are dehumanizing and reductive. They don't tell the whole story of an individual, yet they lead to a lot of assumptions and judgments—in other words, stereotyping.

Despite all our complaints about labels, this is how the world works right now. As such, you have to be able to navigate the system (as faulty as it is) so you can be your own advocate throughout your treatment. Here are some ways to do that:

- Understand your diagnosis and what it means (this chapter will help with that).
- Become familiar with the mental health lingo (don't be afraid to ask your health care provider to explain terms you don't know).
- Do not allow people to make assumptions about you based on your diagnosis.
- Make sure people involved in your diagnosis and treatment are asking you lots of questions; otherwise they *are* making assumptions about you.
- Ask questions—as many as you need.
- You are the expert on you, so if something doesn't sound or feel right, speak up.

We can't emphasize enough how crucial it is to know and understand your "label." Important decisions, including medication and other treatment plans, are made based on your diagnosis; however, it is our experience that most (if not all) anxiety sufferers are atypical and don't fit so neatly into a particular category. We're all a little bit of this and a little bit of that, and we all have symptoms that vary over time. Perhaps what matters is to identify the symptom or behavior that is disrupting your life the most; in other words, what is chipping away at your agency and connection?

> *Because I was having panic attacks, my first psychiatrist diagnosed me with panic disorder and prescribed medication accordingly. My current doctor, however, asked a lot more questions—like, for over an hour— and he decided that my obsessions and compulsions were, in fact, much more disruptive, so he diagnosed me with OCD and prescribed a different medication. Not only do I feel so much better, but the panic has decreased a lot. (Abs, age 52)*

To get you started with the mental health vernacular, what follows is a description of the most common anxiety diagnoses. This section is by no means exhaustive or clinical, but we think it's a good foundation. Let's begin with the most common diagnosis:

Generalized Anxiety Disorder (GAD)

Remember that Worry Cloud we talked about in chapter one? Well, our GAD folks live under it. In other words, they spend a large percentage of their waking hours worrying about something, and the worry is disproportionate to the threat. But worry is only half of the story. Individuals diagnosed with GAD typically experience more than two of the following symptoms: (1) edginess or restlessness, (2) fatigue, (3) insomnia, (4) irritability, (5) headaches, (6) muscle tension or soreness, and (7) difficulty concentrating.

> *I have a hard time concentrating at work, which is ironic because I am always worried about whether I am going to lose my job. You would think that I would focus more with all this worry, but the opposite seems to happen. (Scarlet, age 38)*

GAD sufferers worry about the same things we all do—money, work, relationships, and health—but much more intensely and over longer periods of time. No matter how hard they try, they cannot pull themselves away from the Worry Cloud.

> *When either of my children gets fevers, I go nuts. I really believe that the fever will get so high we will need to go to the hospital. I end up moving the sick kid into the family room, where I sleep right next to him. I actually don't sleep at all because I am up all night checking that he is*

still breathing and not getting sicker. Everything else in my life stops.
(Mags, age 52)

Other GAD delights include catastrophizing (envisioning the worst-case scenario) and hanging out with the what-ifs. You know what we mean. What if I lose my job and then I lose my home? What if my partner leaves me? What if this dizziness is a brain tumor? If you are a GAD sufferer, odds are good that you've spun off quite a few of these.

If the symptoms of GAD sound a lot like the symptoms of all anxiety disorders, you are not wrong. Generalized anxiety is a bit of a catchall; as a result, this diagnosis fits pretty much everyone with anxiety. While there are some anxiety sufferers who are just GAD people, many of us with this diagnosis also have another (or two).

Panic Disorder

If you're a Panic Sister, you know it! We certainly don't have to tell you that you experience panic attacks, which are just about the most terrifying thing on the planet. But to be an official, card-carrying member of the Panic Disorder Club, just having panic attacks is not enough. Two criteria for inclusion in this designation are (1) you enter a Panic Loop, and (2) you become an "avoider" in an effort to stave off panic.

The Panic Loop is just like the Anxiety Loop we've mentioned—it's when your fear of having another panic attack fuels a panic attack. For this reason, panic sufferers experience huge life disruption, which is what the second criterion encompasses. Basically, you are doing your very best to avoid panic attacks at all costs. As panic sufferers ourselves, we would rather clean the bathroom of a fraternity house with a toothbrush (on a Sunday morning) than go through a full-fledged panic attack again.

I had a terrible panic attack in Kroger's, where I usually shop. I didn't go back to that supermarket for a really long time. I also found going to any big supermarket really rough because I would get such bad anxiety thinking about it. (Yolanda, age 42)

While many Anxiety Sisters suffer from panic attacks as part of other disorders, what makes Panic Disorder so special is that, at least at the onset, the attacks are what is called "uncued." This means that they come out of the blue, with no warning or explanation. Because you can't find a source for the panic, these attacks are as shocking as they are scary. "Cued" panic attacks, on the other hand, have a traceable trigger.

When I am driving on local streets, I feel fine. But as soon as I get on the freeway, I have a panic attack. I feel so light-headed that I can't control the car. I keep envisioning the car just skidding out of control. I start to sweat and shake so much that I have to pull over. (Denise, age 33)

Often, cued attacks are caused by other anxiety disorders (such as social anxiety or phobias), which can make the whole panic diagnosis tricky. A really good diagnostician will ask lots of questions to find out whether your panic attacks are cued or uncued, because the treatment for them can be quite different. Regardless of the nature of the panic attack, it is always frightening and exhausting. If you've managed to get through life without experiencing one of these, fortune has smiled upon you.

Social Anxiety Disorder (SAD*), a.k.a. Social Phobia

Before we start talking about this disorder, let's get one thing straight: SAD is not the same thing as shyness or introversion. Introverts derive energy and

---

* Not to be confused with seasonal affective disorder, which is also referred to as SAD.

satisfaction from time alone—in fact, they often prefer it. SAD sufferers, however, abstain from social situations because of the *anxiety* they experience around other people. This is not the sufferer's preference; many Anxiety Sisters we've met have told us that the worst part of SAD is the loneliness and isolation that results from avoiding social situations.

> *Everyone thinks I'm antisocial because I tend to avoid group situations. It's not that—it's that I get so anxious when I'm around more than a couple of people. Last week at the company picnic, I was so nauseated. I left after a half hour. Which was longer than I thought I'd make it. Still, it didn't help me look less like the hermit people think I am.* (India, age 47)

At its core, SAD is a fear of being judged. SAD sufferers worry about humiliating themselves in public—that, for example, they will say the wrong thing or that they will do something stupid. They fear drawing attention to themselves and therefore are extremely self-conscious. It's like a nasty case of stage fright, minus the stage. Common situations that SAD sufferers avoid are interacting with strangers, dating, parties and other gatherings, public speaking, using public restrooms, eating in front of others, and performances of any kind.

I find eating in restaurants really difficult. I'm sure I will spill something on myself and everyone will notice. I just avoid it at all costs.
(Margaret, age 61)

My parents don't understand why I won't make phone calls for them— like ordering pizza or something. They think I'm being lazy but I'm not. I get really nervous when I have to talk to a stranger and I forget what to say. I worry that I'll start stuttering and they'll just hang up.
(Regan, age 18)

I don't speak up in department meetings and it often comes up on my evaluations. The thing is I do have ideas but I am terrified of the sound of my voice. When I hear it, I turn beet red, which of course everyone notices and asks me if I'm okay, which only makes it worse. I end up getting completely tongue-tied. I just can't do it. (Suzanne, age 34)

SAD symptoms, on the whole, are similar to panic symptoms, which makes sense because the sufferer actually experiences a cued panic attack in response to fear of judgment. Not all SAD sufferers have panic attacks; however, all SAD folks experience tremendous discomfort and anxiety. Some of the most common sensations associated with SAD are racing heart, flushing, sweating, clamminess, shaking, dry mouth, feeling out of breath, dizziness, and light-headedness. While they are experiencing these symptoms, SAD sufferers worry about other people noticing them. And that makes the symptoms even worse. As a result, SAD folks often either avoid social situations altogether or bring someone along to do the interacting.

I don't go anywhere by myself. I had to go to the dry cleaner and my husband was sick, so I went on my own. I turned around halfway there and made him come with me. He was really upset with me—he just doesn't understand. (Patti, age 70)

The onset of SAD is often around thirteen years old, that wonderful age when just about everyone is feeling (and looking and acting) awkward. It is the beginning of adolescence, the developmental stage when we are already obsessed with how we are perceived by our peers. Parents might think their children are just being moody teenagers when they prefer to stay in their rooms rather than socialize. And while sometimes this is the case, often the parents are unknowingly observing the start of social anxiety disorder.

> *My daughter has always been on the shy side, so I didn't worry too much when she didn't want to go to high school parties or dances. Truth be told, I never liked that stuff either. But then I noticed she didn't seem to enjoy hanging out with her friend group anymore. They called for her, but she wasn't interested in going out. By the time she got to her senior year, she spent most of her time in her room. I took her to see a therapist, who recommended she take some medication for her anxiety. For the life of me, I never thought it was that, but within a few weeks, she started coming out of her room.* (Audrey, age 49)

Interestingly, SAD also has cultural underpinnings. In collectivist societies like those found in Asia, India, China, and Latin America, there are low rates of social anxiety disorder. However, in individualist Western cultures such as the United States, SAD is quite prevalent. This makes sense because "we" cultures discourage individualism, whereas "I" cultures promote it, which results in more pressure on each person to make it on his or her own.

Phobias

First things first: fear and phobia are *not* the same thing. Fear is a rational emotional response to a real or perceived threat, whereas phobia is usually an irrational response to a non-threat or, less typically, a greatly exaggerated response to a real threat. In other words, a rattlesnake in your bathroom and an alligator in your swimming pool (shout-out to our Florida peeps) both inspire fear, and for an excellent reason. That fear will keep you from trying to pet or even approach either reptile. Fear is protective—it is a basic survival mechanism.

Phobia, on the other hand, is a persistent and irrational fear of an object or a situation that causes the sufferer to go to great lengths to avoid it. Phobic reactions are often extreme and cannot be controlled. As a bonus, phobia sufferers typically experience the full range of panic symptoms, including fainting and dizziness. Phobia is restrictive—it encourages avoidance behaviors that can actually compromise survival.

If you are still a bit confused about the distinction between fear and phobia, here's what our resident phobia expert (Mags) has to say:

> The only thing worse than my flying phobia was listening to everyone explain how flying is statistically safer than driving. During my most phobic years, I always wanted to turn to these Good Samaritans and say, "Listen, you idiots, I am a semi-intelligent adult; I know planes are the safest mode of transportation and I also know that what I am feeling isn't rational, and listening to you yammer on about survivor statistics is making my anxiety worse." Now, however, I understand why so many people insisted on that line of reasoning: they didn't understand that I wasn't just *afraid* of flying—it was a genuine phobia, which is a very different animal. Had I been afraid to fly, commentary about the safety of airline travel could have been helpful because fear is a rational response. However, since I was suffering from aerophobia, which by definition is irrational, all attempts to use logic were useless (and even more anxiety provoking).

Everyone experiences fear at one time or another—it is a normal human emotion. Phobia, however, is experienced by only 9.1 percent of the population—it is considered an anxiety disorder.[2] We know that phobias can be caused by traumatic events. A person who was attacked by a dog as a child may develop a severe phobia of dogs. Likewise, someone who witnessed 9/11 (either in person or over and over on TV) may find herself with a flying phobia. These phobias typically cause a crippling physical reaction (read: panic attack) that makes it impossible to function.

Another way phobias can develop is through parental modeling. If a child witnesses a parent's phobic reactions, he or she may adopt the same behaviors. But there is also a strong genetic component. Identical twins are more likely to experience the same phobias even when they are raised separately, thus pointing toward shared DNA as an explanation.[3]

I am terrified of choking to death—it's my biggest fear and I worry about it all the time. I'm also afraid of vomiting, which I think will cause me to choke. It's so bad I don't even let myself burp because I'm afraid it could lead to throwing up. And if someone throws up near me, I get all worked up because I'm afraid I'll start to gag. The weirdest part of it is that my sister has the exact same phobia. (Mikaela, age 28)

Anything can cause a phobic response. The most common causes include any kind of animal, thunder and lightning, transportation, anything related to doctors or dentists, enclosed spaces, heights, and public speaking. Less frequently reported phobias include clowns, falling asleep, cheese, trees, and bathing. But we have heard so many stories. . . .

I have had an intense fear of mushrooms for as long as I can remember. Of course, I can't eat them or eat a dish that they are in. But I also really can't be at the table if someone else is eating them. (Ruth, age 55)

All phobias are not created equal. There are some that, as terrorizing as they are, don't interrupt your general functioning on a daily basis. You may remember Abs's phobia of cockroaches we mentioned in chapter one (her heart just started thudding when she typed the word). Luckily, she lives in a place where she doesn't come into contact with them and therefore has not sought treatment. Her life isn't compromised by this particular phobia. Other phobic folks are not as fortunate; trying to avoid their phobic triggers really disrupts their lives.

> *I cannot drive over bridges, which is a real problem because where I live in Northern California there are a lot of them. As soon as we approach a bridge I start to sweat and have that dizzy feeling like I am going to faint. I stopped driving myself over bridges eleven years ago and it makes my life very difficult. I am totally dependent on my husband or a friend to drive me a lot of places.* (Judith, age 64)

Another phobia worthy of discussion (due to its destructive and life-altering nature) is agoraphobia, which is a fear of not being safe outside the home or a familiar place. When we say "not being safe," we mean that the agoraphobic person is worried she will experience anxiety or physical illness and will be unable to cope or get help. We talk more about agoraphobia in chapter six, but suffice it to say, it's paralyzing.

Illness Anxiety Disorder (IAD)

Time for a survey: Raise your hand if you have ever wondered if that weird sensation you felt in your stomach the other day was actually the beginning of a fatal illness. Okay, next question. Raise your hand if your doctor gave you a clean bill of health—but you are sure she missed something. Last question. Raise your hand if WebMD is in the top three of your most frequently visited sites. If you raised your hand at least once, you may have IAD.

Formerly known as hypochondriasis, IAD is basically irrational obsessing about your health, which is one of the most common activities for anxiety sufferers. Here are some of the telltale signs of this disorder: (1) a preoccupation with having or developing a serious medical condition, (2) hyperawareness of every bodily sensation or twinge, (3) constant googling of symptoms and causes or hanging out in medical forums, (4) disbelieving negative test results or a doctor's reassurance that you are not ill, (5) compulsive checking for signs of illness, and (6) constantly thinking or talking about topics related to your health.

> *Every time I feel something in my body, I get really scared and think I have something big going on. For a couple of months, I had these sharp pains in one of my breasts and it started to get itchy. I thought either I am having heart symptoms or it's the beginning of breast cancer. It went away, but other things pop up.* (Hope, age 45)

> *Since my dad had a stroke, I am paranoid that it will happen to me. I bought a blood pressure kit so I can track my pressure several times each day. Every time it's higher than usual, I call the doctor. They always tell me that changes in pressure throughout the day are normal, but I am worried that it might not be—that if I stop doing it, I'll miss the signs.* (Vicky, age 27)

IAD sufferers have a special relationship with medical professionals—either they see them as often as possible or they avoid them like the coronavirus (more on that in a moment). Because of their need for constant reassurance that they are not sick, many IAD sufferers spend a lot of time with their doctors. In fact, they will often seek out specialists and testing in order to accurately diagnose what they are sure other experts have missed.

On the other hand, some IAD sufferers are too frightened to go to medical appointments for fear that tests will confirm what they already suspect—that they are ill. These folks prefer to put their heads in the sand, but this strategy doesn't give them any peace. They still worry about their health all the time.

> *I am really far behind on the routine tests I am supposed to get, like my mammogram and colonoscopy. I am too afraid of what they might find, and I keep avoiding making the appointment. The thing is, I think I might really have something wrong with me—I think about that every day.* (Willa, age 56)

Some IAD sufferers have bona fide ailments but exaggerate them to life-threatening (or at least life-consuming) status. We recently met an Anxiety Sister who is convinced her IBS is really stomach cancer. She has been to many specialists, been scoped several times—even swallowed a few cameras—but despite all their reassurances to the contrary, she is sure she is dying.

This subject is strange to write about as the peak of the coronavirus pandemic fast approaches us and we are all sheltering in place on the advice of medical experts. Some with IAD avoid people, places, or situations *they* think pose a risk to their health. We are not talking about smart and necessary precautions here but rather excessive vigilance. Their terror at the idea of becoming hurt or ill overpowers reasonable judgment about what is truly dangerous. Certainly this pandemic has made IAD sufferers out of all of us to an extent—we are all wondering if each sneeze or odd sensation in our chests is the beginning of a battle with COVID-19. True IAD sufferers, however, experience this even when there is no pandemic.

Obsessive-Compulsive Disorder (OCD)

Most people, when they think of OCD, imagine someone scrubbing her hands up to her elbows or frantically organizing the cans in the pantry. These images are brought to you by Hollywood and the media but do not capture the complexity of this very serious disorder. In fact, the way OCD is portrayed in popular culture means that lots of folks with other presentations get misdiagnosed (or not diagnosed at all). Although much fun is poked at the symptoms of OCD, there is nothing funny about living with this anxiety disorder.

OCD sufferers typically experience frequent uncontrollable and distressing thoughts, which are known as obsessions. In order to relieve the anxiety caused by these thoughts, sufferers create rituals or behaviors, which are called compulsions. These obsessions and compulsions are very time-consuming and exhausting; on top of that, they soothe the anxiety only temporarily. Therefore, people with OCD can become stuck repeating their compulsions so that they are unable to move on to the next activity.

> *Every time I leave my house, I always worry that I left the garage open, even though I know I didn't. I'll drive for a while thinking about it, but I always end up going back. I have to touch the door and say "closed." Sometimes I'll go back two or three times. (Isabel, age 24)*

> *My daughter has OCD, which makes it tough to get out of the house in the mornings. She has to touch certain things in each room before she leaves, in a particular order. If she doesn't do it "right," she has to start all over. It can take an hour on bad days. (Gerri, age 47)*

Although most OCD sufferers experience both obsessions and compulsions, the National Institute of Mental Health reports that about 20 percent of sufferers have obsessions only and 10 percent have compulsions only.

We've heard so many different stories about various obsessions or intrusive thoughts experienced by OCD sufferers. A major study led by Concordia University found that 94 percent of *all* people have some intrusive thoughts or impulses.[4] What's different about these thoughts for those with OCD is their frequency, their intensity, and, most important, how much anxiety they create. (The anxiety is what makes the thoughts obsessive.) The most common kinds of intrusive thoughts are (1) aggressive thinking about self-harm or violence toward others, (2) worrying about contamination (both emotional and physical), (3) superstitious thinking or focusing on good or bad luck, (4) sexually explicit and taboo thinking, (5) hyperawareness of bodily sensations, and (6) doubt generation, which is a lack of confidence or even certainty about one's perceptions and actions, causing sufferers to question themselves incessantly.

> *Before I started treatment, I used to think that I could "catch" certain personality traits from other people. Like in the same way you could catch a cold. For example, I used to refuse to go within a few feet of this girl who bullied other kids because I was afraid I could become a bully too.* (Yasmeen, age 18)

Common compulsions include but are not limited to checking behaviors, reassurance seeking, counting, tapping, repeating (often nonsensical) words, arranging things "just so," hoarding, and excessive prayer.

> *I don't like odd numbers. Everything has to be even. Like when I'm eating fries, I have to eat an even amount. It sounds crazy—and it is! But it's easier to keep doing it than trying to stop it. That just makes it worse.* (Petra, age 29)

> *My hoarding is so bad, my house looks like the ones on that TV show. I hate it, but I can't throw stuff away because it might be important. And if I do [throw it away], it'll be gone forever. Once, my daughter tried to clean out my kitchen. As soon as she left, I went through the trash for hours.* (Sylvia, age 74)

One paradoxical and nasty thing about OCD is that the sufferer usually understands that her thoughts or behaviors are irrational and excessive. The problem is, the compulsion can be so powerful that it overrides reason—much like all anxiety disorders. Perhaps the best description of OCD we've ever come across was written by science journalist and *Vice* senior staff writer Shayla Love: "At its core, for me and others, OCD is a disorder of doubt. . . . They're not sure about their safety, their intentions, their motives, their realities. And yet, most people with OCD are painfully aware that what they're thinking isn't true. A person with contamination obsessions, for instance, knows deep down that they don't need to wash their hands for the 100th time, but they are haunted by the reality that they can't be *sure* that there aren't still germs lingering."[5]

Many OCD sufferers experience what we call an "obsession within an obsession." This occurs when the sufferer is afraid she won't be able to stop obsessing and becomes obsessed with that thought.

> *I have this mole on my neck that I touch constantly. I know I look weird doing it, but it's almost unconscious at this point. I'm so scared this will make me go insane—that I won't be able to stop thinking about the mole.* (Ornella, age 40)

OCD often begins in late adolescence (most sufferers receive their diagnoses by the time they turn nineteen) and has been shown to have a strong genetic component. Many family studies have revealed that having a first-degree relative with OCD predisposes you to the disorder. Sometimes children may develop OCD symptoms after contracting a streptococcal infection—this is called pediatric autoimmune neuropsychiatric disorders associated with streptococcal infections (PANDAS). Also, some research has found a link between childhood trauma and OCD.[6] OCD frequently overlaps with other anxiety disorders, depression, ADHD, autism, and tic disorders like Tourette's syndrome.

Post-Traumatic Stress Disorder (PTSD)

During World War I, because of the huge number of veterans experiencing symptoms, the diagnosis of combat stress reaction was created. As we now know, however, war is not the only way to traumatize the human brain, so the diagnosis has changed to PTSD. Being exposed to trauma is not the whole story because not everyone who is exposed to trauma develops PTSD. The diagnosis is actually more complicated.

Of course, PTSD starts with a situation or event that threatens to cause death, serious injury, or sexual violence. The exposure, however, doesn't have to be direct: you could be a witness to a trauma (e.g., seeing a terrible car accident), you could learn of a trauma experienced by a close friend or relative (e.g., a violent death), or you could be exposed to someone's trauma through your work (e.g., a medical professional during the COVID-19 pandemic).

> I left college in my sophomore year after my roommate was sexually assaulted in our room. I wasn't there at the time, and I felt so guilty about that. I just couldn't cope with any of it—I had horrible dreams and panic attacks. I know it happened to her, but it feels like it happened to me too. (Kim, age 52)

The second criterion for a PTSD diagnosis is that the sufferer repeatedly reexperiences the trauma through nightmares, flashbacks, involuntary memories, or reminders of the trauma, which often cause panic symptoms such as a racing heart. In addition, PTSD Sisters develop avoidance behaviors in response to the trauma. For example, in Kim's story, she had to go home midsemester in order to avoid the scene of the trauma.

Another hallmark of PTSD is negative thoughts and emotions that either begin or worsen after the trauma. Some examples of how this appears include (1) forgetting details about the trauma, (2) self-blame or shame, (3) lack of desire to connect with other people or take part in activities, and (4) a generally pessimistic outlook.

> *My husband died three years ago after a very long illness. I had taken care of him for so many years, not just physically but emotionally. Since he died, I keep thinking about what I could have done better. . . . I often have these flashbacks to terrible times in the hospital. I don't enjoy anything. I don't taste food anymore. Worst of all, I feel so alienated from everyone and so alone. (Esther, age 80)*

Another component of the PTSD diagnosis is behavior change as a result of the trauma—for example, becoming aggressive, difficulty concentrating, feeling on high alert, sleep problems, startling easily, irritability, or recklessness.

> *My sexual activity and issues with drugs were very much tied into the years of sexual abuse I experienced growing up. Whenever I was anxious, depressed, or scared—which was pretty much all the time—sex and drugs numbed those feelings; they stopped me from having to feel or think. The hardest part of recovery is having to deal with all those feelings I was able to block out. (Celia, age 37)*

PTSD itself is sorted into categories, the most salient of which is complex PTSD (CPTSD). CPTSD sufferers have experienced prolonged or repeated trauma, often as a result of difficult, abusive, or unstable childhoods. Because of the long-term nature of the trauma, CPTSD sufferers live on a shaky foundation, which makes healing that much harder.

> *My mother was an alcoholic and had a lot of trouble holding on to a job. We moved around quite often. I would walk into the apartment unsure if the lights would be on, if there would be food in the refrigerator, or even if she would be home. I spent a few years in and out of foster care,*

which was really rough for me. I ended up getting married quite young—I was probably searching for some form of stability—but my marriage has been abusive. I can't seem to find my footing in the world. I'm so anxious all the time. (Ursula, age 56)

For most PTSD sufferers, symptoms tend to show up within a few months of the trauma; however, for some, symptoms don't manifest for several months or even years. For these folks, diagnosis is particularly tricky, as they might not associate what they are experiencing with the trauma. Regardless of time of onset, these symptoms can be either ongoing or sporadic, or they can pop up as a response to a newer trauma.

My father died in a car accident when I was twelve. Many years later, I had a miscarriage. My doctor said there was an excellent chance I would get pregnant again, and that miscarriages were very common. But I was inconsolable—not just for a while, but for months. I finally was diagnosed with complex PTSD. Turns out that I was having a delayed reaction to losing my dad. (Karen, age 64)

As is the case with all anxiety disorders, women are twice as likely to experience PTSD as men. (According to the US Department of Veterans Affairs, one in ten women will develop PTSD in their lifetimes.) Additionally, women's PTSD symptoms tend to last longer than those of male sufferers.

Women are also much more likely than men to be sexually traumatized. According to the National Sexual Violence Resource Center, one in five women will be raped in their lifetimes. We are continually astounded by the number of women in our Anxiety Sisterhood who report having experienced sexual violence.

In addition to the sexual violence, women deal with being disbelieved, often by members of their own families, and are further victimized by the judicial system. Our society does not protect girls or women from sexual violence.

That *has* to change. After all, you are less likely to develop PTSD if you receive support following the trauma.

As is probably obvious by now, all of these diagnoses are not so separate, which is why you may recognize yourself in several of the disorders. If you have a phobia, for example, you likely also experience panic symptoms and maybe obsessive thinking as a result. Keep in mind your symptoms can change over time, so it's really important for your mental health provider to ask lots of questions in order to get an accurate picture of your current situation. Most important, pay attention to whichever symptoms are most disruptive in your life, regardless of the label or diagnosis you are given.

As we mentioned earlier in the chapter, we don't pay much attention to our diagnostic labels. We leave that for the insurance companies to wrangle with. Instead, we conceptualize our anxiety as on a continuum—ranging from mild to severe—that reflects how much our anxiety is affecting our daily lives. Are we letting our worlds shrink? If so, to what degree? And when we focus on managing our disorders, the individual symptoms and diagnoses hold less sway. In the end, no matter how our anxiety shows up in our bodies and minds, we are all facing the same challenges. None of us should go it alone.

five

How Did This Happen?

I have a hard time letting things go. If someone criticizes me or gives me a funny look, I go over and over it in my head, trying to figure it out. It drives my family crazy. They say I'm ridiculously sensitive. Why do I think that way? (Samira, age 38)

Because Anxiety Sisters are such gifted (over)thinkers, we spend a lot of time asking ourselves why we have anxiety. We love assigning blame—especially to ourselves—but the truth is, we are not anxious because we are weak or lazy (contrary to popular belief). Anxiety is not a character flaw: it is a disorder, not a decision.

Anxiety is not a character flaw

Anxiety is seldom caused by just one thing. Human behavior is very complex—even scientists don't fully understand it. That said, there are good reasons for knowing the reasons. It is human nature, particularly for anxiety sufferers, to want to make sense of the world. Which explains why the therapy business is booming. Also, addressing the root cause can often alleviate the symptoms. There's plenty of debate about what does cause anxiety. Here are the main culprits (in no particular order) that keep showing up in the literature:

Genetics

If one or both of your parents suffer from anxiety, you are statistically more likely to as well. What's difficult to determine is whether the inheritance of anxiety has more to do with genes or modeling (the way you are taught by your parents to handle anxiety).

> *Nervous stomachs run in our family. Both of my sisters, my brother, and my mother—we all feel everything in our stomachs. Whenever we have any kind of family crisis, we are all in the bathroom!* (April, age 24)

Recently, there have been several studies investigating the existence of an "anxiety gene." In 2015, researchers identified a gene that predisposes carriers to generalized anxiety disorder.[1] A review of studies in 2016 confirmed this and also suggested that both social anxiety and panic disorder have genetic components.[2] Particularly fascinating are the results of another 2015 study, at Weill Cornell Medicine, in which researchers discovered a gene variation, present in approximately 20 percent of the population, that decreases a certain fatty acid in the brain. The result of this reduction is an increase in available anandamide—one of our body's "bliss" chemicals. People with this gene variation are not only more relaxed but also less likely to hold on to prior negative thoughts and experiences.[3] Most recently, in January 2020, Yale researchers conducted a study with two hundred thousand military veterans and determined that there are six genetic variants linked specifically with anxiety.[4]

Rachel Yehuda, an epigeneticist at the Icahn School of Medicine at Mount Sinai, has conducted research using Holocaust survivors and their descendants that suggests trauma can be biologically passed down from generation to generation via genetic and hormonal changes.[5] Similar research is being conducted with African Americans who are descendants of slaves.[6] This new understanding of trauma and the possibilities for the treatment of anxiety disorders in general are cause for hope.

Brain Chemistry

As we discussed in chapter three, anxiety sufferers have trigger-happy amygdalae (part of the brain's limbic system) that cause us to perceive threats even where they don't exist. In addition, we have substances called neurotransmitters (e.g., serotonin, norepinephrine, dopamine) that are responsible for enabling our brains to send messages. When they don't do their jobs or there aren't enough of them, our message wires get crossed. This explains why our brains perceive great danger in relatively safe places (why you suddenly feel the need to escape from your office, the movie theater, your favorite restaurant, or your best friend's wedding).

Gender

Bad news, sisters. Once again, we're the lucky ones. It turns out that we're twice as likely as men to develop an anxiety disorder. Estrogen and progesterone, the female hormones, are most likely to blame for this disproportion (more on this later in the chapter), but there is also some evidence that the female brain doesn't process serotonin—one of the feel-good neurotransmitters—as efficiently as the male brain.[7]

Childhood Events

It is often deeply painful to come to terms with the effects of childhood events on our adult selves. Many people with anxiety have faced significant trauma during childhood (e.g., loss of a parent or significant person, bullying, high-conflict divorce, family dislocation, serious illness, sexual or emotional abuse, and so on). It seems so unfair that a rough childhood translates into increased risk for anxiety, depression, and a whole host of other illnesses in adulthood. However, as we learn more about the growth and structure of our brains and our emotional and cognitive development, the connection between adverse childhood experience(s) and anxiety becomes even clearer.

In chapter three, we mentioned that the brain isn't considered mature until we're around age twenty-five. When we experience trauma before our brains are fully developed, the impact can be lasting. Children exposed to trauma have been found to have changes in the size and thickness of various parts of their brains and alterations in their neurotransmitter systems, which in turn elevates their stress responses.

Of course, a traumatic childhood causes more than brain changes. We learn so much about how to navigate the world from watching and interacting with the people around us. Whether the world feels like a safe place is often determined by how we experienced it as a child. As social learners, we also tend to re-create and copy behaviors we became accustomed to as children, which explains why we so often repeat painful patterns. If you suffered a traumatic childhood, your anxiety is likely connected to that experience. But don't despair: the brain is elastic and can be rewired (through various habits, behaviors, and treatments) throughout the life span. We also want to note that some of the most creative and empathetic people we know come from traumatic backgrounds.

I was sexually abused as a child by a family member. Now I get awful panic attacks and have been diagnosed with agoraphobia. I have a hard time being more than five or ten minutes from home because I am afraid of having a panic attack and not being able to get home. I have been in therapy for a long time and know the root of my panic is the abuse, but knowing does not always help with the panic. (Emily, age 31)

I was bullied a lot as a child. Kids did really cruel things to me. But back when I was a kid, you just had to deal with it. Only as an adult did I realize how much it affected me. I have so much social anxiety and so many issues trusting other people. (Rochelle, age 48)

Medication

All drugs (yes, even aspirin) come with potential side effects. Certain medications, particularly steroids, decongestants, antihistamines, and stimulants, can cause anxiety, as can combinations of otherwise benign medications, including vitamins (such as high doses of B) and herbs (such as ginseng and Saint-John's-wort). Ask your doctor or your pharmacist if anything you are taking may be a contributor to your anxiety. Surprisingly, some common drugs prescribed to treat anxiety and depression may themselves cause anxiety. You'll read more about this in chapter eleven.

I had really bad tendinitis, so my doctor put me on prednisone for the inflammation. About a week after I stopped the prednisone, I suddenly felt really short of breath and dizzy. I went to the ER and they checked me out, said it was a panic attack. Apparently, anxiety is a common side effect of prednisone. (Beth, age 46)

Diseases and Medical Conditions

There are several diseases known to cause anxiety attacks, including hypertension and heart disease, thyroid issues, lupus, Lyme disease, and diabetes. This does not mean that you have any of these ailments—chances are you don't. But this is all the more reason to stay up-to-date with your regular medical check-ups in order to rule out other conditions.

Hormones

Hormones are your body's chemical cruise directors—their job is to coordinate key processes such as growth, reproduction, and metabolism. And as any woman who's ever experienced PMS can attest, hormones gone awry can wreak havoc. The primary hormones that can affect anxiety are (1) sex hormones (estrogen, progesterone, and testosterone), (2) stress hormones (cortisol, adrenaline, and norepinephrine), and (3) thyroid hormones. The interplay between sex hormones—particularly estrogen—and anxiety is very complex, but the widely accepted belief is that if your sex hormones are unbalanced or low, anxiety can result. Thus, it makes sense that at times in a woman's life when those hormones are in a state of flux (puberty, pregnancy, menopause), she is particularly susceptible to anxiety. In fact, for many middle-aged women, menopause can bring on never-before-experienced anxiety. Just another perk of female aging!

> *I never considered myself anxious until I started going through menopause. I went to see a gynecologist with a specialty in menopause-related issues. She told me that the anxiety was actually a result of hormonal changes, so she prescribed hormone replacement therapy (I wear an estrogen patch) and anxiety meds. (Fernanda, age 56)*

The relationship between stress hormones and anxiety is a direct one: the more cortisol and adrenaline surging through your body, the higher your anxiety level. Unfortunately, that relationship is also cyclical—each reinforces the other. This means that if you get anxious, your body naturally releases more stress hormones, which in turn elevate your anxiety level. The cycle can also start with an excess of stress hormones, which can be caused by inflammation, blood sugar issues, chronic stress, and some medications.

Before we go into the thyroid-anxiety connection, let's first discuss what the thyroid is and what it's supposed to be doing in your body. The thyroid is a butterfly-shaped gland located in your neck above the collarbone. Its job is to produce hormones that regulate lots of bodily functions, such as temperature, metabolism, and protein synthesis. Thus, the thyroid affects just about every organ in the body. It makes sense, then, that if your thyroid is malfunctioning, you will experience a systemic response.

One way the thyroid can malfunction is when it doesn't produce enough hormones to serve your body's systems. This is called hypothyroidism or, more commonly, underactive thyroid, which causes the body to slow down. Some of the typical symptoms of hypothyroidism include fatigue, weight gain, lowered libido, reduced cognitive functioning, and slowed reflexes. If you have suffered from anxiety or particularly depression, these symptoms may sound familiar. Another symptom of hypothyroidism is anxiety, which seems logical when you consider that one of the thyroid's duties is to regulate the neurotransmitters serotonin and norepinephrine—the brain's feel-good chemicals. If the thyroid is underperforming, those neurotransmitters will be less available to the brain, which is a direct cause of anxiety and depression.

> When I was finally diagnosed with hypothyroidism it explained so much. Not only about why I was so anxious but also why I was always exhausted and could not lose weight. I took Synthroid and in three days my anxiety all but vanished. I feel like a human being again. (Laura, age 29)

Another way the thyroid can malfunction is when it produces *too much* hormone—when it is overactive. This is called hyperthyroidism, which speeds up the body's systems. Symptoms include rapid heart rate, increased blood pressure, insomnia, shaking, and weight loss. Doesn't this sound like an anxiety attack? Indeed, having hyperthyroidism can feel like being in a constant state of panic. In fact, panic attacks are another symptom of the disorder.

A third way the thyroid can malfunction is called Hashimoto's thyroiditis, which is an autoimmune condition whereby the thyroid is attacked by your own body's immune system. The constant onslaught of antibodies causes the thyroid to break down and greatly inhibits its ability to function, which in turn brings about anxiety and depression for some of the same reasons as in hypothyroidism.

So here's what's tricky about thyroid disorders: they are frequently undiagnosed or mistaken for mental health issues, thus leading to improper treatment. According to the American Thyroid Association, approximately twenty million Americans suffer from thyroid disorders, a whopping 60 percent of whom may not even be aware of their condition. Given this information, it should not be a surprise that doctors often overlook the thyroid as a possible culprit in the development of anxiety disorders.

Because women are much more likely to suffer from thyroid dysfunction than men, and because the risk increases as we age, we encourage all Anxiety Sisters to be proactive. If you have anxiety, ask your doctor to order the thyroid panel (simple blood test) so you can see how well your thyroid is actually functioning. For many women, correcting thyroid hormone imbalances alleviates their anxiety completely, so it is worth checking out. One caveat: Make sure your doctor orders the whole panel (TSH, T3, and T4)—not just the TSH (thyroid-stimulating hormone) test. Abs frequently has a "normal" TSH level even though her thyroid is completely out of whack.

One more hormonal issue to cover: polycystic ovary syndrome (PCOS). PCOS is the most commonly diagnosed endocrine issue in women of childbearing age (fifteen to forty-four)—between 7 and 10 percent of women develop this condition, which is an imbalance of reproductive hormones (e.g., estrogen and progesterone).[8] Because of this imbalance, the ovaries do not function effectively, thereby creating irregular menstruation and fertility issues as well as the growth of cysts.

One of the principal symptoms of PCOS is the development of anxiety or depression. A January 2017 study found that women diagnosed with PCOS are three times as likely to report anxiety symptoms compared with women without PCOS. The numbers are similar for depression.[9] This strong correlation makes sense—not only do PCOS sufferers have hormonal imbalances (which are known causes of mood disorders), but they also have to deal with the stress of body image anxiety resulting from physical changes (such as weight gain and facial hair growth) that accompany PCOS. And while there are medications (hormones!) that are used in the treatment of PCOS, there is no easy fix for this condition.

> *When I was younger, nobody believed how painful my periods were. They thought I was making it up. I struggled a lot with depression and anxiety. Then, when I had trouble getting pregnant, I got diagnosed with PCOS, which explains why my periods were so awful and why I have so much anxiety.* (Tracy, age 36)

Pregnancy and New Parenthood

Hopefully, most new moms are aware of postpartum depression and are screened for it during postpartum visits to their ob-gyns. But an increasing focus is now on postpartum anxiety (PPA), which sometimes starts during pregnancy. About 6 percent of pregnant women and 10 percent of new moms are diagnosed with a pregnancy-related anxiety disorder.[10] Of course, many women probably go undiagnosed, so these numbers are likely to be much higher.

Let's face it, being a new mom is terrifying and exhausting. Most new moms are pretty worn out from childbirth and experiencing a roller coaster of hormones in extreme flux. (During pregnancy our progesterone and estrogen levels increase ten- to a hundredfold, and they fall to almost nothing right after delivery.) All of a sudden, we are responsible for a dependent human being. Anxiety is a normal and healthy response.

However, moms with PPA find that motherhood does not get less frightening as the weeks go by. For some, this means that hypervigilance becomes the norm (which makes it hard to sleep, think, or function). Moms with PPA may also develop postpartum panic attacks, which are pretty awful at any point in life. But put them on top of the demands of new motherhood and the situation can feel unbearable.

Sometimes new moms find themselves doing rituals to soothe their obsessional thoughts, which may point to postpartum obsessive-compulsive disorder. Not wanting to risk being labeled a danger to the baby, mothers often hesitate to share these thoughts. However, postpartum OCD is not associated with violence, and it is highly treatable, so let your doc know if you are experiencing obsessive thoughts or compulsions.

> *I don't think anxiety was really an issue for me until I got pregnant. I had a lousy first trimester, throwing up all the time and feeling exhausted. Then I stopped being able to sleep through the night. I didn't know it was anxiety at the time—I just was really short-tempered and every little thing bothered me. And then, after he was born, things got really, really bad. I constantly worried that the baby would stop breathing if I wasn't watching him all the time. I would check on him all night long, so I didn't sleep at all. Even when I took him in the car, I would have to pull over and check him every ten minutes if he wasn't making any noise. I was a complete wreck. I had heard of postpartum depression, but not this. (Angelina, age 33)*

Vitamin and Mineral Deficiencies

Vitamins (and minerals) are a significant factor when it comes to anxiety. In fact, the production of stress hormones, the ingestion of SSRIs (Prozac, Zoloft, etc.), and our favorite anxiety soothers (caffeine, sugar, alcohol) all actually *deplete* our stores of key vitamins and minerals. (Note: Lots of meds deplete vitamins—aspirin, Advil, antibiotics, antacids, and H2 blockers such as Zantac and Pepcid, just to name a few.) To add insult to injury, anxiety slows down digestion, thus inhibiting the absorption of vitamins and minerals we get from our diets. So if you are an anxiety sufferer, there's a good chance you're lacking in important vitamins and minerals that protect your brain, heart, and other crucial organs. In a nutshell (a great source of vitamin B and magnesium), here are the three most important vitamins and minerals for anxiety sufferers:

VITAMIN B

Vitamin B is the brain vitamin: it provides the body with energy (it's hard to feel good without energy) and, more important, helps the body create serotonin and norepinephrine (which antidepressants are designed to boost). While there are eight vitamins in the B complex, the ones to watch in terms of mood stabilization are B_6, B_9 (also known as folate), and B_{12}. If you are interested in raising your levels through diet, you can find B_6 (pyridoxine) in poultry, fish, organ meats, potatoes, starchy vegetables, and non-citrus fruits. B_9 (folate or folic acid) is abundant in green leafy vegetables, liver, yeast, black-eyed peas, lentils, asparagus, and brussels sprouts. B_{12} is found in all animal foods as well as in nori (seaweed). If you are a vegetarian or vegan, it is hard to get enough B_{12} without supplementation; even if you are a carnivore like us, you can be severely lacking in B, so hurry up and check it out. This is one situation that may actually have a quick fix.

VITAMIN C

Probably best known for boosting immunity, vitamin C is actually more important for fighting stress and anxiety, which it does in three ways: (1) it suppresses the production of the stress hormone cortisol, (2) it lowers blood pressure, and (3) it is required by the body to produce and synthesize serotonin and norepinephrine. Several studies have shown that people lacking in vitamin C are more likely to suffer from mood disorders like anxiety and depression and that people diagnosed with generalized anxiety disorder saw a substantial reduction in symptoms when they took vitamin C daily.[11] The best sources of vitamin C are citrus fruits, strawberries, pineapple, papaya, and kiwi. Peppers of all kinds (red, green, and yellow bell peppers, hot peppers), tomatoes, and cruciferous vegetables (broccoli, brussels sprouts, cauliflower, kale) also contain vitamin C, but you'd have to eat quite a lot of them to get the recommended daily allowance.

MAGNESIUM

The connection between magnesium and anxiety is so strong that researchers can induce anxiety in lab animals simply by depriving them of magnesium. This mineral stimulates the production of GABA, often referred to as "nature's valium"—a neurotransmitter that calms the brain when it is overstimulated, as is the case when it is experiencing a panic attack or having obsessive thoughts. Magnesium also suppresses the production of stress hormones and acts as a barrier to keep them from entering the brain. As a bonus, magnesium regulates blood sugar levels, which decreases anxiety often caused by sugar highs and lows.

In terms of dietary magnesium, there's good news and bad news. The good news is that you can find magnesium in lots of healthy stuff such as avocado, black beans, legumes, whole grains, spinach, nuts, seeds, and soy products. The bad news is that our soil has been largely depleted of magnesium, so foods don't contain as much as they once did. Also, more than two hundred drugs block the absorption of magnesium, so if you take any meds, you probably are lacking in the magnesium department.

There are other vitamins and minerals that when lacking are connected with brain disorders such as anxiety and depression. These include zinc, iron, calcium, vitamin D, and omega-3 fatty acids. But the big three—B, C, and magnesium—are the first ones you should investigate. Ask your doctor to prescribe the blood work, and discuss the results with him or her.

One more piece of advice: use pharmaceutical-grade supplements, if at all possible. There is a lot of variation in nutritional products, and with few exceptions, you get what you pay for. Here's our argument for using pharma-grade: (1) they are made with the highest-quality raw materials, (2) they have been purified to eliminate contaminants, and, most important, (3) they are formulated to optimize absorption.

Caffeine

Caffeine causes our bodies to release adrenaline and norepinephrine, the fight-or-flight chemicals that trigger the anxiety response: rapid heartbeat, shaki-ness, nausea, and so on. It's a stimulant, and we're already pretty stimulated. Caffeine can also cause sleep disturbance (particularly when ingested closer to bedtime), and we all know that lack of sleep worsens anxiety. That said, we find it too anxiety-provoking to contemplate giving up our morning coffee, so we could never recommend that to anyone else, even though many experts counsel people with anxiety disorders to eliminate or greatly reduce caffeine consumption.

If you are watching your intake, it is important to know that caffeine is hid-den in lots of strange places. So while one large cup of morning java may be fine, we need to take into account the caffeine we may unwittingly be getting throughout the day. Keep in mind that herbs such as echinacea and medica-tions such as decongestants, some pain relievers, and antihistamines interact with caffeine to intensify its effects. And caffeine can show up in your yogurt, granola, chocolate, or ice cream if it is coffee-flavored or labeled "energy."

When it comes to caffeine intake, there are no hard-and-fast rules. Each person has a very different body chemistry and has to find out what works for them. The recommended daily maximum intake of caffeine is 400 milligrams (four eight-ounce cups of home-brewed coffee or two large Dunkin' coffees). Some people, like Abs, find that they can have only about half that amount before anxiety symptoms set in. Others can comfortably have more. You are the expert on your own body. If you suspect that caffeine may be causing (or exacerbating) your anxiety, you may want to experiment with reducing your intake. One solution is to have caffeinated coffee in the morning and decaf later in the day.

Alcohol

So sorry, sisters, but the news here is not good. Alcohol's effect on the brain is to alter the levels of our feel-good neurotransmitters (serotonin and norepinephrine) so that they become unbalanced, resulting in—you guessed it—anxiety. *But my wine relaxes me,* you might be thinking. *I feel better after a few drinks.* This makes sense, as alcohol is a depressant and thus has a sedating effect, but the initial calm and buzzy feeling you get after consuming a serving of alcohol will eventually wear off; when it does, you may feel more anxious than you did before you drank. Excessive drinking causes dehydration and low blood sugar (more on this next), both of which exacerbate anxiety. We are not telling you to become a teetotaler. Just pay attention to how you feel a few hours after you drink to see if your anxiety levels are affected. And as always, seek out help if you think you have a problem.

Sugar

Confession: we cried when we wrote this part. Which tells you that sugar and anxiety are not a winning combo. Like alcohol, sugar can be soothing at first but anxiety-provoking later. And unbalanced blood sugar makes the body work so hard to release insulin and get everything back to normal that we feel shaky, irritable, and jittery. Not a welcome constellation for anxiety sufferers. For panic sufferers, blood sugar spikes can actually bring on an anxiety attack. And yet we can't seem to put down the Chunky Monkey. Sigh.

Depression

When we think about anxiety, we often imagine our bodies "freaking out" and "revving up." Depression, on the other hand, causes us to feel "flat" and sapped of energy—sometimes unable to get out of bed. So it's tempting to assume these disorders are opposites. While these characterizations may be broadly true, many of us are both freaking out *and* stuck in bed. We are really the Anxiety and Depression Sisters (not as catchy, we know), because the two disorders are so closely related.

According to a study in the *Archives of General Psychiatry*, depression often precedes anxiety. In that same study, almost 50 percent of those with ongoing depression also experienced ongoing anxiety.[12] A similar or higher incidence of overlap has been reported in much of the literature: if you have experienced clinical depression, you have an 85 percent chance of developing generalized anxiety disorder (GAD), and a 35 percent chance of developing panic disorder.[13] This association means that if you have been or are depressed, buckle your seatbelt because anxiety may well be around the corner. For those who develop anxiety disorder first, there is a slightly lower correlation but the association is still strong. Fighting anxiety all the time is exhausting, and the ensuing hopelessness can certainly feel depressing.

What we know is that these disorders are located in the same areas of the brain, with many of the same hormonal and chemical reactions and nerve responses, and they are often treated with the same drugs. In other words, whether a person has an anxiety disorder or depression can sometimes be a matter of very subtle differences in symptoms, and many people have what is called co-occurring disorders (both at the same time). In fact, there has been a push to come up with a mixed anxiety/depression disorder in the latest *Diagnostic and Statistical Manual of Mental Disorders* (*DSM*), which is the handbook of psychiatric diagnoses that all clinicians use. For technical reasons, a new co-diagnosis has not been adopted here in the United States, although they do use it in Europe.

> *I have battled depression on and off since childhood, though lately I have been much more anxious. Some days I have the more typical depressed feelings like crying, but other days are more anxious and irritable. I guess they go together. (Alena, age 19)*

Grief

It is very common to develop an anxiety disorder (or to have a preexisting one intensify) after a death or loss. You may have heard of Elisabeth Kübler-Ross, a psychiatrist who came up with what is now known as the five phases of grieving: (1) denial, (2) anger, (3) bargaining, (4) depression, (5) integration/acceptance. Although we know these phases are not the same for everyone (nor do they always happen in this order), they definitely give us a framework with which to make sense of the most common feelings associated with loss. In our experience, confirmed by many grief counselors, anxiety is a glaring omission from Kübler-Ross's taxonomy. To us, it is pretty obvious where anxiety fits into this framework: it may be part of each of the phases and often becomes its own.

We live in a culture that often tries to pretend death is avoidable and therefore pushes it out of mainstream conversation. We try not to think about it and act like youth and immortality are something we can hold on to forever (if we just buy the right products). The death of someone close to us forces us to confront our own mortality, which again prompts our fear response: *Am I next?*

Our culture also shortchanges us when it comes to the grieving process. Bereavement leave, when offered at all, is often just a few days; we are expected to be "over" our loss and ready to get back to work by week's end. Our grief vocabulary is lacking, to say the least, and we receive little guidance on how to process loss. Often, bereaved Anxiety Sisters tell us that people are afraid to even mention the names of their lost loved ones, which not only isolates them further in their grief but also provokes tremendous anxiety.

Likewise, there is no place in our society for grief when the loss is not someone in our immediate family. If we lose a close friend, a beloved aunt, or another important person in our life, we aren't even granted time off to deal with the grief. The "rules" around for whom we should grieve and for how long are very limiting and therefore invalidate meaningful relationships and connections. Often, in these instances, we are forced to hide our feelings, which creates even more anxiety.

> *I've lived alone since my husband left, so Elsa was my constant companion for the last twelve years. When she died, I felt like my world was ending. I was so devastated, I could barely function. I called in sick to work for a whole week because I knew I couldn't tell them the real reason—nobody makes room for grief over a pet.* (Kai, age 63)

> *I lost my brother a year ago and he was my best friend. It is the worst thing I have ever been through. I understand the sadness, but I am also so anxious that I feel like I could jump out of my skin. Some days the anxiety is just unbearable.* (Nina, age 44)

Interestingly, Eastern cultures, which incorporate death and grieving into their lives much more organically, have little experience of anxiety surrounding loss. This is not to say they do not experience profound sadness and grief—only that anxiety and the fear response are generally absent.

PTSD (Post-Traumatic Stress Disorder)

Many Anxiety Sisters with PTSD experience anxiety, particularly panic. In fact, one of the primary symptoms of PTSD is some form of anxiety. In popular culture, PTSD is associated with veterans returning from war; however, it can be caused by a single traumatic event (violence, rape, loss, accident, natural or man-made disaster, etc.) or ongoing trauma (war, prolonged abuse, illness, etc.) over a long period of time. Many people who have been abused physically, sexually, or emotionally may also develop PTSD. Complex PTSD, also a cause of anxiety, is often diagnosed when sufferers have dealt with trauma over a long period of time rather than a more isolated event.

In his fascinating book *The Body Keeps the Score*, Bessel van der Kolk explores how the trauma associated with PTSD not only changes our brain's wiring but also manifests in bodily symptoms and sensations. Anxiety sufferers with PTSD may try to put aside or "get over" traumatic experiences, but they often find that their bodies remember what their minds would like to forget.

> *My neighborhood burned down in the Paradise fires. We were lucky enough to get out in time, but we lost our house. I never had panic attacks before, but boy do I get them now. (Nancy, age 61)*

> *I was in an abusive marriage for a long time. Now, even several years later, my whole body gets stiff and my heart races when a man touches me. I mean, even when a guy goes to shake my hand, I become really anxious. (Tiffany, age 42)*

Stress

We're not talking about your garden-variety life challenges here. We mean chronic, intense, overwhelming stress—like that brought on by divorce, illness, death, or a really demanding job (shout-out to the Newark air traffic controllers). We live in what many authors have dubbed "the age of anxiety"—one in which our safety, economic security, and environmental stability are constantly threatened. Soaring health care costs, joblessness, and mass shootings are our reality. It's no wonder that so many of us struggle with anxiety—our world breeds it.

> *I'm going through a very difficult divorce and it's starting to affect me physically. I can't sleep, which makes me exhausted and incredibly anxious. Even small decisions overwhelm me. And now I get headaches.*
> (*Julie, age 57*)

Societal Expectations

This is a different kind of stress, but it's mentioned enough by Anxiety Sisters that we decided to include it. For most of us, from the time we hit puberty (and sometimes before), we are, thanks to the media and often the people closest to us, acutely aware of our bodies and how they differ from the "ideal female specimen." Although men deal with their own societal pressures, it is the female body that is co-opted for public consumption. In this sense, we are always under scrutiny. This constant judgment leads many women to feel uncomfortable in their own skins (or certainly their bathing suits). Add to this the professional and caregiving responsibilities that surround us and you have a perfect storm of unrealistic expectations, which we have become convinced are not just realistic, but required. Perhaps this explains why so many women feel a sense of shame surrounding their anxiety—society just doesn't allow us to buckle under the enormous weight of its demands.

Systemic Racism

In her extraordinary book *Caste: The Origins of Our Discontents*, Pulitzer Prize winner Isabel Wilkerson explains how the term "racism" does not adequately capture the structure of oppression that this country was built on and still has in place to this day. "Racism" implies a personal preference or prejudice. "Casteism," however, reveals the bigger picture—the way all systems and institutions in the United States are based on a hierarchy that determines who gets resources, privileges, status, and even basic human kindness. There is plentiful evidence that the system is rigged against Black people, who occupy the bottom rung of our caste system in this country. And while, as white women, we are in no way experts on this topic, as anxiety experts we understand how systemic oppression causes anxiety, depression, and other health issues.

Compounding the situation is the rightful distrust that some members of the African American community feel toward our health care system, which neglects their needs and is often culturally insensitive. Of further consequence is the lack of access to high-quality health care in general and mental health care in particular that is experienced by most Black people.

I am a physician and live in Boston. But I still get followed in stores. When I walk into a room at the hospital, people still express surprise that I am the doctor. I constantly deal with these assumptions about who I am and how capable I am. I always have to prove myself. It's exhausting. (Deja, age 56)

I am in a program to become a therapist. I am one of two Black people in my class and most of the other participants are white. This worries me because the African American community has a mental health crisis. We need therapists who personally understand the unique needs and concerns of our community. We need professionals that look like us and experience what we experience in our daily lives. (Kiara, age 29)

As a Black woman, I am always in fight-or-flight mode. It astounds me when people ask why I'm anxious. (Michele, age 51)

Discrimination

Being part of a marginalized community is anxiety-provoking for obvious reasons. Members of the LGBTQ community have the highest suicide rates, in part because of the discrimination they experience not only within our culture but also within their own families. Immigrant communities, certain ethnic and religious groups, people with disabilities, and so many others face enormous challenges in their everyday lives, and even greater difficulty gaining access to quality mental health care. We need to do better. Now.

> When I was in college, I was beaten severely because I'm openly gay. You wouldn't think it could happen in an Ivy League school, but it did and it does. This incident was almost ten years ago, but I still have nightmares about it. I won't walk alone at night. I think I have PTSD. (Frankie, age 27)

> After 9/11, I decided not to wear my head covering outside anymore. Being Muslim and Pakistani is an unsafe combination right now. (Safah, age 36)

> I am deaf and use sign language to communicate. When I was training to become a therapist I had a sign language interpreter with me most of the time. One day a classmate and I were assigned to do a project together, and instead of asking me when I would be available to work, she asked my sign language interpreter when I was free. He had to remind her that he was not answering for me—that he was just interpreting the conversation. This kind of thing happens all the time. People talk to my interpreter as if I am not there. It is incredibly frustrating to be treated like a young child whose parent has to answer questions. (Samantha, age 44)

Anxiety

It seems really chicken-and-egg, but a major cause of anxiety is, well, anxiety. During the anxiety response, your neural pathways are altered; in other words, you get rewired for anxiety. So the more anxiety attacks you have, the more your brain gets "trained" to reproduce them. It's like muscle memory: the more you practice, the better you get.

> When I started to have panic attacks, my whole body chemistry changed. Even when I'm not having an attack, I am always hot and flushed, where before I was often the one wearing heavy sweaters. My body feels hypervigilant. I can't relax it. It's like I'm always ready for battle. (Marta, age 30)

Remember, anxiety can and often does have multiple causes, which may even interact with one another. Like we said, causation is complicated. It's a little like trying to figure out which ant bit you when you were standing on an anthill.

Lastly, we would be remiss if we didn't mention a few things that, although absent from the clinical literature, *absolutely* cause anxiety, including:

- Having one or more teenagers living with you
- Having in-laws (not necessarily living with you)
- Bathing suit shopping
- Tenting for termites (or any other extreme pest-control measures)
- All forms of hair removal
- Spanx
- Living through a pandemic

SIX

The Fallout

We called this chapter "The Fallout" because the effects of unmanaged anxiety are so disastrous and far-reaching. Remember in chapter one we said that having agency (making your own decisions) and connection are prerequisites for happiness? Well, it's awfully hard to have those things when your anxiety is out of control.

> *I hate that my life is no longer my own. There are so many places I won't go, so many things I won't do. It doesn't even feel like a choice.*
> (*Lola, age 65*)

When your anxiety is in charge, you may not even realize how much you are giving up—it's often a slow, sneaky process. For that reason, we are going to spend some time talking about the damage anxiety can inflict.

When your anxiety is in charge, you may not even realize how much you are giving up—it's often a slow, sneaky process

Shame

When our anxiety is making our choices for us, we feel ashamed and power-less. Add to that the judgment of the people around us and we've got what au-thor Brené Brown calls a "shame shitstorm."

Despite anxiety's biological underpinnings and genetic links, our culture still views it as a sign of personal weakness or failure. Most Anxiety Sisters have had the experience of someone saying to them, "Just relax." Those words are themselves quite shaming. They suggest that your anxiety disorder is some-thing you have chosen and could wave away if you were so inclined.

The stigma surrounding mental health issues, although markedly less than it was even twenty years ago, is still pretty robust in our culture. Since the be-ginning of history, people with mental illness have experienced prejudice and unfair treatment. In the Middle Ages, mental illness was thought to be a curse from God; sufferers were greatly feared and even burned at the stake. Through the years, the mentally ill were ostracized for being possessed by the devil and were treated like criminals. Often, they were tortured, imprisoned, and exiled. Many were killed. To this day, there is still a lot of fear and misinformation around the topic of mental health, the legacy of which is stigma and shame.

The medical establishment certainly hasn't helped eradicate the stigma. Ac-cording to Dr. Jerome Groopman, professor of medicine at Harvard Medical School and bestselling author of *How Doctors Think*, physicians often question the validity of symptoms that originate in the mind. In fact, patients with psychiatric complaints are frequently dismissed as neurotic or even delusional. Groopman goes on to report research that shows that internists, gynecologists, and surgeons are especially prone to shrug off patients with psychological disorders.

> At my first checkup [after the baby was born], I told my ob-gyn about
> my anxiety. I told him about the panic attacks and the lack of sleep
> making it so much worse. He kind of shrugged and said it's normal to

feel "hormonal" and that the good news was I was cleared to have sex.
(Jasmine, age 31)

The shame is so powerful and pervasive that many sufferers won't admit to having anxiety, much less taking medication to manage it. One person even puts her Celexa in a Tylenol bottle so that nobody will discover her "secret." The notion that one should be able to muscle through a legitimate illness is utterly ridiculous. That antiquated way of thinking serves only to exacerbate the suffering.

Hypersensitivity

Many Anxiety Sisters, including us, have been told, "Get out of your head." That's like telling the Pope to get out of the Vatican. He can't—it's where he lives. And anxiety sufferers live in our heads. Studies have shown that people who suffer from anxiety are more self-preoccupied than people without anxiety.[1] Which means they spend significantly more time pondering their feelings than most. Our response: What was your first clue, Sherlock?

The result of all this introspection is a focus not only on feelings but also on physical sensations. Every single physical sensation. One anxiety sufferer we know can feel her digestive process, from the moment she swallows her food all the way through both intestines and out the other side. This awareness of every heartbeat, every tingling, every unusual pain leads to a hypervigilant state in which we are constantly asking, "Is this normal? Am I okay?" And all this hypervigilance is time- and energy-consuming to the point of exhaustion.

From time to time, my legs get shaky and I start to feel hot and cold—like I have a fever. Even though I don't. I keep thinking—no, believing—that I am having the first symptoms of COVID. Rationally, I know this is just my anxiety making me feel this way. (Ellie, age 58)

Depression

We mentioned depression as a cause of anxiety in chapter five, but it also belongs in this list of the fallout we experience from anxiety. Here's why: When you suffer from anxiety, you feel crappy. You often don't want to even get out of bed, and certainly not out of your home. Your energy is sapped; you may experience insomnia, appetite changes, and, of course, a feeling of hopelessness and despair. In other words, you display many of the symptoms of depression. Which comes first is largely a chicken-and-egg debate, but the literature in general supports a strong association between anxiety and depression. Interestingly, Europe recognizes the intertwined nature of anxiety and depression by having a diagnosis of mixed anxiety and depression (MADD), because so many anxiety sufferers experience depression and vice versa.

Motivation and Performance

Two psychologists named Yerkes and Dodson came up with a law expressing the relationship between arousal and performance:[2]

The following graph illustrates that some arousal is needed to have the motivation to complete a given task—indeed, if we had no anxiety at all, we'd spend all our time napping (no judgment—been there, done that). There is an optimal level of arousal, which varies individually, during which we perform the best and feel the sharpest. When there is just enough pressure to motivate you, but not so much that it paralyzes you. Say you are running a race. You need enough anxiety to get the adrenaline going so you want to start moving quickly, but not so much that you hyperventilate.

In chapter three we referred to the amygdala hijack, which is when you are so anxious that your limbic (emotional) system takes over and your cognitive abilities are stymied. But, as we've been saying, you need *some* anxiety to fuel

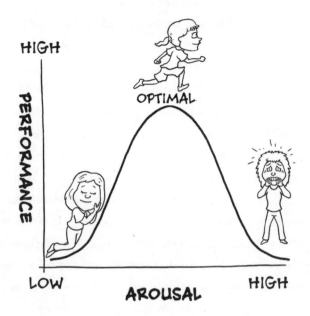

motivation. So it's important to figure out what your optimal level of arousal/anxiety is, because if you exceed that threshold, you become too overwhelmed with stress to perform well. For many of us Anxiety Sisters, any arousal sends our brains right into fight, flight, or freeze mode, so untreated anxiety absolutely leads to reduced motivation and poorer performance.

Shrinking World Syndrome

According to the *American Journal of Psychiatry*, Americans lose 321 million days of work annually because of anxiety and depression. An earlier report from the US Bureau of Labor Statistics suggested that individual Americans who suffer from anxiety disorders miss approximately twenty-five days of work per year. That's five workweeks. From looking at our own track records, this seems right on target. Absenteeism, however, doesn't tell the whole story—missed opportunities and diminished confidence to move forward professionally are the long-term effects of living with unmanaged anxiety.

Another effect we can attest to is the toll anxiety takes on relationships. We can no longer count the number of weddings, baby showers, parties, graduations, holiday celebrations, and even a few funerals we have had to skip because of anxiety. Needless to say, we pissed a lot of people off. Many other sufferers have shared their stories of how anxiety impacted (and sometimes destroyed) their relationships.

Missing work and dealing with relationship struggles are part of what we feel is the most challenging consequence of unmanaged anxiety: "shrinking world syndrome." In a nutshell, SWS occurs when you eliminate activities from your life because you believe they may provoke anxiety. It starts quietly—you stop going to the mall or maybe to certain restaurants. Then you find yourself not wanting to go on a trip. Before you know it, you are reluctant to go anywhere. It feels like your world has gotten so small—like you can take only a few steps that are safe before you plunge into icy unknown waters.

It started with a panic attack at the movies—suddenly I couldn't breathe and my heart was racing. The walls were closing in on me, so I just left

right in the middle. The next week, my boyfriend wanted to go see an-
other movie. I got panicky just thinking about it. So I avoided the mov-
ies. When I got that claustrophobic feeling at a party, I stopped going to
crowded places altogether. (Marisa, age 35)

SWS sufferers don't retreat only from the places they feel anxious; they avoid places they *think* might make them anxious. This very quickly casts a pretty wide net. As more and more places become off-limits, home becomes the one place that feels safe. The danger in retreat is that you believe everything will be okay if you can just get home. As a result, you spend much of your time either trying to get home or trying not to leave home. What we are talking about here is not just a geographical shrinking but an emotional one as well. You convince yourself that you simply cannot handle being out in the world, and you prove it to yourself when you stay isolated at home.

I was heading to a friend's wedding feeling nauseated and achy. As we
were driving, I remember feeling worse and worse. Finally, after about
two hours, we made a pit stop. At that point, I felt too sick to continue on
the drive, and we decided to head home. As soon as we made the U-turn,
I started to feel better. After about an hour, I was fine. (Kyla, age 32)

Like Kyla, many Anxiety Sisters have told us about this U-turn phenomenon. Even though you may feel a sense of relief when you make that U-turn (and we have made so many of them), you are actually strengthening your anxiety response. (Damn those neural pathways!) We are not suggesting that you never go home and dive into bed after an anxiety episode. (We're not hypocrites.) Sometimes that is all you can do. However, if you're doing the U-turn on a regular basis, it's time to get some help. Most anxiety sufferers with SWS need medication, the expertise of a mental health professional, or both. (We needed both.)

You may be thinking that SWS is pretty extreme, but you don't have to be agoraphobic to suffer from this syndrome. Like many things, it's on a continuum.

On one side there are folks who never leave their homes. At the other end of the spectrum (where many Anxiety Sisters we've talked to seem to be), SWS sufferers are a lot more functional, but they feel safe only at home. So don't assume you are free of SWS just because you go to work and run errands. The real issue is whether you or your anxiety determines how far from home you'll go.

Ask yourself this question: Have you stopped letting yourself do (or even think about) things that take you out of your geographic comfort zone because you are worried you'll feel anxious? If the answer is yes, or if you can't think about it right now because you are so focused on getting home, then you probably have SWS.

> When I was in peak anxiety mode, I stopped traveling anywhere farther than a couple of hours from home. I convinced myself I didn't want to go away, and I believed it until a friend gave me a book of travel essays. I wouldn't even look at the book because I felt so bad about how small I had let my world get. (Judy, age 55)

One more thing about shrinking world syndrome: as lousy as it can be for the person who has it, SWS doesn't just affect the anxiety sufferer. Obviously, others are impacted by your shrinking world as well. One Anxiety Sister we know will not get on an airplane, even if it means she is forever limited to wherever she can drive. She may have accepted the loss of weekend getaways and traveling opportunities, but her children—who also must miss family events because of distance—don't get a choice. Her anxiety shrunk not only her world but also her kids' worlds.

> My sisters and I always used to get together at the lake in the summer for a long weekend. We did it for years until I stopped driving on highways. Now it's been a few years since I've gone. It was awful that first year, but I'm kind of okay with it now. It's just not something I can do. But my kids really miss seeing their cousins. (Nadia, age 53)

Agoraphobia

Perhaps the most extreme form of SWS is agoraphobia, which is the fear of having a panic attack in a public place and not being able to get help or get to a "safe zone." It's not about being afraid to leave the house—it's the fear of dealing with our phobias, panic, or physical illness when we do. Mags's agoraphobia stemmed from her worry that her panic attacks would cause her to pass out or vomit (or both) on the subway. She didn't need to stay home as much as she needed to avoid the subway and a long list of places that might make her feel trapped.

In all but the most severe cases, people with agoraphobia do leave home—as long as they are in a safe zone, where they feel relatively comfortable. For some, this means they will go anywhere in their own town but will be too fearful to venture farther away. For others, the safe zone can be even wider (or smaller).

Many people with agoraphobia dislike being alone and are quite dependent on friends or family members, especially when venturing out of their safe zones. In fact, agoraphobics often have trouble going places alone because they are scared that if something happens to them, nobody will be there to help them. When agoraphobics withdraw from loved ones, it may be because they feel that they are a burden to family and friends, which can cause profound loneliness and bouts of isolation.

We are not doctors, and we would never feel comfortable diagnosing anyone; however, experts say that people with agoraphobia tend to avoid at least two of the following for at least six months:

- Trains, buses, and planes (public transport)
- Open spaces like malls and parking lots
- Enclosed spaces like movie theaters, smaller stores, restaurants, and meeting rooms
- Waiting in lines or being in crowds
- Leaving home alone

Although most sufferers start to experience agoraphobia in their twenties, people of any age can become agoraphobic. As is true of anxiety disorders in general, women are twice as likely to become agoraphobic as men. Also, feel free to blame it on your parents: in about 60 percent of cases, agoraphobia has a genetic component.[3]

> *I haven't left my house—other than to go to the corner market or to the doctor—in three years. It just got too hard to do it. I used to get dressed, eat breakfast, get ready for the day. But when I got to the front door, I felt like I was going to throw up. Sometimes I pushed through it, forced myself to go out. But I felt so dizzy and sick I couldn't do it anymore.*
> *(Jan, age 66)*

Anxiety Contagion

Another consequence of anxiety is that, like the coronavirus we were dealing with at the time of this writing, it is very contagious. Human beings are, as we've said before, social animals with a pretty strong herd instinct (a nice way of saying we often behave like sheep). When Abs was a college professor, one of her favorite exercises to do with her Group Dynamics seminar was to take her students to an outdoor mall for a little experiment. When they arrived, she would ask the students to look up at the sky as if something spectacular were happening there (i.e., lots of pointing and gaping) while she observed from across the street. It took all of thirty seconds for swarms of people to join her students in their sky watch. After a few minutes, she would call the students away from the ever-enlarging crowd, who not only were looking at the sky but also were pointing and gaping, thus proving the point that shoppers, if not all humans, tend to mimic one another's behaviors without question. Like sheep. Or lemurs (for those of you who watch Animal Planet).

I never had anxiety until I moved in with my roommate, who has panic attacks. After living with her for two years, I started having panic attacks too. I guess your period isn't the only thing that gets in sync when you live with someone! (Alex, age 22)

Similarly, anxiety is transmittable. Your anxiety is contagious, particularly to the people most likely to imitate your behaviors—those closest to you in proximity (your spouse, your partner, your kids, your coworkers, etc.). This means your mini-me will try on not only your shoes but also your anxiety for size.

Anxiety contagion can explain why we don't always get the reaction we want from those around us. While some people simply cannot relate to the experience, others become very threatened (often subconsciously) by it. Our experience is that many people try to distance themselves from a loved one's anxiety because on some level it triggers their own anxiety—whether or not they admit it (there are lots of anxiety deniers out there).

My husband and I were on a small plane during a storm. It was very bumpy, and I started to panic. I might have been making a bit of noise—somewhere between a moan and a yelp. Instead of trying to calm me, he told me to be quiet because I was "infecting the entire plane." (Lori, age 44)

Before we put Lori's husband in the ejection seat, we need to look at what may have motivated his insensitive (but true) remark. Most likely, he was feeling pretty nervous himself, and Lori's audible expression of fear confirmed his own. His snarky remark served as a buffer that allowed him to contain his own anxiety.

Fran, an Anxiety Sister in her sixties, told us about her life partner, Lynne, who completely shuts down whenever Fran has a panic attack. "I'm losing it," she told us, "and she acts as if nothing is going on." Fran and Lynne came to us for advice because this was causing a great deal of tension in their relationship. After getting to know the couple a bit, we were able to help Fran see that Lynne felt so overwhelmed by her panic that ignoring it was all she could do to keep herself together. Lynne told us if she had been more responsive, she would have been sucked into the panic herself.

Just as your anxiety is contagious, so is everyone else's. Particularly if you are living with another anxiety sufferer, it can be very difficult to keep it from "going viral." We know this is much easier said than done, but it is important to follow the advice offered by the airlines: "Place the oxygen mask over your own nose and mouth before you attempt to help others." In other words, take care of your needs first. Sometimes we can't be the ones to listen to and reassure a spouse or even a child. We might need a therapist to help us figure out containment strategies.

> *My daughter can talk to me about her anxiety for twenty minutes a day. Often we spend the time writing down the things she is anxious about (which can be anything from homework to the possibility of me dying). We talk about the specific worries and put them in a worry jar. She can, on her own, add to the worry jar, but I'm only involved for the twenty minutes. This not only helps her to move on, but it keeps me sane. Our anxieties tend to merge and grow—feeding off each other. By limiting the time we spend talking about it, it reminds us both that we do not want it to overtake us. (Tina, age 46)*

If you are suffering from SWS or any of the other consequences of unmanaged anxiety, you're carrying a heavy weight around with you, and chances are you're not connecting as much with others as you might like. We aren't blaming you—this is not your fault. Still, it's a problem that needs attending to, and we have some solutions we hope you'll try. One is called riding the wave. Read on to see how it works.

seven

Riding the Wave

et's go to the beach. It's a private beach—one where you don't have to shave your legs or be seen in a bathing suit. (We're trying to tame anxiety.) It's a blustery day and there is a sign posted that reads BEWARE OF RIPTIDES. For those of you not from the coast, riptides are strong, narrow currents that move away from the shore so that anything (or anyone) that gets caught in them is dragged out to sea. Riptides are notoriously dangerous for swimmers because when you find yourself swept into one, your instinct will be to try to swim back to shore against the current. This is a big mistake. No matter how strong you are, the current is going to be stronger. Fighting against it will only deplete your energy and pull you farther away from shore. Not even Michael Phelps can outmatch a powerful riptide.

So what do you do if you are caught in one of these currents? As counterintuitive as it sounds, you want to swim parallel to shore. If you try to swim directly toward the beach, you will be challenging the rip current, and you will not win. If you don't fight the riptide, it will eventually release you and allow you to swim back to the beach.

We use this riptide analogy to illustrate our philosophy of anxiety management. Anxiety—especially acute anxiety—is a lot like a rip current in that it completely overtakes you and your first instinct is to struggle against it. Which makes a whole lot of sense considering that anxiety makes you feel like you might die, so you wil¹ do absolutely anything to stop it. As is the case with riptides, however, fighting against your anxiety will only serve to exhaust you. Truth be told, anxiety seems to get stronger the more you fight against it because, as Deepak Chopra points out, what you pay attention to grows. If you are laser-focused on your anxiety symptoms and trying to stop them, you will become even more aware of them.

So how do you manage your anxiety if you can't fight it? Just as the experts recommend with riptides, you swim with it until it releases you. Which it will. It doesn't seem like it during the throes, but it always eventually lets you go. We call this strategy "riding the wave."

Riding the wave means your goal is to make yourself as comfortable as possible while you are getting through your anxiety, as opposed to desperately trying to make the anxiety go away. Riding the wave also means recognizing that your anxiety is not going to last forever—that it will let you go. It means understanding that you cannot, through willpower or personal strength, defeat your anxiety. You have to learn to swim with it.

At one time, I used to try to stop my anxiety attacks and found that they only became more entrenched. I realized I couldn't stop the dizziness and nausea (by trying, I would only make it worse), but I could go for a walk and talk myself through it. Saying "I am okay" over and over did make a difference. (Mags, age 52)

So what exactly does "swim with it" entail? We have a three-step approach to riding the wave—which, by the way, is how you begin your journey to anxiously happy:

1. EXPECT
2. ACCEPT
3. BE KIND

Expect

Expecting means saying to yourself, *Of course I'm going to experience anxiety—I am an Anxiety Sister!* It's normalizing the experience of anxiety because, let's be honest, anxiety *is* a normal experience for anxiety sufferers. If you expect anxiety, it can't sneak up on you, which is a lot of its power. If you expect anxiety to be a part of your life, you take away its shock value. As an added bonus, you won't waste all that energy wondering, *What is going on? Why is this happening?* You will know because you expect it.

Once I realized that I was going to get panic attacks, they were a lot less scary and intense. I benefited so much from realizing that so many people were experiencing all of the same symptoms. It helped me to remember that this was just anxiety and it was normal. (Cynthia, age 62)

Another component of expecting is figuring out *ahead of time* things to do to help you get through the episode. Yes, we believe in planning for panic. One great tool to help you plan for your anxiety is what we call a Spin Kit, which is, very simply, a portable first aid kit for your brain. There are three types of soothers in a Spin Kit: (1) grounding tools, (2) distracters, and (3) symptom relief.

When in the grip of anxiety, many folks report feeling overwhelmed and disoriented—some even float (which is our term for dissociate). Grounding tools typically engage the senses in order to reorient you so that your feet are firmly planted on the ground. Examples of grounding tools include things with a strong smell or taste (e.g., peppermints, eucalyptus oil, cinnamon gum), things to engage your tactile senses (e.g., soft fabric, beads, worry stones), music or soothing sounds, and visual soothers such as photos of loved ones (including pets), serene scenes in nature, or art you enjoy.

Distracters are exactly what they sound like—a way to keep you occupied so that you don't try to fight your anxiety. Some of our favorites in this category include coloring, needlework, audiobooks, and blowing bubbles. Really any activity that's portable will do.

> When I'm feeling really anxious, I find the most helpful thing to be this kaleidoscope my grandson made for me. I get lost in all the colors and shapes. (Harriet, age 74)

> I have knitted away my anxieties since I was eight years old, billions of stitches. (Eileen, age 92)

> I keep some meditation playlists on my phone. Seems to always help when I get that "spinny" feeling. (Darcy, age 38)

The idea behind symptom relievers is to make you more physically comfortable while you ride the wave of your anxiety. Examples can include pain relievers, sedatives, fans, cool compresses, and the like.

I never go anywhere without my ginger tea. It calms my stomach right down whenever I'm upset, and the warmth is very soothing.
(Wendy, age 47)

Because everyone is soothed and distracted by different things, each person's Spin Kit will be unique. For example, here are a few items from Abs's Spin Kit:

• Lavender-infused eye pillow
• Cooling towel
• Picture of her cats (Phoebe and Quincy)
• Douglas the Chicken (stuffed animal with very soft fur)

While the photo of her pets soothes Abs tremendously, they might actually cause Mags to panic. As such, her Spin Kit is different:

• Gas-X
• Crochet
• Lemon drops
• Essential oils

You can keep your Spin Kits in a cosmetic bag (those Ipsy glam bags work great), a box, or even a Ziploc. As long as you can take it wherever you go, any container will do.

Another technique to help you ride the wave is "bookending," which involves creating a positive activity on either end of a potentially triggering event. In other words, planning for your anxiety. For example, if you know that going to the doctor will cause you to feel panicky, you might bookend the visit with something more pleasant. It's kind of like getting a lollipop at the end of the doctor's visit—a reward for having survived the challenge. But perhaps even more important, bookending also involves a "lollipop" before the appointment even occurs. We think this is the more important bookend because if you don't have one in place, your dread can really overcome you and may even cause you to cancel the appointment altogether. (No judgment—been there, done that.) Coming up with rewards for surviving the doctor's appointment or whatever event is triggering your anxiety is a piece of cake (literally). If sweets aren't your thing, perhaps a pedicure, diving into a Netflix show, or window-shopping will do the trick. The pre-bookend might be talking to a supportive friend, a calming meditation, or a soothing music listening session.

Bookending is a way of managing something called anticipatory anxiety, which occurs prior to a triggering situation.

> *About a week or ten days before going on a plane, I find myself having trouble sleeping and feeling really overwhelmed. Sometimes it takes me a while to even connect my insomnia with going on the flight because I don't feel anxious—at least not consciously. (Cory, age 27)*

Sometimes it's obvious that our anxiety is being caused by a particular stressor. Cory's story, however, illustrates why anticipatory anxiety is such a slippery bugger. It is often difficult to connect the dots, so to speak. We don't always know why we're feeling anxious or even *if* we're feeling anxious. We know something's not right—that we are feeling "off" or "heightened"—but we don't realize that what we are experiencing is actually connected with a future happening.

Symptoms that used to baffle us have since become easily identifiable responses to anticipatory anxiety. Making anticipatory anxiety part of your vocabulary will help you start to recognize your anxiety response patterns, which goes a long way in helping you ride the wave.

Accept

Let's do some free association. We'll mention a word and you write down the first thing that comes to your mind. Ready? Here's the word: anxiety. We're willing to bet that most of you wrote down any number of words with negative connotations, such as "attack," "terrible," "overwhelming," "scary," and so on. This is because we have been trained to think of emotions as either good or bad, positive or negative. Happiness and excitement would fall in the positive category, while sadness and anger would be in the negative group. Guess where anxiety is.

But what if we reframe this paradigm? What if emotions are neither positive nor negative, but instead are part of the full range of feelings included in the human experience? In other words, what if we stop judging our emotions? This is what accepting is all about— it's letting yourself feel whatever it is you are feeling at the moment. It's recognizing that we all experience a wide range of emotions and, even more important, that these emotions come and go. There is an impermanence to what we feel at any given moment; the fact that our emotions are fleeting (even if they don't feel that way) makes it possible to accept them and ride the wave.

What if we stop judging our emotions?

When we think about anxiety in this way, we realize that we don't have to fight against it, because either way, it will come and go. We don't *expect* to be anxiety-free, and when it inevitably shows up, we *accept* it by not attempting to shut it down.

Accepting is no easy feat—it takes patience and practice. We find that the tool that is most helpful when it comes to acceptance is self-talk. In fact, most of us talk to ourselves all the time. Research has shown that the most powerful voice we hear is our own—we believe our own voices above anyone else's (for better or worse . . . and often it's worse, because our unconscious voice can be a negative one). For this reason, we not only promote talking to yourself but also recommend that you do so *aloud*. This helps reinforce the message you *want* to send your brain.

To start, explain to yourself (out loud) what is happening by labeling the experience. For example, "What I'm feeling is anxiety. It is very uncomfortable, but that is what anxiety feels like." Or: "I know what this is; I've had it before. It's not pleasant, but I can ride it out." Or maybe: "This is how I'm feeling right now; it is part of the human experience. I don't need to make it go away—it will subside on its own."

Closely related to labeling the experience is a technique we call Naming Your Monster. The idea here is to visualize as vividly as possible what your anxiety looks like. Is it big or small? Thin or fat? Does it have teeth or claws? What color is it? Human or animal? What's its name?

This may seem a bit juvenile to you (and, in fact, it is a great technique to use with kids, who often don't have the vocabulary to discuss their anxiety issues), but if you are the imaginative type (and let's be honest, some of those worst-case scenarios we come up with are quite imaginative), Naming Your Monster can be pretty powerful. Through visualization, you make an intangible feeling like anxiety very concrete, and in doing so, you take away its invisibility. Giving your anxiety a distinguishable form and a way of addressing it is a great way to accept it as part of your life. If we treat our anxiety as a living thing, if we can yell at it or send it to its room, we take away its leverage—we regain the upper hand. Plus, it can't plan a surprise attack if you know what it looks like (unless your anxiety wears camouflage). So, in addition to helping you ACCEPT, Naming Your Monster goes a long way in helping you EXPECT.

My anxiety is dark gray and swishy with lots of wrinkles. It's male and just hangs over me. It stabs me without moving, without knives or claws. (Bella, age 23)

If I wake up anxious, I say to my anxiety, "Oh, you're here? Fine. But you're not driving." (Abs, age 52)

My anxiety's name is Ruby because she's deep red and very loud. The last time she showed up, I actually yelled at her. I said, "You're not the boss of me!" during a panic attack. That made me laugh, which helped me feel better. (Kamryn, age 34)

Sometimes, when we imagine our anxiety, it resembles a person in our lives—a parent, sibling, spouse, child, or other person. Although these instances are a bit trickier, the fact that a specific person comes to mind is very good information when it comes to anxiety management. It is truly helpful to know who triggers you and under what circumstances. When you examine the triggering behaviors more closely, you may realize that you need to find a new way of relating to your trigger person. We advocate being prepared with a set of strategies so that the anxiety you feel in reaction to your trigger person is not a surprise, and so that even if you are anxious, you know what to do to manage the relationship. This process takes a lot of time and energy, and sometimes requires the help of a good therapist.

My husband becomes really argumentative when he is anxious. I used to fight with him, but that never went well for either of us. Now I know that if I can stay very calm myself, he seems to calm down too. I can't say I do it all the time, but when I can manage it, it really takes the edge off. (Miriam, age 68)

Another pathway to acceptance is the use of mantras, which are short phrases that you repeat to yourself in order to calm your mind. Interestingly, if you disassemble the word "mantra," you get "man," which in Sanskrit means "mind," and "tra," which means "transport." Thus, a mantra is a way of transporting the mind through self-talk. There are many types of mantras, but the most effective when it comes to riding the wave are soothing suggestions such as:

- Breathe in, breathe out
- This too shall pass
- I'm okay
- Ride the wave
- Let it go

Any gentle command or phrase will do; the idea is to provide your brain with something to focus on other than your anxiety. Whether you are repeating a mantra, labeling your experience, or just having a conversation with yourself, keep talking until the anxiety subsides.

> *I say to myself, "Peace, be still," whenever I'm feeling anxious. I can't always remember all the techniques I've learned when I need them most, but "Peace, be still" stays in my brain. I don't even have to think. It just pops into my head.* (Vivian, age 58)

Be Kind

When we say, "Be kind," we're not talking about being nice to others (although that's always a good idea); we're talking about being kind to *yourself*. This is no easy task—we are often much quicker to be kind to everyone else but ourselves. Recognizing this, Kristin Neff, a researcher and professor at the University of

Texas, Austin (and with whom we were fortunate enough to have trained), developed the concept of self-compassion, which is giving ourselves the same kindness and understanding we would offer a friend who is experiencing difficulty.

Typically, when we're having a hard time, we tend to beat ourselves up about it. Our inner critics are all too eager to remind us how we've failed (once again):

> *I've allowed my anxiety to take over my life. I should have gotten treatment years ago, but I let this get out of control. I am so mad at myself.* *(Deborah, age 71)*

> *I feel like a terrible person because I always blow up at my kids when I'm anxious. I let the worst parts of me take over.* *(Gillian, age 44)*

> *I really want to visit my son, but I am too afraid to make the drive. I feel like such a failure.* *(Reyna, age 55)*

Self-compassion is all about turning our inner critics into our inner advocates. Instead of reprimanding ourselves, self-compassion suggests we offer ourselves unconditional acceptance and supportive self-talk. For example, Deborah, Gillian, and Reyna could practice self-compassion by saying something like: "Anxiety is a real struggle for me, and this has been really painful."

Self-compassion, as conceptualized by Dr. Neff, comprises three components: (1) self-kindness, (2) common humanity, and (3) mindfulness. We've already covered self-kindness, which is all about treating yourself gently and compassionately, as you would a good friend. Common humanity is the understanding that we all struggle with challenges and that none of us live a life without pain. Suffering is part of what it means to be human—nobody gets out unscathed. When we truly accept our common humanity, we realize how connected we all are. Our trials are not unique, and we are not alone.

Self-compassion, then, allows us to transform a sense of isolation into connectedness when we are suffering. Common humanity is such a valuable notion because we all know how lonely it is to live with an anxiety disorder.

> *I thought I was the only one who had trouble leaving the house. I was so embarrassed about it—I wouldn't talk about my anxiety with anyone. When I learned that agoraphobia was an actual thing, and that other people had it too, it was like the weight of the world was lifted off me.*
> *(Natalie, age 63)*

> *I was really upset about screwing up a major presentation in school. I kept having to look at my notes and I left out a really important part. It was pretty much a disaster. I went to the instructor expecting him to say how unprepared I was and that I deserved the bad grade. Instead he told me I should be more compassionate with myself and that he too had messed up a presentation when he was in grad school. And when he went to his professor, she told him that every professor has screwed up at least one presentation. I guess it's easy to forget that everybody makes mistakes. Especially in such a competitive environment.*
> *(Premila, age 19)*

The root of self-compassion is mindfulness, which is defined as being completely open to whatever it is you are feeling or thinking in a given moment. Many of us are uncomfortable sitting with our emotions because we are scared they will swallow us whole. Mindfulness teaches us not to push away or try to suppress our emotions. We've been told by more than one therapist (and our yoga teacher): "What we can feel, we can heal. What we resist, persists." This is why we are such big fans of labeling your emotions and experiences.

What we can feel, we can heal. What we resist, persists.

Another aspect of mindfulness is recognizing that your thoughts and feelings are not a permanent state—that they too will pass. Understanding the transient nature of thoughts and emotions helps us stay off the hamster wheel of exaggeration—when your mind goes right to "This is the worst thing ever" or "I'll never feel better." If we believe that no emotional state lasts forever, then we are better able to tolerate pain and suffering. Once we can tolerate our pain and suffering (by using self-compassion), we can proceed to soothe ourselves.

Self-compassion is not only about making yourself feel better. It's also about empowering yourself to take action. When we aren't caught up in the denial spiral or stuck on the exaggeration hamster wheel, we free up our rational brain to help us problem-solve. For science wonks, once the limbic system is calmed, the prefrontal cortex can be engaged.

You might be thinking that self-compassion is self-indulgent; it lets you off the hook. Worse, it doesn't help you change your behavior. Regarding the self-indulgence complaint, if you really understand self-compassion, it is more about connecting with the universality of human experience (common humanity). When we are compassionate with ourselves, we are more able to be compassionate with others. Similarly, when we are not spending so much time judging ourselves, we spend far less time judging others. As such, self-compassion dissolves our sense of separateness and makes us less self-focused.

Regarding the idea that self-compassion makes us less accountable, it actually allows us to own our mistakes without assigning blame to ourselves or to others. This in turn permits us to move forward instead of getting stuck in the blame-shame cycle.

In terms of motivation to change behavior, self-compassion is a far better choice than self-criticism, which releases stress hormones and lowers resilience. How has berating yourself helped you manage your anxiety? We're guessing not so well. Self-compassion allows you to be less afraid of failure and judgment, which results in your being better able to take risks.

Here's what the research says about self-compassion:

- Soldiers who practiced self-compassion experienced less PTSD and were less likely to die by suicide.[1]

- After failing an exam, students who practiced self-compassion spent more time studying than their non-self-compassionate peers.[2]

- Self-compassionate people are better able to handle tough situations like divorce,[3] illness,[4] and chronic pain.[5]

- Self-compassion is correlated with a stronger immune system and overall well-being.[6]

- Self-compassion reduces the harmful effects of stress on the body.[7]

- People who practice self-compassion are more willing to compromise in relationships and are generally more forgiving and less judgmental of others.[8]

- People who practice self-compassion are more likely to apologize and less likely to repeat offensive behavior.[9]

Studies show that self-compassion makes us less self-indulgent, more accountable, and more likely to change our behavior. It also makes us more resilient. But most important for us, research shows that self-compassion is correlated with decreased anxiety and depression.[10]

So how can we use self-compassion to manage our anxiety? As we said earlier, we start by talking very gently to ourselves and disengaging our inner critics:

INNER CRITIC'S VOICE ⟶	INNER ADVOCATE'S VOICE
I can't get anything right.	This is hard, but I am capable of growth.
All I do is worry.	Anxiety is painful, but I am working toward letting my worry go.
Things will never get better.	I'm suffering right now, but I won't always feel this way.
I'm a total mess.	Anxiety is part of the human experience. Sometimes it feels messy.

After you have silenced your inner critic and given yourself some compassion, you can then ask yourself, "What do I need right now?" In other words, do you need to be alone? With others? An action plan? A hug? A bath? A walk? Do you need to enlist other resources, like a therapist or the advice of a close friend?

Finally, remind yourself that *everyone* experiences suffering—that what you are going through is valid and very human. Give yourself permission to feel anxious, because all humans feel anxious sometimes; then, with the love and compassion you absolutely deserve, tell yourself you will be okay.

My dad was very critical of us when we were kids. He was in the military and had such high expectations of everyone. As a result, I grew up internalizing his perfectionism and am now super-critical of myself. Practicing self-compassion helps me push away his voice in my head when I make a mistake—I tell myself instead that everyone makes mistakes and that I am only human. (Sheila, age 67)

My mother was not a very warm person, so we didn't get a lot of affection growing up. Learning self-compassion has allowed me to give myself the comfort I never received as a child. It's kind of empowering. (Opal, age 36)

Recap

Riding the wave is the foundation of your healing journey. In order for other techniques and treatments (including medication) to be most effective, you have to first learn to expect, accept, and be kind. We realize that this is a tall order and requires tons of practice. We're still practicing, and on some days we find it excruciatingly difficult to do. But we do it because it works—better than anything else we've ever tried.

Remember those neural pathways we talked about in chapter three? At this point, your default neural pathways—which have become quite well worn—encourage you to fight against your anxiety, avoid anxiety-provoking situations, and beat yourself up for your perceived weakness or failure to manage your disorder. Neuroplasticity allows us to create new pathways, which can over time become new habits. In other words, we can retrain our brains to ride the wave (expect, accept, and be kind) in response to anxiety. We hope you'll give it a try.

eight

It's Hard to Be Happy
When You're Gasping for Air

We don't know about you, but together, we've swallowed enough air during our anxiety journeys to blow up all the balloons at the Macy's Thanksgiving parade. Hyperventilation is such a part of the anxiety experience that often we aren't even aware that we're doing it. But we're sure as heck aware of the light-headedness, shortness of breath, and dizziness that results. Why does this happen?

We all have this thing called the autonomic nervous system (ANS), which is responsible for everything our body does automatically. We're talking about breathing, digestion, temperature, heart rate, blood pressure, and finishing the entire pint of Ben & Jerry's (okay, maybe not that last one). In other words, you don't have to tell your heart to beat—it does it all on its own. (You don't need to check—it's beating.)

Your ANS provides two types of responses: (1) the sympathetic response and (2) the parasympathetic response. The sympathetic response, also known as the stress response, is that whole fight-or-flight thing we've talked about. It's your body getting ready to face imminent danger. For example, your heart beats faster, your muscles tense, your pupils dilate, and your breathing gets shallow.

The parasympathetic response, or peace response, is all about resting and digesting. In other words, it is your body's winding down in the absence of any imminent threats. Examples of the parasympathetic response include decreased heart rate, muscle relaxation, increased digestive activity, and constricted pupils.

Many things cause the sympathetic system to react, including hormonal changes (hot flashes, anyone?), chronic pain, stressful situations, and—you guessed it—anxiety. When we experience anxiety, the sympathetic (stress) response is activated, which is why we feel all "revved up" and hypervigilant. It makes sense, then, that in order to decrease the anxiety, we have to get our bodies to move into the parasympathetic (peace) response.

How do we do this?

The easiest, cheapest, and most legal way to get your parasympathetic response to kick in is through a process called diaphragmatic breathing. Now, you're probably thinking, *Really? Breathing? That's your big antianxiety tool?* Yes! And here's why.

When your sympathetic system is in charge, your breathing is shallow and rapid (think of a dog panting). You are inhaling and exhaling so quickly that you are using only a fraction of your lung capacity, which also explains why we often hyperventilate when we panic. This process is called chest breathing because that's the part of the body that moves when you inhale.

When you slow down your respiration—really, really slow it down so that your stomach fills up with air when you breathe in—not only are you using more of your lung capacity, but you are using your diaphragm (the muscle that separates your chest from your abdomen). Thus the term "diaphragmatic breathing," although we prefer the more alliterative "belly breathing."

If you deepen and lengthen your breaths by inhaling through your nose and exhaling through your mouth, you will automatically activate a parasympathetic response. Your brain assumes that if you have the time to breathe slowly and deeply, you must not be in any immediate danger. As a result, your ANS

You are always only ten breaths away from reduced anxiety

starts to decrease your blood pressure and heart rate and allow your muscles to relax. Just ten belly breaths can engage the parasympathetic response, which means that you are always only ten breaths away from reduced anxiety!

The following are some of our favorite belly breathing techniques. Don't get nervous—you already know how to breathe. We're just going to add in some rhythm. You can do breathing exercises in any position (we usually lie down), but we find it helpful to place your hands on your belly so you can feel it rise with your inhale. If your belly isn't rising, you need to inhale more slowly and deeply.

One little warning (maybe not so little): some folks may find breathing exercises during a panic attack make them hyperventilate more. If this happens to you, stop the breathing exercises and wait for a calmer time to try again.

Incremental Breathing

Research has consistently shown that in terms of engaging your parasympathetic response, the exhale is where it's at. In other words, the longer the out breath, the more relaxed you'll be. Remember to breathe in through your nose and out through your mouth. Feel free to make a whooshing noise on the exhale—it's really satisfying. The most important part is to do only what feels comfortable. Just like with stretching, some people are more breath-flexible than others. You do not want to push yourself to the point of hyperventilation. As is true for so many things, practice makes all the difference.

1. With your first breath, inhale for a count of 2 and exhale for a count of 3. (Inhale, 1, 2, exhale, 1, 2, 3.)
2. Repeat.
3. If you feel comfortable, inhale for a count of 3 and exhale for a count of 4.
4. Repeat.
5. If you feel comfortable, inhale for a count of 4 and exhale for a count of 5.
6. Repeat and keep adding beats, one at a time, until you've lengthened your breath as much as you *comfortably* can.

4-7-8 Breathing

This technique was developed by Dr. Andrew Weil and has been used to treat not only anxiety but also insomnia. If, like so many anxiety sufferers we've spoken with, you have trouble falling or staying asleep, this technique may just do the trick. Find a comfy position and give it a try:

1. Empty your lungs of air by exhaling.
2. Count to 4 as you inhale through your nose.

3. Hold your breath and count to 7.
4. Count to 8 as you exhale forcefully (whoosh).
5. Repeat 3 times.

> *My therapist recommended the 4-7-8 technique to help me manage my anxiety. The first time didn't do much for me, but after a few days, I definitely noticed that I felt much more relaxed. And when I do it before bed, I fall asleep so much faster. (Desiree, age 28)*

Imagery Breathing

If you aren't a numbers person or if counting feels cumbersome, you can try this technique instead:

1. Create a picture in your mind of a big balloon. Be sure to make it real by giving it color, shape, and texture.
2. As you inhale, imagine filling the balloon with air. Watch it expand in your mind.
3. As you exhale, imagine the balloon deflating.

You can do this exercise with any image. Abs likes to imagine a fire-breathing dragon, while Mags focuses on a whale's blowhole. Hmmm. Explains a lot . . .

Alternate Nostril Breathing

This sounds so much better in Sanskrit, where it is called *nadi shodhana pranayama*. (Translation: subtle energy clearing breath technique.) Arising from various yogic traditions, nostril breathing is a great relaxation tool. It also is helpful for enhancing concentration and clearing nasal passages (unless you have a bad head cold—trust us, it's not pretty).

Generally, it is advised that you do this one seated, either on the floor or in a straight-backed chair. You will be using your thumb and any finger on one hand. If you are a righty, use your right hand; if you're a southpaw, use your left. Start by taking a few deep, easy breaths.

1. Inhale through your nose.
2. Close off the right nostril with your thumb.
3. Exhale through your left nostril.
4. Inhale through your left nostril.
5. Close off your left nostril with your finger and open your right nostril.
6. Exhale through your right nostril.
7. Inhale through your right nostril.
8. Close off the right nostril with your thumb.
9. Repeat.

It takes a while to get the hang of it, but once you do, the pattern will be clear: exhale and inhale with one nostril, then exhale and inhale with the other.

> *For a long time, I could not do breathing exercises without starting to hyperventilate. My PTSD would kick in and I would start to panic. But my yoga teacher taught me the alternate nostril breathing exercise and it was so helpful. I think being able to use my hands and not worrying about breathing so deeply was key. (Isla, age 38)*

Meditation

Before you skip this section, here's a surprising truth: if you are consistently doing any of the breathing exercises we mentioned (or others), you're already meditating. Like breath work, meditation focuses you on keeping yourself in the present moment, which is important for anxiety sufferers, who spend a lot of time ruminating about the past or worrying about the future. We also tend to be very harsh self-critics, and meditation is about observing *without* judgment. When we meditate, we notice our thoughts and feelings, but we learn not to judge them, in much the same way we watch clouds move across the sky. We watch them as they pass by—we don't try to hold on to them, stop them, or change them. We may decide which animals they resemble, but we don't judge them.

The benefits of meditation are astounding. Researchers have found strong and persuasive evidence showing that a regular meditation practice decreases anxiety, depression, and chronic pain.[1] In 2014, a study in *JAMA* found not only that eight weeks of meditation reduced anxiety and depression, but that these effects lasted anywhere from three to six *months* after the study ended.[2] Other investigators found that meditation was just as effective as cognitive behavioral therapy (CBT) or antidepressants in treating anxiety and depression.[3] Brain scans of meditators have shown changes in their amygdalae (the fear center) and other parts of the brain connected with anxiety.[4] And these changes were long lasting.

You're probably convinced meditation is a good idea, but, as with eliminating sugar, very few of us seem to be able to do it on a consistent basis. There are a few reasons why we think meditation can feel so difficult. First, there's that whole business about "quieting the mind," which, from where we sit, seems an impossible task.

Before we go further, we're going to ask you to close your eyes for one minute and think about a white polar bear. Focus only on the bear—nothing else—for just one minute.

How'd that go? If you are like us, your mind started imagining the bear, and then remembered that polar bears are in such trouble because of climate change, which reminded you how warm this winter was, which got you worrying about how hot the summer is going to be, and on and on.

Okay, now try this: let your mind wander anywhere it wants to go for the next minute. Just don't think about the polar bear.

How was that? If you are like us, you thought about nothing but the polar bear!

We just replicated an experiment done by Dr. Daniel Wegner, a psychology professor at Harvard who was studying thought suppression. What he found will not surprise you at all. Data from his work showed that (1) the human mind is easily distracted, and (2) the more you try to push a thought away, the more it will enter your mind.[5] Sort of like dieting—as soon as you tell us we can't have a particular food, it's the only thing we can think about.

The takeaway for meditation is this: allowing your mind to wander is perfectly okay. You don't need to try to quiet anything. That part will happen on its own. In fact, some research has shown that a wandering mind actually promotes creativity (as long as the mind is truly wandering and not perseverating or ruminating, which we anxiety sufferers tend to do).[6]

The second thing that makes meditation hard for some folks is just how uncomfortable it can be to sit like a Buddhist monk—legs crossed, back straight, arms resting on knees with fingers joined in the universal "ohm" position—for even five minutes. Breaking news: you don't have to sit like that. In fact, you want to be as comfy as possible. So make yourself a pillow pile, wrap yourself in your favorite blanket, and sit or lie down in a position that you know you can stay in for a while. If sitting or lying down is not your thing, there are plenty of great walking meditations you can try. Really, anything goes.

A third reason some folks struggle with meditation is that it becomes just another thing on their already impossibly long to-do list. Both of us treated meditation like a chore that we put off all day long, until we were finally in bed and then: *Oops.* Another day we didn't get around to meditating. Or giving up sugar.

Any amount of time you spend meditating counts

But we don't have to think of meditation as a task. It can be something we integrate into our day, like when you're on the carpool line, sitting at your desk at work, or commuting. Any amount of time you spend meditating counts—it doesn't even have to be five minutes.

I started my meditation practice by taking four to six deep breaths at some time during the day—usually when I was at work. I ended up doing some in the car before I drove home too. The more I did, the better I felt, and that is really how I started to meditate. I craved feeling that calm. (Hallie, age 59)

There are lots of ways to meditate, but breath meditation is a good way to start. Basically, the goal is to focus on your breath, and only your breath, for a few minutes each day. You can achieve this by repeating a mantra like "Breathe in, breathe out," or you can count as you inhale and exhale (breathe in, 2, 3, 4, breathe out, 2, 3, 4). You can also use any of the exercises we presented earlier in the chapter. As you focus on your breath, other thoughts may pop into your head. Like a white polar bear. No big deal—this is normal. Just notice the thought and then return to your counting or mantra. Don't force anything.

When a distracting thought comes into my head, I say "later" to myself. I don't try to push the thought away forever. I just let myself know that I can think about it at another time. (Lourdes, age 35)

Other ways to meditate include walking meditation, progressive muscle relaxation or body scanning, prayer, chanting, and certain types of yoga. Really, there are no rules to follow. The goal is to hang out in the present for a while and try to push aside judgy thoughts.

I meditate by walking around the track at the local high school. I just focus on my steps. Sometimes, if I'm distracted, I'll even say, "left, right," to myself, just to get it going. (Colleen, age 62)

I often wake up in the middle of the night anxious and sweaty with my heart beating so fast. I find it really hard to calm myself down, much less fall back to sleep. Now I listen to a guided meditation on one of those

*apps when I wake up and it helps so much. I usually fall back to sleep
with the meditation on. (Yvonne, age 78)*

If you have been diagnosed with PTSD or are dealing with trauma, you may
want to take the process of meditation very slowly. Some anxiety sufferers find
that they experience flashbacks during meditation and feel more distressed
afterward. If this is the case, please do not push yourself to continue to meditate. There are many ways to reap the benefits derived from meditation practice without exacerbating your PTSD.

Visualization

Closely related to meditation is visualization, another tool for activating your
parasympathetic nervous system. Scientific studies have shown again and
again how powerful visualization can be in reducing anxiety, boosting immunity, enhancing creativity, and managing pain.[7] Here's how it works: You create
a vivid picture in your mind's eye, which your brain interprets as reality. (Yes,
it's that easy to trick your brain.) Then your autonomic nervous system re-
sponds accordingly. There are lots of ways to practice visualization, but our
favorite method is "serene scenes."

SERENE SCENES
Think of a place—anywhere in the world (or in the galaxy—we don't want to
discourage the astronauts among us) that makes you feel safe and calm. It can
be a beach, your grandmother's living room, a mountain cabin, or anywhere
else. The important thing is that your scene is a place where you feel comfortable and relaxed.

Once you have picked your serene scene, you can add imagery from all your
senses (in order to make the scene feel real). Imagine what you can smell or

hear or taste or see. What are you doing in this scene? What is the temperature? What are the textures? The goal is to do such a good job creating the scene that your brain believes you are there.

Hang out in your serene scene for a few minutes and allow your body to start to relax. Notice how your heart rate has decreased, your breathing has deepened, your muscles have slackened. Enjoy the sensation of complete safety and comfort.

Ideally, you should visit the same serene scene in your mind as often as you can so that you create a neural pathway that becomes easy to access anywhere. That way, if you begin to feel anxious in the grocery store, you can close your eyes and go right to your serene scene until you are feeling calmer. The more you practice, the quicker and easier your access to your special serene place.

> *My serene scene is a lake in the Berkshires that my family used to visit when I was a child. I jump into the water and it is slightly chilly, but the day is sunny and the sky is bright blue with clouds gently moving through. I get on top of my favorite orange raft and my skin is warmed by the sun. I float on the water and see the trees all around the lake and the mountains in the background. I am totally safe. My body just relaxes right into the raft. My hands are skimming the cool water. The birds are chirping and the wind is rustling against the trees. I am at peace.* (Mags, age 52)

Let's review. When you are anxious, your nervous system goes into sympathetic, or stress, mode; when you are relaxed, your nervous system goes into parasympathetic, or peace, mode. Your goal is to learn how to flip the switch from stress to peace. To be clear, we are not suggesting you try to avoid the sympathetic mode altogether—remember, there's no such thing as a life without stress. But you can manage your anxiety if you learn how to activate your parasympathetic response.

Breathing, meditation, and visualization are three methods of flipping from the sympathetic to the parasympathetic mode. Remember, you are not using these techniques to *stop* your anxiety—that would be struggling against it, which only exacerbates your sympathetic (stress) response.

Instead, you employ these methods to actively redirect your brain toward the peace response. They also serve the very important purpose of keeping you distracted from your anxiety symptoms. Breathing, meditation, and visualization are not passive endeavors—as such, you benefit from feeling some control or agency in a typically out-of-control situation.

> *Having something to do when I get caught in a worry spiral has been so helpful. At first I had to keep reminding myself to do the visualization exercise, but now it comes pretty naturally. I'm getting really good at calming myself down. And I like feeling like I have some power to control my mind.* (Vanessa, age 27)

There is yet another advantage to using these techniques. With practice, you learn how to become less reactive in all stressful situations. In other words, you are able to pause between your thought or emotion and your behavior. This is particularly helpful for those of us who experience angry outbursts.

> *Since I have started to meditate, I am less likely to just react to situations "on the fly." I have so much more of an ability to understand what I am feeling and to pause while I think about how I want to respond.* (Dahlia, age 70)

You may have noticed a common theme in the stories in this chapter: what made people feel better was not that they were able to get rid of their anxiety (they weren't) but that they could do something in the moment while they were riding the wave. That sense of agency is so empowering—it is such a big part of being anxiously happy.

nine

Don't Believe Everything You Think

Thoughts are not facts. We'll say that again: thoughts are not facts. Just because your mind suggests it doesn't mean it's true; however, we give our brain so much credit (it is the top organ, after all) that we believe whatever it tells us. Those of us with anxiety disorders really buy into our thoughts—hook, line, and sinker. And sink we do, into a spiral of anxious assumptions because our thoughts are often untrue and lead us wildly astray.

Just because your mind suggests it doesn't mean it's true

This chapter, based on the principles of cognitive behavioral therapy (CBT), is all about checking the accuracy of your thoughts and challenging your assumptions as a way to manage your anxiety. If we don't blindly accept as true every thought that pops into our heads, we won't fall into so many rabbit holes—where lots of Anxiety Sisters spend the bulk of their time.

My brain goes into overdrive and I imagine all these terrible scenarios. They play out in my head until I'm in a panic. (Fiona, age 54)

Go-To Thoughts

In order to question your thoughts and assumptions, you first have to identify them. One place to start is with beliefs you go to automatically in response to stressful situations and events. We all have these Go-To beliefs we carry with us, and they become our default explanations for when the going gets rough.

> *I got into a car accident that was my fault. All I could think was I always screw up and this is just another thing to add to my list of screwups. A friend pointed out how harsh I was being to myself. She also reminded me that I have been driving for many years without incident, so the word "always" was not really true.* (Mindy, age 63)

Mindy's "I always screw up" is an example of one of these Go-To beliefs. We Anxiety Sisters tend to be pretty self-critical, so what we tell ourselves in times of stress is often unkind, even cruel. On top of that, these Go-To thoughts are often untrue. In Mindy's case, she made a mistake. It was an accident—not intentional, as the active verb "screw up" implies. Also, by using the word "always," Mindy assumes facts not in evidence. She doesn't have car accidents daily, weekly, or ever before, for that matter. Thus, her Go-To belief is inaccurate.

> *Growing up, my siblings got a lot of attention from my parents when they excelled at sports or got good grades. I did neither of those things, so I always felt that nobody really understood me or paid attention to me. As an adult, I still get easily upset if I feel like someone is not really "getting" me. I tend to assume that nobody cares about me, which of course isn't the case. I just seem to think that people will always let me down.* (Rebecca, age 32)

In this case, Rebecca has already figured out that her Go-To belief is not true. Even still, it's so powerful that it keeps coming up. Her assumption that nobody cares about her makes connection with others really difficult, which in turn reinforces her assumption. Which then increases her sense of isolation. It's a bit of a vicious cycle.

Where do we get these Go-To thoughts? Many times, they originate in childhood and stay with us through adulthood. We recite these scripts over and over until they have carved a neural pathway—until they are our default thoughts in times of uncertainty or challenge. Go-To thoughts that started in childhood are very deeply ingrained.

Another place Go-To thoughts are born is during a traumatic experience. Trauma is so terrifying and overwhelming that we feel completely out of control when it occurs. This is the perfect breeding ground for Go-To thoughts.

> *I was raped by an ex-boyfriend, and it changed so much about me. I no longer think I read people well or have an ability to understand them. I now don't trust my gut. (Zena, age 24)*

Societal messages, like the ones that prescribe how our bodies should look or the quick-fix mentality we described earlier, are also sources of Go-To thoughts. What we consider a success or a failure is often determined by culturally mandated voices and values. We learn to judge ourselves based on this external lens.

> *Being thin was such a big deal when I was growing up—gaining weight was, like, a major sin. It's no shock to me that I now have an eating disorder. (Barri, age 26)*

Identifying Go-To Thoughts

So how do you go about pinpointing your Go-To thoughts? Start by thinking about the critical things you say to yourself all the time, especially in difficult situations. Do you call yourself names? Do you disparage your abilities or your appearance? Do you blame yourself for everything? Do you undercut your achievements? The following is a sample of Go-To thoughts we've heard from Anxiety Sisters in the past few years:

- I'm a loser, an idiot, etc.
- I never get things right or I always get things wrong.
- I don't deserve this (for good things).
- I deserve this (for bad things).
- I always say the wrong thing.
- I'm not smart, competent, capable, etc.
- Nobody understands me.
- I can't get a break.
- Things will never get better.

Do any of these sound familiar?

Another way to spot your Go-To thoughts is by asking yourself whose voice are you hearing. In other words, is the recurring thought your voice or someone else's? If you can pinpoint someone else's critical voice in your head, chances are it's a Go-To thought.

> *My dad was a sergeant in the army. He expected a lot from all of us, particularly me. His big line was "Don't bother doing it if you aren't going to do it right." He drove himself and us pretty hard, even with the smallest tasks. For instance, if I did the dishes, he would do a spot check to make sure I did them right. If things weren't up to his standards, he*

would say, "Is this your best effort?" To this day—and my dad died six years ago—that's the voice in my head. I'm such a perfectionist— nothing is ever good enough. (Stephanie, age 57)

In high school, I had a math teacher who called me "dummy" every time he called on me because I had a hard time learning algebra. I don't think he realized how much influence he had over me, but now, twenty years later, I still believe I'm stupid. And it's not just with numbers—I call myself dumb anytime I do something wrong. (Felicia, age 38)

A third way to detect Go-To thoughts is to scan your beliefs for the words "always" or "never." If you say to yourself that you *always* or *never* do a particular thing, that is a signal that this thought is not only scripted but also faulty. Absolutes are rarely true. (Notice we didn't say "never"!)

Disrupting Go-To Thoughts

Now that you know how to identify your Go-To thoughts, let's talk about how to counteract them. First, locate your "always" and "never" beliefs and reframe them. For example, if one of your Go-To thoughts is "I never get a break," you can change it to "Like all human beings, sometimes I have bad luck." Feel free to choose your own words, but the idea is to recognize the universality of human experience as well as the temporary nature of the situation at hand. When we acknowledge our common humanity, we normalize our challenges and difficulties. Using a phrase that connects you with all of human nature lessens the burden of going it alone. It makes us remember that nobody is perfect and that struggle is part of what it means to be human.

A second way to defuse your Go-To thoughts is to consider talking back to them, especially if the voice in your head is not your own. For example, if your mother's voice is bothering you about your weight, tell her respectfully (or not so respectfully) to mind her own business.

Agency, one of our essential components of happiness, is about listening to your own voice. It's important to know what your opinion is and to feel entitled to it. Some folks find writing a letter to whoever has been behind their Go-To thoughts to be a great method of exorcism. However you choose to do it, kick unwanted voices out so you can be in control of your thoughts and assumptions.

> *I was bullied a lot in school. Kids would call me stupid and tell me that I was ugly. So I was surprised that when I got to college, I made friends and boys seemed interested in me. But no matter how many friends and boyfriends I had, I still held on to the idea that I was stupid and ugly. One thing that has helped me was to write letters to the kids that hurt me back in school. In those letters, I would say how hurt I felt and that I am actually smart and attractive. I never mailed any of them, but just confronting those people on paper made their words less powerful.* (Allison, age 41)

A third technique for addressing Go-To thoughts is the Three Questions: (1) Is it true? (2) Is it helpful? (3) Is it compassionate? As we've said ad nauseam, Go-To thoughts are seldom true, especially if the words "always" or "never" come up. In addition, if you are ascribing negative personality traits to yourself, that is another clue that the belief may be distorted. For example, saying "I'm a disorganized mess" is untrue, just by the virtue of the implied "always." You may struggle with organization, but not in every single aspect of your life.

Aside from it being untrue, calling yourself a disorganized mess (or any pejorative label) is also not helpful. Painting yourself with a negative brush does nothing for the growth process because it doesn't leave room for you to see yourself any other way. Trust us when we tell you that people don't typically flourish while being berated. And, as a bonus, calling yourself names puts your nervous system in fight, flight, or freeze mode.

You may remember our discussion of self-compassion from chapter seven, in which we explained how it is correlated with reduced anxiety and depression. Likewise, self-compassion has a direct relationship with problem-solving skills and a capacity for personal growth. The more kindly you speak to yourself, the more likely you will be able to engage your rational decision-making skills.

> *I had been calling myself a loser for so long, I really believed it to be true. And whenever I called myself a loser, I would shut down. Now I am trying to change my thoughts by not calling myself names. After all, I wouldn't call anyone I cared about a loser.* (Destiny, age 26)

Challenging Other Assumptions

Now that we've learned how to dismantle our Go-To thoughts, let's zoom out and use the same skills to question other thoughts and assumptions—especially when it comes to our interactions with others. When we make assumptions about other people's perceptions and motivations, we create a lot of misunderstandings and subsequent anxiety for ourselves. Here is a true story illustrating how this works.

A school counselor (we'll call her Daphne) occasionally would meet parents at a local diner during the evening when they could not get out of work to meet with her during the school day. One such evening, she was in the middle of a meeting with a parent when Daphne's friend Leslie walked into the diner. Leslie came over to say hello but felt slighted when Daphne did not respond to her enthusiastically or invite her to sit down. Leslie walked away thinking that Daphne was being cold—even rude—toward her and, as a result, felt hurt and angry.

Of course, Daphne was deep in conversation with the parent about a very serious matter, and she wanted to make sure she maintained confidentiality;

thus, she did not introduce Leslie, nor did she realize that her friend was upset. Leslie, in her anger, refused to call Daphne, believing that Daphne owed her an apology. And Daphne couldn't understand why Leslie was avoiding her.

As you can see, we assign meanings to situations that affect how we feel and act, but these meanings do not always reflect the reality of the situation. If Leslie avoids Daphne because she is hurt or angry, she is reinforcing her own thoughts that Daphne treated her unkindly. Thus, Leslie enters a vicious cycle of assigning (faulty) meaning to a behavior, feeling hurt, and avoidance. This habit of jumping to negative thoughts and interpretations without questioning their validity is a common attribute of those of us who suffer from anxiety.

We aren't suggesting that you stop making assumptions—all humans do that. What we are advising is that you learn to question these assumptions before you act on them, which will go a long way in reducing anxiety. Here are some ways Leslie might question the assumptions she has made about Daphne's behavior in the preceding example:

- "Wow, that behavior isn't like Daphne. I wonder what's the matter."
- "I do feel slighted by Daphne, but since she is usually so kind, I wonder if she was just having an off day."
- "It feels like Daphne is mad at me, but am I sure that is true? Is it like Daphne to be angry without talking to me about it?"

Leslie would then reserve judgment and keep an open mind about her friend's unusual behavior. Once she postponed making a judgment and instead became *curious* about the why of the interaction, she probably wouldn't jump to feeling hurt. She would then have no reason to avoid contact with her friend, so she could check in with her to find out what actually happened.

This technique works with all kinds of thoughts. For instance, if you suffer from illness anxiety disorder (IAD), you probably have done your share of catastrophizing your symptoms. Say you're feeling really dizzy. If you are a bona fide Anxiety Sister, your first thought is that you must have a brain tumor. (Or a potentially deadly virus. The choice is yours.) Now is the time to start questioning your assumptions. Before you go any further, stop and ask yourself if there are alternative explanations for your dizziness. In fact, you should make a list of possibilities: (1) I'm hungry, (2) it's too hot in here, (3) I'm wearing new eyeglasses, (4) I stood up too fast, (5) I'm dehydrated, or our personal favorite, (6) it's my hormones. If you cannot come up with a list on your own, feel free to phone a friend to help you brainstorm.

At this point, you can go through your list and find the explanation that makes the most sense, but honestly, just the act of writing a list of options will halt your journey down the IAD rabbit hole.

Common Stumbling Blocks

For anxiety sufferers, the ability to recognize distorted thought patterns is a very important skill to practice. There are so many of these patterns, but we think the following are the most frequently encountered.

BLACK VS. WHITE

This is a very either-or way of looking at the world, which, of course, is not an accurate perspective considering all the shades of gray out there. Most things in life fall between all and nothing; the inability to see this causes frustration because the bar is set too high (and the floor is too low).

> I was very upset when my fundraiser didn't meet its goals. We only missed by a few hundred dollars, but I saw it as a total failure. I cried all the way home in my car. (Ella, age 41)

Obviously, any money raised for a good cause is a success. Ella has a right to feel disappointed about not reaching her monetary goal, but her deep distress is a result of erroneous thinking.

INSUFFICIENT EVIDENCE

This thought pattern occurs when you generalize from one specific incident (hint: the words "always" and "never" tend to result). The problem with this way of thinking is that you are making a blanket statement based on very little evidence—certainly not enough to make probable cause.

> *When I didn't get my dream job, I got really depressed because I believed that I would never get a job that I really wanted. I saw myself as completely stuck in my career, unable to do anything about it.* (Penny, age 32)

Can Penny really say she'll never get a job she wants based on one missed opportunity? That doesn't seem likely. Yet she really believes this distortion, which can then become a self-fulfilling prophecy, only confirming her erroneous thinking. This is a nasty cycle, but one we hear about all the time. We need to be able to say the words "this time" or "in this case," as opposed to generalizing so broadly.

IT'S ALL ABOUT ME

This way of thinking makes the assumption that you are the subject of everyone else's thoughts and actions—that everything is directed at you. If it sounds a little paranoid, it kind of is in the sense that, very often, what other people think or do has nothing to do with you.

> *I was in the parking lot at school when I saw my friend by her car. I called her name and waved, but she just stared at me and didn't wave back. I was so upset. Then I found out that she had gotten some really bad news that day—that she didn't even know it was me waving.* (Riley, age 19)

So often, people's actions and reactions have nothing to do with you—it's about what's going on in their own heads. But it is so easy to misinterpret a gesture, a behavior, a facial expression, or even words when we assume it's about us. Even when someone is behaving rudely, we have to remember that we don't know their story and it is erroneous to decide it's directed at us. The only person whose world you are the center of is your own (unless you have a dog).

THE NEGATIVE LENS

This distorted thought pattern magnifies the negative and minimizes the positive. It's a brand of persistent pessimism that filters our worlds through soot-colored glasses. Like waiting for the other shoe to drop. Anxiety Sisters unwittingly use the negative lens to reinforce their fears and worries, which it does very effectively.

> *I recently read some of my work at a poetry slam. This one guy told me he thought it was heavy-handed. Even though so many others came up to me and said they loved my writing, all I could think about was that one guy. When I got home, I told my boyfriend the reading had gone really badly.* (Mira, age 23)

Imagine if Mira had focused on all the compliments she'd received. . . .

FORTUNE-TELLING

This distorted thought pattern assumes you have the ability to (1) read other people's minds, or (2) predict the future. Unless you're the Long Island Medium, this is erroneous and creates a lot of unnecessary strife. As we've said before, we really can't know what's in someone else's mind. It's hard enough to know what's in our own minds! So it is not very fruitful to base your own actions on what you *assume* someone else is thinking or feeling. Similarly, we cannot know what the future holds. Just because something is a certain way today does not mean it will be that way tomorrow. Because anxiety is often a future-oriented disorder (we worry about what might happen), fortune-telling is particularly appealing to sufferers. In fact, it is the root of most catastrophizing.

I went through a really bad divorce a few years ago, and now I'm con-
vinced I'll never find someone to love. The thought of spending the rest
of my life alone makes me so anxious. (Valerie, age 45)

It goes without saying that Valerie cannot know that she will never again find love. If getting divorced (or having a bad breakup) designated the end point in someone's romantic life, there'd be very few couples left on the planet. Not only is Valerie fortune-telling, but she is using the negative lens to do so—a distorted-thinking double whammy and a huge source of anxiety.

We would encourage Valerie to use the words "right now" or "at this time" when she is talking to herself about her love life; doing this emphasizes that we do not know what the future holds.

SHOULDING

Albert Ellis, the famous psychologist, was known for saying "Don't should all over yourself," which basically means stop making so many rules and expectations that even Wonder Woman couldn't live up to (and she has an invisible plane and supercool wristbands that can do magic things). This is a tall order, because we live in a world of "shoulds." We tend to internalize all those things society demands of us, and as a result, we become tyrannical with ourselves. Of course, anxiety is the result.

I have a long list of things I think I should be doing in order to be a good
mother: I should make more money. I should volunteer at their school. I
should make healthy home-cooked meals. I should keep my cool when they
push my buttons. Most of all, I should make sure my kids never see my
anxiety. My therapist often points out how impossible it would be to do all
these things, but a lot of moms I know seem to pull it off. (Carrie, age 36)

Treat yourself kindly and recognize that the shoulds are the problem—not you. Unrealistic expectations are impossible to fulfill, so you are setting yourself up for failure. Also, don't let social media fool you—nobody has it all under control (even the folks who want you to think they do). Remember, all humans struggle. Because anxiety can be so debilitating, it is important to give yourself a break. Sometimes just brushing your teeth is a big win.

Disputing these distorted thought patterns is the next step. One of our favorite techniques to counteract faulty thinking, especially if you are a catastrophizer (and who among us isn't?), is something we call best-case scenario. Since catastrophizing, by definition, is creating the worst-case scenario, it makes sense to flip our perspective by envisioning the opposite.

> *My dad was really sick for many years and died when I was a teenager. Now that I have kids of my own, I worry that I will get sick too and won't be around to see them grow up. One thing that really helps is to imagine being at their graduations or playing with my future grandkids. I do a 180 in my head and it stops the worry from spiraling out of control. (Tara, age 40)*

The key to this technique is to imagine the scene as vividly as you can. This will help transport you out of your catastrophe more convincingly. Best-case scenario can be really helpful if you are worried about getting bad news. Abs always imagines getting good test results before going to a dreaded doctor's appointment—it really calms her down.

Another great way to challenge catastrophic thinking is by playing the "possible versus probable" game. Is the situation you are imagining conceivable (possible) or likely (probable)? How possible or probable is it? (You can even assign a percentage, if it helps you.)

> *My husband has to drive a lot for work. Whenever the weather is bad, I always worry that he will be in a terrible accident. It really affects me to the point where I can't breathe right until I know he's safe. My therapist explained to me that while it is possible for anyone to have an accident,*

my husband having a fatal crash is unlikely. This really shifted things for me. (Georgia, age 50)

What *can* happen is very different from what probably *will* happen

The idea behind this technique is to remind you that what *can* happen is very different from what probably *will* happen. To wit: How many times has the worst-case scenario actually occurred?

By now, you know how much we believe in talking to ourselves as a way of managing anxiety. What your brain hears you say, it believes. So when your mind offers up distorted or catastrophic thoughts, you have the ability to override them with your voice. Some really great things to say to yourself are:

- I have anxiety, which is causing my faulty thinking.
- This is just a Go-To thought.
- Where's the evidence to support this thought?
- Am I shoulding on myself?
- I cannot read other people's minds.
- I cannot predict the future.
- Not everything is about me.
- Thoughts are not facts.
- DON'T BELIEVE EVERYTHING YOU THINK!

ten

The Spin Cycle

R eady for another field trip? This time, we are headed to the laundry room (during the COVID-19 lockdown, this counts as a field trip). Stay with us—we're onto something here. Now, imagine you are in your washing machine during the spin cycle. You're probably feeling disoriented, dizzy, nauseated, overheated, scared, claustrophobic, exhausted, and wet. Also, you are thinking there is a very good chance you might die. If there's a better metaphor for a panic attack, we haven't yet found it. Because we find the words "panic" and "attack" very anxiety-provoking, we like to call it the spin cycle, or spinning for short. (If spinning is anxiety-provoking for you, feel free to pick another metaphor.) In this chapter, we are taking a deep dive into panic and what to do about it when you are stuck in the spin cycle.

What makes panic so excruciating is the combination of physical discomfort and mental disorientation that makes us feel like we are dying (or like we've been thrown into a washing machine). For most anxiety sufferers, when we panic, our worlds go upside down and we don't know how to right ourselves. In fact, some folks dissociate and leave their bodies altogether (we call this floating). Of course, this discombobulation compounds the already awful physical distress, kind of like when you tug on a loose thread and the whole sweater unravels. Ugh. Our hearts are starting to thud just thinking about it.

> *When I start [to panic], it's like I'm underwater. Everything is fuzzy, and I can't tell which end is up. And I'm just flailing around, waiting to pass out.* (Donna, age 37)

So what's an Anxiety Sister to do? Unlike worry, which is a cerebral activity, panic is completely somatic. Therefore, strategies for managing it must engage our bodies. We need a way of reorienting ourselves so that our feet are firmly planted on the ground. Which is where grounding comes in. Simply put, grounding restores your equilibrium by employing your senses, promoting activity, and providing a distraction. Remember we talked about Spin Kits in chapter seven? Those are really Grounding Kits you can take with you wherever you go.

> *I was having a panic attack on a plane, and the flight attendant gave me this peppermint oil to put on the tip of my tongue and rub on my wrists. It really helped bring me back to myself. Plus, it gave me something to do. Now I always carry a little bit of essential oil with me.* (Faith, age 72)

Panic is a state of unreality: it results from an erroneous command from the brain to get ready to fight or flee an enemy that doesn't really exist. Grounding is a way to help your brain see its error and allow your body to resume a more relaxed state. The following are a few of our favorite grounding techniques.

The Five Senses

1. Describe (talk to yourself) or write down five things you can see right now.

2. Describe four things you can touch right now.
3. Describe three sounds you can hear right now.
4. Describe two things you can smell right now.
5. Describe one thing you can taste right now.

By the time you finish the last step, you will have distracted yourself from the panic and brought yourself back into the current moment.

Splish Splash

Water is a fantastic grounding tool. If you have access to it while you are in the spin cycle, here's how you can use it to calm down:

• Turn on the faucet and run your hands under the water. Pay close attention to how the liquid feels on different parts of your hand—your fingers, the back of your hand, your palm, etc.
• Alternate temperatures from cold to hot and back again. Notice the varying sensations.
• Get a piece of ice and rest it in the palm of your hand. Notice the sensation as the ice melts.
• Splash cool water on your face.
• Take a cool or cold shower.

> I carry a small washcloth and when I am anxious I wet it with cold water and put it on my wrists, my neck, and my face. Sometimes I even take a cup of cold water and pour it over my head. (Nieve, age 28)

Body Touch

Start by placing your hands on the top of your head. Feel the texture of your hair as you move toward your face. What do your ears feel like? Your nose? Your chin? Is that a beard hair?

Other methods of body touch include rubbing your hands together (that warm sensation from the friction is very grounding), giving yourself a hug, or placing one hand on your heart and the other on top. You can also massage your temples, your neck muscles, or your feet.

Reality Jolt

This particular exercise jolts you back to reality through your senses. You can create lots of variations of this exercise to wake up your senses, such as:

- Suck on an ice cube, an Altoid, or other bracingly refreshing mint, ginger candy, or lemon drops (unsweetened is best—then you really pucker).
- Inhale a strong smell such as eucalyptus, lavender, or green apple.
- Snap a rubber band or hair elastic against your wrist.
- Take off your shoes and walk barefoot—literally connecting your feet with the ground is enormously helpful.

Concentration Games

Another way to ground yourself is by putting your brain to work. Choose an activity that requires some concentration, but not too much. You want to spark your brain, not light it on fire.

- Count backward from 100 by 8 (Mags says this would cause her brain to smoke; she recommends counting backward "like a normal person"—99, 98, 97, 96 . . . and so on).
- Recite the words of a favorite poem (we like The Raven by Edgar Allan Poe for this task, but anything you were forced to memorize in middle school will work).
- Create a shopping list using items from each letter of the alphabet.
- Say aloud the words to a song you used to love but haven't heard in a while.
- If you have a large family, list all your cousins by age.
- Recite the capitals of the United States—by the time you get to the tenth one, you'll be out of the spin cycle.

By the way, panic is not the only thing grounding helps. Many PTSD sufferers use it as well, especially in dealing with flashbacks.

> *When I was a child, I was the victim of sexual abuse. Now certain situations trigger flashbacks and dissociation—which is how I coped with the abuse. It is especially bad when anything is put into my mouth and I feel like I am going to gag. Going to the dentist is really rough: I get flashbacks, which send me into a panic. In order to get through the visit, I wear earphones and blast my music really loud. My dentist also lets me bring a diffuser so that I can use aromatherapy during the appointment. I also take frequent breaks to splash water on my face.* (Emma, age 47)

TLC

In addition to the aforementioned techniques, we have our own strategy for dealing with panic. It's called TLC and is based on the principles of grounding, distraction, and self-talk.

Talk to yourself
Loosen all constraints
Cool down

What does this mean, exactly?

Talk is about saying words to yourself *aloud*. These words can be anything soothing or a particular mantra you like. But you must at least whisper the words, so your ears can hear them.

Why? We have said before that there is copious evidence for the effectiveness of self-talk, but here's another interesting factoid: an educator named Edgar Dale, who conducted research on how we learn and retain information, discovered that while we typically remember only 10 percent of what we read and 20 percent of what we hear, we retain 70 percent of what we *say out loud*. So it seems that saying is believing. Also, speaking engages your auditory sense, which is grounding in and of itself.

When you talk to yourself aloud, remind yourself that what you are feeling is panic. Your physical symptoms are the result of anxiety and they will pass. It's very important to talk to yourself in a calm and reassuring tone—like how you would address a scared child or another Anxiety Sister. Here are some suggestions:

- "Breathe in, breathe out."
- "This too shall pass."
- "This is unpleasant, but I can handle it."
- "This is temporary; it is just how I am feeling now."
- "Ride the wave."
- "I am okay."
- "Serenity now!"

Loosen is about freeing your body of anything restrictive or tight. Many of us experience a choking or claustrophobic feeling during a panic episode. One of the things we have found very helpful is to get as physically "free" as possible. If you are home, get naked. This, of course, might not work as well in your office or in the dairy aisle of the supermarket, so what we suggest is feeling as close to naked as possible. Undo your seatbelt, pull out hair clips, ditch the bra and pantyhose, get rid of the belt, unbutton your jeans. Give yourself as much breathing room as possible. For most people, feeling unbound gets their blood flowing again and allows their muscles to relax.

Cool is about bringing your body temperature down. Anxiety causes your blood vessels to constrict, which heats the body. Our fight-or-flight response has released all that adrenaline, which serves to rev up our system (thus the rapid heartbeat, flushing, muscle tightness, and sweating). Coolness reverses the process and resets your body so it stops sending out all that adrenaline. You know the saying "hot and bothered"? Well, we are trying for the opposite sensation.

One of our favorite ways to cool down is to go for a walk on a cold day or go for a drive with the windows down. If it's hot out (shout-out to our tropical sisters), consider using a cold washcloth, cooling towel, or ice pack on your head and neck, blasting your car's air conditioner, jumping into a cool shower, or even drinking some ice water.

Interrupting the Buildup

What brings on your panic attacks? For many of us, ironically, a common cause of our panic is, well, panic. Since the spin cycle is so physically and emotionally difficult, we often become most anxious about the idea of dealing with another episode. We become panicked about our panic. This is a nasty loop.

It is very difficult to halt panic once it takes over

We become panicked about our panic

your body. Suddenly, you are no longer a thinking being, but only a reacting and feeling one. It's all physical symptoms and spinning. But if you can somehow also stay a thinking being—even while your body is starting to freak out—you can break the cycle. We call this technique "interrupting the buildup." Remember, you are not trying to stop the panic; you are simply trying to change a thought.

What follows is a diagram of a typical panic sequence. It starts with a thought—not even a momentous one, just a little notification from the old memory bank (box 1). That thought triggers symptoms (box 2). The next thought (box 3) triggers even more physical symptoms (box 4), which really sends your mind into overdrive (box 5). Notice how the thoughts and feelings get bigger and scarier with each step.

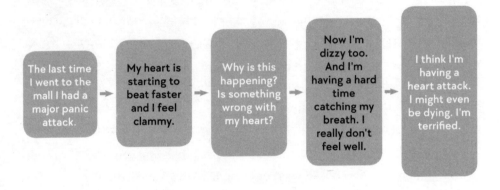

You cannot hope to stop the crescendo when you are in the feeling mode (boxes 2 and 4), but there are some possibilities in the thinking mode—particularly early on when the thoughts and feelings are smaller and more manageable. If you can interrupt or question your thoughts, the resulting feelings become much less intense. And once you start doing that, you get stronger and your panic weakens. Here is another diagram of the same panic sequence that highlights places where the thoughts can be interrupted.

Notice how changing your thoughts (or questioning their validity) results in

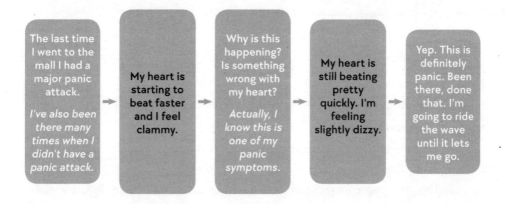

changes to the feelings, and how the feelings deescalate. Of course, this thought-altering strategy takes some practice to master, but it absolutely works. If you would like to take a crack at it and it won't cause you to become anxious, try diagramming one of your panic sequences. First, diagram what happened, then rewrite your thoughts. Visualize the feelings getting less intense while your thoughts take control.

By drawing the diagram when you are *not* anxious, you are creating a new neural pathway that will lessen the intensity of future panic. Plus, you can always pull out your diagram when, in a moment of panic, you are too anxious to think one up.

Phobias

The Panic Loop can lead to the development of a phobia. If you have either a traumatic experience or a panic attack (or both) in a particular situation or place, it makes perfect sense that you would not want to revisit the scene of the crime. Thus, when you even think about that situation or place, you experience anticipatory panic, which then reinforces your fear. In some cases, this becomes a full-fledged phobia.

A few years ago, we were on the highway when a truck hit our car. After that I became really frightened to drive on highways and I did every-thing to avoid them. (Kay, age 60)

After a major panic attack during a concert, I can no longer be in crowds. I get so panicked I feel like I can't breathe. And I always have to be near the exit. (Quinn, age 25)

While some panic loops lend themselves to thought interruption, you abso-lutely cannot think your way out of a phobia. When we have an irrational fear, we naturally do our best to avoid whatever it is that scares us. This avoidance, however, only makes our anxiety more intense. The most effective treatment for phobias is called exposure therapy, which re-quires us to stop avoiding what we fear. It asks us to do the very thing that feels the most impossible and to keep doing it until it no longer feels so difficult. By exposing ourselves to our fears over and over again, we gradually develop a tolerance for the anxiety, and ultimately we stop feeling fearful altogether.

This avoidance, however, only makes our anxiety more intense

Obviously, this type of treatment is highly anxiety-provoking in the short term, but it is usually very helpful—if not curative—in the long term. Both of us benefited tremendously from exposure therapy; although it took some time and quite a lot of discomfort, we both overcame our phobias.

One of my phobias was of elevators. Since I lived on the sixteenth floor of an apartment building, this made it difficult to go in and out of my home. Because of how disruptive this particular phobia was in my life, my therapist suggested exposure therapy. She told me to ride my eleva-tor up to the top floor and back down to the lobby without getting out. When I started working on this assignment, I felt like I was going to pass out each time I got in the elevator, and I was extremely nauseated.

The first time I could only stay on for five minutes. Imagine my door-man's surprise as the door opened in the lobby and there I was, huddled in the corner of the elevator trying to breathe deeply. Slowly, over the course of a few weeks, I built up from five minutes to a whole hour. After riding for an hour a few times, I was no longer afraid of elevators—I was just bored. (Mags, age 52)

A few things we've learned about exposure therapy:

• Exposure needs to be repeated consistently. This is not a quick fix, and it takes a lot of practice.
• You may start by doing only a few minutes of exposure, but you are aiming to build up to an hour (e.g., an hour of driving).
• Because of the discomfort that inevitably accompanies exposure, you may have to take meds (we did!), at least in the beginning. It's not impossible to do exposure therapy without meds, but it's pretty hard.
• Sometimes having an anxiety buddy or therapist with you helps. If you have a nonprofessional with you, make sure they know what they're doing.
• If you do exposure therapy for one phobia, you may find that it helps with other phobias. How's that for a perk?

One final thought about phobias: like bunnies, if left to their own devices, phobias tend to grow and multiply. Also, they are the quickest route to SWS (shrinking world syndrome). So it's super-important to get help because phobias are so treatable. It's no trip to the spa, but its contributions to your well-being are enormous.

At first it was only heights, which was pretty easy to avoid. Then I noticed that I started to become fearful of places that weren't especially high. We went hiking to a waterfall with some friends. I started

panicking on the first rock and had to go back down the hill. After that
I wouldn't hike except on flat terrain. My roommate teases me that soon
I won't be able to go up a flight of stairs without panicking. What's scary
is that doesn't seem so impossible. (Stella, age 20)

We recognize that any situation can result in panic, but there are a few specific scenarios we get asked about all the time:

Night Panic

Nighttime panic attacks are incredibly frightening and disruptive to our sleep cycles. Of course, not getting enough sleep can easily lead to more anxiety. It can feel like a never-ending cycle. The treatment for middle-of-the-night panic is pretty similar to the treatment for daytime panic. You can use TLC and grounding techniques to help you manage.

There has been some research suggesting that how you speak to yourself before you go to bed influences your sleep experiences. This is why we encourage night anxiety sufferers to repeat a mantra like "I am at peace," "Breathe in, breathe out," or something equally soothing. Some people find it helpful to do a guided meditation before going to sleep. One Anxiety Sister has told us she likes to listen to the sounds of the rain forest as she falls asleep. Soft music is another idea. You can download free recordings of all types from the internet. Another really helpful intervention is aromatherapy or essential oils that you can diffuse while you are sleeping.

Note: It is important to rule out other medical issues such as sleep apnea, thyroid imbalances, gastrointestinal distress, and other conditions that can wake us up and mimic the symptoms of panic attacks. Some doctors suggest sleep studies and other tests to rule out a variety of causes.

Morning Panic

While some people find their worst time for panic is at night, others really struggle in the morning. There are many possible reasons for this. One is that the stress hormone cortisol is at its highest level in the first hour after you wake up. Another is that your blood sugar is at its lowest because you presumably haven't eaten since the night before (unless you are like Mags and raid the snack bar in the wee hours). And if you are a night panicker or experience disrupted sleep, that doesn't help either.

Some morning panickers do so at the thought of having to get out of the house and go to work. Anxiety sufferers quickly find themselves in the Panic Loop when confronted with the possibility of a day fraught with spin cycles. Agoraphobics may panic at just the thought of leaving home. Whatever the reason, morning panic is especially miserable because of the time constraints and responsibilities that are not typically there at bedtime.

To counteract the higher levels of cortisol in your body, one thing you can do is something called progressive muscle relaxation (PMR). A form of meditation, PMR requires you to lie flat on your back (you can put a pillow under your legs if your back is sore) and then systematically tense and relax each muscle in your body.

We like to start with our foreheads, but you can start anywhere you like. To tighten your forehead muscles, raise your eyebrows as high as you can and hold it for five seconds (you can count aloud if you like). Then release your eyebrows and feel your whole upper face relax. Pause for a few moments to take a nice, deep breath. Then do your lower face by smiling as hard as you can and holding for five seconds, feeling your cheeks tense up. Once again, release. Pause for a breath, then move to your eyes—squeeze them shut for five seconds and then release. Your whole face should feel so much softer and more relaxed.

Moving on to your neck, look up at the ceiling, letting your head slide back. Hold for five seconds and release. Next, tighten your shoulder muscles by trying to get them to touch your ears (by shrugging) and hold for five seconds. Then move to your upper back: tighten the muscles by pulling your shoulder blades together and holding. Once again, release. Continue progressing down your body, tensing each muscle group for five seconds and releasing. Pause between body parts to take a nice, deep breath. Go all the way to your toes, which you should flex for five seconds and release. Then point them for five seconds and release. By the time you are finished, your muscles should be pretty limp. As a bonus, you will be focused on your body (due to the grounding effects of PMR) and not on your mind, so your anxiety should be on hiatus, even just for a short while.

Another effective morning "icebreaker" is 4-7-8 breathing, which we discussed on pages 118–119. As with PMR, you can do this breathing exercise as soon as you open your eyes, without even having to get out of bed. Chamomile tea and certain essential oils are also very helpful.

It's a really good idea for morning panickers to have a simple but consistent routine so they can be on autopilot and not have to think too hard about the day ahead. You don't want to have to organize yourself (or anyone else) when you are in the spin cycle.

Car Panic

One of the places people often panic is in their cars. If you are in your car, in addition to giving yourself some TLC you can:

- Unbuckle your seatbelt.
- Roll down your windows (if the outside air is cool and fresh).
- Turn on the air conditioner and aim the vents directly at your face.
- Listen to soothing music.
- Play a light but engaging audiobook (David Sedaris works really well).
- Tune in to an inane but comical radio show.

- Suck on a peppermint or lemon drop (Mags likes sour apple).
- Pull over and take a walk.
- Phone a buddy to talk you through it.

For some folks, their car panic is due to a driving phobia. If you are one of these people, you may want to look into exposure therapy or medication. You're not going to like this, but the key to managing driving phobias is to drive. The good news is you can start with teeny-tiny baby steps—just a few minutes of driving at a time. Begin with local roads you know well—not during rush hour—and slowly work up to bigger streets. If highways are what scare you, drive in the right lane with your hazards on, one exit at a time. Ideally, you want to work up to an hour of driving, but take your time getting there. It is a difficult process, but it can be done. Just ask Mags, who now regularly takes extended highway rides *for fun*.

Flying Panic

In addition to TLC, we find it essential that you have a Spin Kit with you when you fly because disembarking midway is not a safe option (even though we've both tried). Its purpose is twofold: (1) to help you self-soothe (like a pacifier for a baby), and (2) to provide a plan of action—something to do other than try to crawl out of your skin. You particularly want to bring stuff that smells good (because planes don't) and noise-canceling headphones to block out scary noises. Something to occupy your hands, like needlework or a soft fabric, is also very helpful. We cannot emphasize enough how important it is to carry one of these kits when you travel by plane.

Another great tip: wear the appropriate anxiety wardrobe. You should feel cool and comfortable. Avoid tight waistbands, push-up bras, and turtlenecks. Instead opt for loose layers that are easily removed.

The best solution we've found for a midair panic attack is flying first class (if you can afford to do so). Don't be afraid to tell a member of the flight crew if you are spinning. First of all, he or she can provide help in the form of a cold compress or a cold glass of water. Second, if there are empty seats, a really sympathetic flight attendant may be able to move you up front if you're sitting in another section. In first class, there is tons more air and the seats are way bigger, so no one can touch you. Any way you can get up there, try to do it.

As is the case with driving phobias, the only way to beat a fear of flying is to do it and do it a lot. Start with short trips. If you live in New York, look for a discount fare to Boston or Washington. If you live in Miami, hop on a shuttle to Tampa. L.A. to San Fran is another good phobia-beating route. You don't have to be in the air for very long—even a forty-minute flight counts. The more often you fly, the less panic you will experience.

DIB

This strategy is a last-resort option. We are big believers in not allowing panic to take over our lives. In fact, we spend most of our time trying to teach others how to manage their panic. But we are nothing if not realists. Sometimes no strategy, no amount of effort, no medicine, and no mantras will work. There are days we could breathe deeply while taking an ice bath and repeating "This too shall pass" after taking a Xanax blessed by the Dalai Lama and we would *still* have crushing panic.

Occasionally, it is okay to give in to the anxiety, and ride it out from the safety of your bed. This is especially true in the beginning of your journey, before you have learned what strategies work for you. Even we panic veterans still need to dive into bed (DIB) on occasion. In fact, as long as you follow some DIB guidelines, a few hours or even a full day in bed can be incredibly therapeutic.

Why do we have DIB guidelines? Because if not used with caution, DIB can be a segue to persistent avoidance behaviors, which can result in SWS. Yes, we like to use initialisms. LOL.

1. Do not DIB two days in a row. Or even two days in a week. It's too easy to make it a habit. (We know this from experience.) If you cannot stop DIBing, you need to seek help ASAP (there are those initials again).

2. Reserve DIB as your emergency option—when all other options have been exhausted (or will be useless).

3. Try not to DIB during important life events—a friend's wedding (or your own), a funeral, the day of a trip departure, and so on. These are the times we most feel like DIBing; however, if you DIB on those days, it becomes much harder to "get back to normal." If at all possible (and we know this is no small task), drag yourself out of bed and show up, even if you feel and look like a wreck. Being there counts. And it shows you that anxiety does not get to run your life. Of course, if you do need to DIB, try to do it for only an hour and then get going—no matter what you look like. (Mags once wore sweatpants to an important and dressy event with Abs's family—it wasn't pretty, but she was there.) Tell yourself to get to the event and that you can DIB as soon as it's over.

4. Don't feel guilty about diving into bed. It is part of the anxiety condition and happens to all of us from time to time. However, if you are DIBing frequently, take it as a sign that you need more help in managing your anxiety.

Sometimes nothing else helps me but a warm blanket and my sofa.
(Johanna, age 63)

THAT SOUNDS LIKE A GOOD IDEA, BUT . . .

When you are in the spin cycle, many well-meaning people will try to offer advice. The thing is, the advice may not actually be helpful:

• Hot showers (or baths): This is a common suggestion that may backfire. Warmth, while soothing much of the time, can be a disaster if you are already overheated.

- Exercise: While exercise is a great way to manage stress, depression, and various diseases, elevating your heart rate and sweating are not typically helpful during panic. Those famous endorphins are not useful when you are already doused in adrenaline. It's kind of like going to a rock concert to alleviate a screaming headache.
- Alcohol: Particularly if you are experiencing dizziness or stomach upset, this is a bad idea. While there are some folks who report feeling better after having a drink, most just feel dizzier, hotter, sicker, and more out of control. Remember bed spins?
- Massage, wraps, and other body treatments: Since claustrophobia and overheating are hallmarks of panic, you may want to avoid being covered in warm blankets and rubbed by warm hands.

> When I went for my spa treatment, they wrapped me like a mummy in these hot, wet sheets from my neck to my ankles. Then they dripped warm oil on my forehead and started massaging my scalp. Suddenly, I felt like I was suffocating. I got so freaked out that I had to stop the treatment. *(Jessica, 24)*

- Cuddling and hugs: See above. Many Anxiety Sisters have told us (and we feel the same way) that being touched during a panic attack heightens their disorientation and claustrophobia.
- Getting out of the house (shopping, lunch, etc.): No matter how much we wish it were otherwise, a great sale cannot interrupt panic. And don't even think of trying on clothes in a hot fluorescent-lit fitting room the size of an airplane lavatory. Being in a mall or restaurant can add to your sensory overload.
- "Just relax": People love to say this, but our response is something like, "I'm having an out-of-body experience—*you* *@$%# relax!"

We know some of you are saying, "The most soothing thing for me during panic is a hot bath, a glass of wine, and a massage." Certainly, there are many Panic Sisters who swear by weighted blankets and other forms of swaddling. That's what makes horse races, as our grandmothers would say. Of course, do what works for you!

On a final note, it is possible to deal with panic without medication. Possible. But *really* hard. Like walking-a-tightrope-in-stilettos hard. If you aren't a Flying Wallenda, you may need a prescription for meds, at least in the beginning of treatment. We did. And it really helped.

eleven

Better Living Through Chemistry

First things first: *we are not doctors.* As such, we are unwilling to dispense medical advice (although we have been known to hand out the occasional Ativan to desperate sisters). Anything we say about medication is based on experiences other Anxiety Sisters have shared with us, discussions with many psychiatrists and psychopharmacologists, the latest research, and our own trial and error (a lot of error and many trials). Another caveat: The stories you'll read in this chapter are *not* recommendations or medical advice. Every body is different and every person has a unique reaction to medication. It is therefore critically important to consult your own medical practitioner for guidance.

Our general stance is that because anxiety is a medical issue (a brain disorder), treating it with medication may be necessary—much in the same way we treat bacterial infections with antibiotics or diabetes with insulin. Both of us are on an SSRI, which is a medication taken daily, to manage our anxiety disorders for the long term. We have been on these meds (Zoloft and Prozac) for years and probably will be until the end. (Mags always says, "You can pry my Zoloft from my cold, dead hands.") We are very lucky that these meds work so well for us with minimal side effects.

That said, we recognize that medication is not for everyone. There are some very real disadvantages to taking antianxiety meds, including side effects ranging from mild to deal-breaking. As is true for any decision, you have to weigh the pros against the cons. Speaking with a medical practitioner (preferably one who specializes in anxiety medication), your therapist, as well as a good pharmacist (such an underutilized resource) should help you decide what is right for you.

To begin, it is very important to become familiar with the lingo. There are several classes of medication prescribed to treat anxiety.

Benzodiazepines (Benzos)

These meds are muscle relaxants/sedatives. You probably know them by their brand names: Valium, Ativan, Librium, Xanax, and Klonopin (generic names: diazepam, lorazepam, chlordiazepoxide, alprazolam, and clonazepam), to name the most popular. These tranquilizers work immediately—usually within thirty minutes of taking them. Due to their quick-acting nature, benzos are very helpful in managing acute anxiety, such as phobic reactions and panic attacks. Because they slow your nervous system down and relax your muscles, benzos are also prescribed for insomnia. Often they are prescribed "as needed"—that is, whenever you feel panicky, you take one (or two). Many sufferers are prescribed daily doses of benzos as a kind of preventive measure.

> *Maybe once a month I go through a day or two when my heart starts to beat really fast and I get short of breath. The whole thing lasts maybe a minute, but it can happen five or six times throughout the day. My psychiatrist gave me Xanax to take whenever I feel the anxiety coming on. I asked about going on an SSRI, but the doctor felt, because it doesn't happen that much, that the Xanax would be enough. And it has been.*
> (Kristin, age 49)

I take half an Ativan every morning when I wake up to manage my morning anxiety. Even when I don't wake up with it, I still take the pill. I've been doing this for the last ten years, and it has made such a difference in my quality of life. (Doreen, age 66)

Although many benefit tremendously from these drugs, benzodiazepines can be addictive for some people. Thus, they are not recommended for folks with substance abuse issues. We know many Anxiety Sisters (including Abs) who have taken these drugs for years without increasing their dosages or becoming addicted, but it is something to consider and monitor when starting to take benzos. Rarely, some folks with no previous substance abuse problems can become addicted to these medications and face serious withdrawal symptoms.

Benzos are so addictive. My GP started me on them in my twenties— kind of a "mother's little helper." Now I am in my fifties and can hardly stand the nerve ticks and stuttering I experience if I take none. These drugs are very destructive and not worth it. (Heather, age 58)

I never had an addiction problem until I started to take Valium. I ended up in the hospital because I had such severe physical effects from coming off it. I was even suicidal. If people tell you they are not addictive, don't believe them. (Lisa, age 32)

Benzos are often discussed in terms of overdose, especially regarding a number of recent celebrity deaths. Here's the problem: they slow down the nervous system (thus the sedating effect), so if taken in doses higher than prescribed and in conjunction with alcohol or other drugs that also depress the nervous system, they become dangerous. Approximately 30 percent of people who overdose on opioids also have benzos in their systems.[1] This is why benzos are contraindicated for substance abusers.

The opioid crisis is one reason many doctors will no longer prescribe benzos, even though they are not opioids. However, as many as 17 percent of folks who take benzos misuse them.[2] We get that the docs are gun-shy—17 percent is not an insignificant number. But what about the other 83 percent who truly benefit from the responsible use of benzos?

> *I have been taking Klonopin for many years for my anxiety. But when my doctor moved and I went to a new one, she decided I needed to come off it. She tried putting me on SSRIs, but those made me feel awful and even more anxious. I keep trying to tell her that Klonopin works for me—no side effects or addiction—but she just won't prescribe it. It is so frustrating. I had something that helped so much and nothing else seems to work. (Meredith, age 46)*

There have been some studies connecting Alzheimer's and dementia with long-term use of benzos.[3] In all fairness, these studies involved people taking very high doses of benzos on a daily basis. And many other medications—even some over-the-counter drugs—have also been linked with cognitive issues. Food for thought: the risk factors associated with untreated anxiety (e.g., social isolation) are also strongly correlated with higher risk for Alzheimer's and other cognitive impairments as we age.[4]

Selective Serotonin Reuptake Inhibitors (SSRIs)

The first SSRI—Prozac (fluoxetine)—came out in 1987 and was followed by several others, including Zoloft (sertraline), Paxil (paroxetine), Lexapro (escitalopram), Celexa (citalopram), and Luvox (fluvoxamine). These meds, unlike benzos, have to be taken on a consistent basis (daily) and may not be fully effective for a long period of time (up to six to eight weeks). Also, SSRIs are not addictive (more on this later).

We've talked quite a bit about serotonin, which is one of the body's feel-good chemicals thought to stabilize mood. (Serotonin is also connected with appetite, digestion, and sleep cycles.) In order for serotonin to help us feel good, however, it has to be outside the brain's cells (actually, in the gaps between them). Once it is inside a brain cell, it doesn't do anything—bad or good—so the job of an SSRI is to block the reabsorption of serotonin into brain cells. When people say that the brain stops producing serotonin with the use of SSRIs, they are mistaken. Production is not affected by the medication, and 95 percent of our serotonin is actually made in the digestive tract (our second brain).

> *Last year, my OCD got so bad, I almost had a nervous breakdown. So I gave in and tried Prozac because I just couldn't live like that. I'm not exaggerating when I say I got my life back. For the first time that I can remember, I'm not counting every step I take. (Simone, age 31)*

Serotonin-Norepinephrine Reuptake Inhibitors (SNRIs)

Similar to SSRIs but targeting an additional neurotransmitter, this class of meds includes Effexor (venlafaxine), Cymbalta (duloxetine), and Pristiq (desvenlafaxine). These drugs are taken daily and, like SSRIs, may require several weeks to be fully effective.

Buspirone (Buspar)

This drug is a very mild tranquilizer (but is not a benzo), typically prescribed for mild to moderate anxiety, especially for sufferers of generalized anxiety disorder (GAD). Buspar is taken daily and, once again, you may have to wait a month or more for it to fully kick in.

Beta-Blockers

This class of fast-acting drugs includes Inderal and Tenormin, which are prescribed off-label to counteract the physiological effects of anxiety, such as pounding heart, sweating, and shortness of breath. Beta-blockers lower your blood pressure and heart rate by blocking adrenaline, so they can be very effective for performance or public speaking anxiety. Nowadays, thanks to the opioid crisis, these meds may be prescribed instead of benzos.

Antihistamines

Another benzo replacement, antihistamines like Atarax and Vistaril (hydroxyzine) are sometimes prescribed to treat anxiety because of their sedating effects and their effect on serotonin. Some folks take over-the-counter Benadryl, also an antihistamine, to help with anxiety-induced insomnia. Antihistamines are fast-acting drugs, so they are often taken on an "as needed" basis.

> *Nights are the worst time for my anxiety. Even if I can fall asleep, I can't stay asleep. Now I am taking a prescription antihistamine and I really get a good night's sleep—what a relief!* (Iris, age 71)

In no way is this an exhaustive list of antianxiety medications. Many sufferers we have spoken with take other drugs such as tricyclics (e.g., Anafranil, Tofranil), MAOIs (e.g., Marplan, Nardil), NDRIs (Wellbutrin), and antipsychotics (e.g., Abilify, Seroquel, Haldol) to manage their anxiety.

Do I Need Medication?

This is where you need to consult a doctor. Only someone with medical training can determine if you need medication and, if so, what kind you should take. Many anxiety prescriptions come from internists, which makes sense because they are the first people most of us go to when we don't feel well. Here's the tricky part: not all internists are experts on anxiety meds. In fact, the only experience some internists have with anxiety drugs are with the samples dropped off by pharmaceutical reps.

We recommend that you find a professional who is an expert in managing anxiety with medication. Often that person will be a psychiatrist or psychopharmacologist, but not always. It may be a nurse practitioner or even, in some states, a psychologist who has chosen to specialize in this field. Get a referral from someone you trust (*not* the yellow pages)—either another Anxiety Sister or your favorite doc. If you live in a place with limited choices or you don't have insurance, telemedicine may be the way to go.

Buyer beware: You are in a vulnerable position when you are searching for help, and not all practitioners are created equal. If a doctor tries to sell you *anything*, run to the nearest exit and never look back. Abs spent an entire year choking down disgusting vitamin shakes "specially formulated for anxiety sufferers" twice each day to the tune of two bucks a pop—all of this courtesy of a very well-respected local psychiatrist. While the doc raked in the money, Abs continued to panic.

Another red flag: Do not accept a prescription from anyone who hasn't spent a good amount of time (more than fifteen minutes) discussing your medical history. Your first appointment should take no less than forty-five minutes. Be suspicious if you don't feel that the doctor is responding to your specific needs; there is no cookie-cutter approach to anxiety

There is no cookie-cutter approach to anxiety meds

meds. Most of all, trust your gut. It is completely appropriate and probably even smart to get a second opinion.

A dozen psychiatrists ago, when we were first beginning our journey with anxiety meds, we did not know the right questions to ask. Now we do, and we want you to know them too. Take the following questions with you when you visit your practitioner (you can download a checklist from our website). If he or she cannot or will not answer them, find another doctor.

1. **Why are you prescribing this particular medication?** In other words, why Prozac versus Zoloft, Paxil, or others? You want to know how a drug will address *your* specific symptoms. Although the SSRIs (and SNRIs) as a class work in similar ways, there are definitely subtle differences, and those differences can make a big impact on how you respond to them. Your practitioner should be intimately familiar with all the options and which one or combination would suit you the best.

2. **How long will it take to work?** One of the problems with SSRIs and SNRIs is that in order to work, they need to build up in your system over a period of weeks (or months). It is not a quick fix. Although you may start to notice a slight improvement after the first two weeks, generally you will not realize the full effect of the drug until you have been taking it for at least six weeks. No two people react the same way to the same drug, so it is hard to predict exactly when you will start to feel better. Ask your doctor if it is appropriate for you to take a benzo while you wait for your SSRI or SNRI to kick in. If not, load up on TLC and hang tight.

3. **What is the therapeutic dosage for my medication?** This question is really for those of you taking SSRIs or SNRIs; finding the right dosage is a real art with these classes of meds. Typically, sufferers taking SSRIs or SNRIs begin with a "starter dose," which is less than the dosage required for full effectiveness (the therapeutic dose). The idea behind a starter

dose is to ease a small amount of the drug into your system. This allows you to see how well you tolerate the medicine; it also minimizes side effects. Most people, after a period of two or three weeks, will have their dosages upped to a therapeutic level. Why do you need to know all this technical stuff? The following story from a fellow sufferer should shed some light:

When I told my internist about the panic attacks, he put me on Effexor and handed me a whole bag of samples. It took a while, but after a couple of months, I definitely felt better. Over time, though, I noticed more and more breakthrough anxiety, so I went to a psychiatrist my friend had used. When I told the psychiatrist that I thought I needed to switch medications, he told me that I was on a starter dose, which in my case was not enough to be fully effective. He then wrote me a new script for a higher dose. The improvement was almost immediate. (Odette, age 56)

4. **What are my instructions for taking this medicine?** You may think this is a no-brainer; after all, wouldn't any doctor give you specific instructions with your prescription? In a word, *no*. Amazingly enough, our experience has been that practitioners who give explicit directions are the exception and not the rule. The following are some of the specifics you should know about your medication before you leave your doctor's office:

• Should I take this med with food? (Will it upset my stomach?)
• What time of day should I take this med?
• Do I have to take this med at the same time every day?
• What if I miss a dose?
• Can I drink alcohol while taking this med?
• Can I smoke pot while taking this med?

- Will this med make me sleepy? (Or will it cause insomnia?)
- What if I get pregnant?
- Can I take a generic? (Is one available, and if so, will it be as effective?)
- How will this med interact with my current prescriptions, vitamins, herbal remedies, Ben & Jerry's addiction, etc.?

After my bout with breast cancer, my oncologist put me on Tamoxifen. At the time, I was taking Zoloft for my anxiety, and it was working great, but the doctor told me that Zoloft counteracts Tamoxifen, so I'd have to switch to Effexor. I didn't want to switch because the Zoloft was working so well, but there was no way I was going to mess with my cancer treatment. (Gretchen, age 63)

This story was particularly powerful for us because one of Abs's close family members was on both Tamoxifen and Zoloft at the time. When Abs shared Gretchen's story with her relative, the relative immediately called her oncologist. Shockingly, the doctor had no idea of the contraindication, but when he looked it up, he took her off the Zoloft right away. This is a great argument for not only asking your doctor but also asking your pharmacist and doing your own research.

Speaking of pharmacists, they are invaluable members of the Anxiety Sister's care team. Do not underestimate a good pharmacist's knowledge, which can rival that of a doctor. If you don't already know your pharmacist's name, go introduce yourself.

If you are a Suggestible Sister (you responded to the recent reports of a rare flesh-eating bacteria by making an emergency appointment with your dermatologist), you may want to tiptoe around the discussion of side effects. Let's face it—you have the ability to bring on your own symptoms. Accordingly, our recommendation for Suggestible Sisters is not to ask about side effects until *after* you experience them. For those of you who don't have a suggestibility issue, definitely ask your practitioner about the most common side effects that occur with the particular med she or he is prescribing.

But I'm Afraid to Take Medication

So were we. And so were most of the people we've met. If you can manage without meds, great. But for those of us who need more help, fear shouldn't stand in the way of getting it. After all, there's nothing more frightening and uncomfortable than daily spinning. Nobody likes the dentist, but if your tooth is throbbing, you will move heaven and earth to get to her office. Because resistance is such a common issue, we thought we'd mention some of the major stumbling blocks:

- "My personality will change." Thanks to the media and its liberal use of the term "happy pill," many sufferers are concerned that taking meds will make them feel either high or somehow not themselves. Benzos, SSRIs, and SNRIs are *not* personality-altering drugs.

- "I'll get addicted." "Addiction" is a tricky word because people define the term differently. We agree with Dr. Michael Craig Miller of Harvard Medical School, who writes that addiction is a "complex pattern of behavior that involves craving, drug seeking, and needing more and more drug to produce the desired effect."[5] In that sense, SSRIs and SNRIs are not addictive. Nobody craves Paxil or Prozac. That being said, there is no doubt that these drugs change your body chemistry. If you miss a dose or decide to go off the medication abruptly, you will experience physiological symptoms (more on that later). Benzos are a bit different. Because their effects are immediate, there is more potential for abuse. If you have concerns or a history of substance abuse, certainly discuss this with your physician or pharmacist.

• "I've heard that medication isn't necessary to treat anxiety." Some professionals say that medication only alleviates the symptoms without addressing the underlying cause of the anxiety. First of all, as you have read in chapter five, it is often virtually impossible to pinpoint the exact source of your anxiety, especially since there tends to be more than one cause. Second, medication and other treatments are not mutually exclusive. Sometimes medication can be a good place to start because it will calm you enough to allow you to try other coping techniques. If you can't get out of bed, it's difficult to meditate your anxiety away. For some sufferers, medication alone does the trick. Others find nondrug interventions more suitable. And many find a combination of medication and therapy to be most helpful. In any case, there should be no judgment regarding the "best" treatment.

> *I had severe agoraphobia and could barely leave the house. I could not follow through on a lot of things I needed to do for therapy because my panic would become so horrible. When I went on medication, it became easier (but still really hard) to start doing what I needed to deal with the agoraphobia. I was in therapy twice a week and with medication was able to take back my life.* (Kitty, age 45)

• "I want to use a 'natural' remedy." This sounds reasonable until you discover that herbs are not regulated. In addition, even natural substances interact with your body's chemistry and with other medications (including non-pharmaceuticals) you may be taking. For example, if you take blood thinners, you should avoid too much chamomile. If you are going to go the natural route, you really have to do your homework so that you fully understand where the product came from, what its contraindications are, and what other ingredients may be in the product. Finally, as is the case with *anything* you ingest, there can be side effects, some of which are pretty severe.

I was taking Saint-John's-wort for my depression because I wanted to avoid medication. After a few doses, I started getting a racy heart—it felt like I was on speed. It made me so anxious, I had to stop taking it right away. (Devon, age 21)

- "If I just eat a healthy diet and exercise, I won't need medication." Anxiety is a brain disorder. While eating nutritious foods and exercising can certainly improve the quality of one's overall health, plenty of healthy eaters and movers suffer from anxiety. We know lots of vegans and marathoners with anxiety disorders.

If you are dealing with mild to moderate anxiety, we agree that dietary changes (such as limiting sugar and caffeine) and exercise are great first steps. Some folks can rely solely on lifestyle changes to manage the less acute symptoms of brain illness. But panic and other severe forms of anxiety are a different animal altogether.

Exercising while in the throes of panic can often exacerbate your symptoms—after all, cardio gets your heart rate up and your body all flushed and sweaty. Likewise, when we are in a state of panic or acute anxiety, most of us can barely eat—sometimes for days at a time. Following the FDA food pyramid while in the spin cycle may simply not be an option.

We have not read a study that has shown gluten-free diets to be effective in managing anxiety, but we have heard some anecdotal evidence that people have felt that it has helped. There is much more solid evidence to support keeping blood sugar levels stable, staying well hydrated, and sleeping as anxiety management techniques. Although, once again, it is generally extremely difficult to focus on these issues when one is experiencing acute anxiety.

- "Once I start with these meds, I'll be stuck on them for life." This is also a myth. We know so many Anxiety Sisters who have gone off their meds when they felt better and more able to cope. Lots of people have tried anxiety meds and found them helpful without becoming "lifers."

I took medicine for a year. Now exercise is my medicine. But it wasn't until I took meds that I could even think about other techniques. (Joan, age 61)

• "I should be strong enough to beat this on my own." What this statement really points to is the stigma our culture places on mental illness, which it systematically delegitimizes. Our society treats anxiety as a sign of weakness. As a result, there's a cloud of shame surrounding the use of meds.

I have always thought of myself as so competent and together. I shouldn't need to take a pill in order to control my mind. (Jen, age 27)

My mother and father were the types that did not believe in medication. In fact, they didn't believe in mental illness. So I lived with a lot of anxiety but I never talked about it with anyone. Finally, I went to a doctor for help. Even though I was scared, I tried several different medication combinations over the course of a year until I found one that worked. I still have not told my family because they would judge me. (Molly, age 48)

I used to think anxiety medications were the easy way out. But then my daughter started having panic attacks and it was a nightmare. She missed so much school and stopped hanging out with her friends. We tried therapy and yoga and deep breathing and all the natural treatments out there. None of them stopped the dizziness and stomach problems she had every single day. Finally, she begged us to let her take something for the anxiety. Thank goodness we did. She is a different person now. (Arden, age 39)

So let's talk about the bad rap anxiety medication has, because we believe it is a cultural issue more than a medical one. Mental illness has always been stigmatized and treated as less valid than other diseases, so it makes sense that medications used to treat mental illness are stigmatized and treated as less valid than other medications. This is still, after so many years, infuriating to us.

Nobody takes issue with blood pressure medication or cholesterol-lowering medication or diabetes medication. These are all considered legitimate and necessary for the treatment of illness. Society's ignorance notwithstanding, antianxiety meds are just as legitimate.

This is not to say that anxiety meds are benign. They, like all drugs, herbs, vitamins, and anything else you ingest, come with side effects, some of which can be nasty. (More on that in a moment.)

All Anxiety Sisters who are suffering from an illness of the brain should feel comfortable mitigating the effects of their condition using all available options, as needed. Shame should not be part of this process.

Trigger Warning!

This next section contains detailed information about side effects, which may not be healthy for Suggestible Sisters.

Feel free to skip ahead.

Living the Fine Print

Buckle in, folks, because we're addressing side effects, which couldn't be more erroneously named—these guys are front and center. We're trying to be real here, because these cherries come with some serious pits. We don't want to scare you off, but you should be aware of what you are getting yourself into. Most people, when first taking SSRIs or SNRIs, experience a whole new set of physical symptoms unrelated to their anxiety but caused by their anxiety meds.

This is doubly unfair because not only do you have to wait for the medication to work, but in the meantime, you also have to tolerate stomach distress. Or an unrelenting headache. Or dizziness. Or any number of issues ranging from pesky to unbearable. It can take a lot of patience and a very skilled prescriber to help an Anxiety Sister find a medication that relieves her anxiety without causing other serious side effects.

We characterize side effects as either "pimples" or "wrinkles." Pimple side effects, as their name suggests, can be uncomfortable and annoying, but eventually you outgrow them. They typically appear when you first start taking the meds and often subside within a couple of weeks. The most common of these are nausea, diarrhea, queasiness, headaches, drowsiness, insomnia, and irritability.

"Wrinkle" side effects creep up on you over time and tend to stick around for as long as you take the medication. These include long-term sleep disturbance, loss of sexual appetite, difficulty achieving orgasm, dry mouth, and weight gain. Like with real wrinkles, once you discover them, you end up longing for your pimple days.

Each person has a different reaction to these medications, so it is impossible to predict which side effects, if any, you will encounter. What works for one person may not work for another—each person's body chemistry and metabolism is different. Two Anxiety Sisters can have opposite reactions to the same medication. Some folks find they cannot tolerate SSRIs or SNRIs at all.

Side effects, which you can generally tolerate, are not the same, however, as adverse reactions, which you cannot. How do you know what is a side effect and what is an adverse reaction? You make this determination based on your ability to function. For example, one Anxiety Sister told us that upon taking her first SSRI dose, she suddenly felt heart palpitations. "It was like it was beating out of my chest," she recalls. "I was climbing the walls. I knew I couldn't take one more pill." This woman was so unnerved by her reaction that it took her six months (and a lot of spin cycles) to try another med, which turned out to be a great match for her. So if you have an adverse reaction or even a lot of side effects, don't discount the entire class of drugs. Although SSRIs and SNRIs work on the same neurotransmitters, each drug has a different chemical makeup. As such, one person's nightmare is another's nirvana. If at first a med doesn't succeed, try, try again.

> *The first drug I took for my anxiety was Lexapro. After a few weeks, I told the doctor it wasn't helping, so he upped my dose. All that did was make me feel tired all the time, but I still had so much anxiety. So I switched to another drug, which really helped for a while—maybe a year. Then, all of a sudden, the anxiety came back. My doctor said I should switch again. I did and it seems to be working—for now. (Naomi, age 53)*

Weight Gain

We are giving this side effect its own section because of the number of Anxiety Sisters who have shared their frustration with us over the years. Here's what some (of the hundreds) have to say:

> *I gained a ton of weight from SSRIs, mood stabilizers, etc. I am now doing a weight-loss program and am down sixty pounds. It is harder to lose the weight on the meds, but it can be done! (Heidi, age 50)*

> *I gained fifty pounds in total over the first year of taking Paxil. But I had lost a bunch of weight before taking it because I was unable to eat, or when I did, I would have instant diarrhea. My husband says, "Who cares? At least you're healthy now." Gotta love that man! (Jada, age 41)*

> *I have gained over eighty pounds in one year and I was exercising! I can't get the weight off! (Trish, age 65)*

> *Better fluffy than anxious! (Phyllis, age 72)*

My SSRI really helped with my anxiety and depression, but I gained roughly sixty pounds in nine months. I have struggled with obesity my whole life and have worked really hard to get my weight down to a more "reasonable" level. It's hard to figure out which is worse—living with the anxiety or the weight. For now, I'm going to try to do it without the meds. (Reba, age 59)

My biggest pet peeve is to be told by doctor after doctor that I need to diet and exercise more to lose weight when the weight gain has nothing to do with food or exercise habits and everything to do with the medication. (Esme, age 35)

While I am pudgier than I'd like, it's a means to an end to get my dodgy brain back on track and totally worth it. I always drop the weight, or at least a good portion, once I'm off meds again. (Bronwen, age 32)

I gained thirty pounds on my antidepressant. Now I am off it but the weight won't come off. I think my metabolism has changed. (Autumn, age 28)

The one problem I never had is with my weight. But going on medication I gained ten pounds fairly quickly. Since I didn't want to add being overweight to my issues, I went right off. (Chelsea, age 23)

If you ask your MD (and, believe us, we have many times), he or she will probably tell you two things: (1) SSRIs and SNRIs don't cause weight gain—or, at least, not a significant amount—and (2) if someone is gaining weight it is because she feels better and, consequently, has recovered her appetite. As Anxiety Sisters who have battled with the disorder for thirty-plus years, we respectfully disagree. Okay, maybe not so respectfully. Here's the deal.

The first studies of side effects (including weight gain) were sponsored by Big

Pharma. Let's face it, if their studies had shown a connection between America's "biggest sin" (gaining weight) and their incredibly profitable drugs, it would have been a PR nightmare. Big Pharma thus conducted studies with very small samples and over a very short period of time—typically eight to twelve weeks. As you may know, SSRIs take a month or two to get into your system, so not many people reported significant weight gain in the first two or three months. Therefore, the data did not support the idea that people on SSRIs gained weight.

In 2014, Harvard Medical School and Massachusetts General Hospital conducted a study of nineteen thousand people on SSRIs over the course of one year. The researchers found that the average weight gain was one to two pounds ("not significant"). This was a big headline in *JAMA* (*Journal of the American Medical Association*), where many docs get the latest research information. The headline in the publication of Harvard Medical School was: "Antidepressants Cause Minimal Weight Gain." But the authors of the Mass General study suggest in their conclusion that one year may still be too short a time period in which to see significant weight gain.[6]

WebMD researchers, on the other hand, state that upward of 25 percent of people on SSRIs gain ten pounds or more. This is much more in line with reports of significant weight gain that we have heard. We even heard from sufferers who never had weight or food issues (hard for us to imagine) until they started taking SSRIs or SNRIs.

To further complicate this issue, for many of us, our bodies adjust to the higher weight and it becomes very difficult to lose it—even if we go off the meds. Unfortunately, many health care professionals don't understand how hard it is for us to deal with weight gain on top of the mental health issues. This is especially difficult because our culture doesn't treat larger female bodies very well. Contrary to what our culture (and many of those in the medical field) would have you believe, recent research has shown that having a larger-size body does not necessarily make you less healthy.[7] Weight discrimination can be a big source of anxiety in and of itself.

So what can you do about the weight gain? The decision is a very personal one because so many other factors are involved in the equation (such as the existence of an eating disorder, the causes of the anxiety, physical capabilities, etc.), but here are some ideas:

- Use the SSRI or SNRI for only a short stint—six months or less—during which you can find other treatments that work (e.g., therapy, acupuncture, meditation, exercise, herbal supplements). That way you will have gotten on your feet without packing on too many pounds.
- Switch SSRIs or SNRIs. Often just changing from one to another—for example, from Prozac to Zoloft—does the trick. There are subtle differences in each of the drugs within their class, and these can affect your metabolism in different ways.
- Stay on your SSRI or SNRI and accept the plumper but calmer and more-able-to-function you. This is what we chose—we're not always pleased when we look in the mirror, but we are thrilled to be living fulfilling and anxiously happy lives. The trade-off is worth it to us; however, we completely understand and respect that others may view such a trade-off as a deal breaker.

Finally, two don'ts:

- *Do not* take any weight-loss medications (over-the-counter, herbal, or otherwise) while taking SSRIs or SNRIs. Drug interactions are serious business.
- *Do not* let anyone, especially in the medical field, shame you for your weight issues. Fire any health care professional (or anyone else, for that matter) who makes you feel bad about your body size.

Sexual Side Effects

Yup, we're going there. And you should come too (no pun intended) because sexual side effects such as decreased libido and anorgasmia affect more than 70 percent of people taking SSRIs and SNRIs.[8]

> *Before I started taking my meds, I used to be able to climax during foreplay—it took a while, but it usually happened. Now I can't at all—not even with a vibrator. At first I didn't think it was so bad because my anxiety was so much better, but, after a while, I noticed I wanted sex less and less. Like, what's the point? (Delilah, age 43)*

> *My boyfriend is really upset because he can't make me come anymore. I keep telling him it's the drugs, but he doesn't believe me. It's really affecting our relationship. (Kendall, age 19)*

> *I feel pretty flat sexually. It's like I don't even think about sex anymore— I feel sorry for my partner. (Lydia, age 63)*

> *Sex was always really important to me. I have to say that since taking antidepressants, my drive has been cut in half. I can take it or leave it now. (Maya, age 33)*

Sexual health is a very worthy pursuit in the anxiously happy life, so don't ignore it. Also, orgasms can do wonders in the anxiety department. Here are just a few benefits:

• Orgasms decrease activity in the amygdala, the part of the brain responsible for the anxiety fight, flight, or freeze response.

- Orgasms release sleep-inducing chemicals into the bloodstream, thereby staving off insomnia—a known cause of anxiety.
- Orgasms make the neurotransmitter serotonin more available throughout the body, which is exactly what SSRIs and SNRIs aim to do.

So what can you do if your SSRI or SNRI is putting a crimp on your love life? For starters, don't be shy about talking with your prescriber. Unless you are her first patient, she has dealt with this issue quite a bit and should have a few ideas about improving your situation. As we've said before, not all SSRIs and SNRIs are created equal. While they share the same active ingredient, they are different compounds and thus can affect individuals in various ways. Your prescriber may want you to try a new medicine in the same class. For Abs, that was all it took. If you do not want to or can't change meds, your prescriber may lower your dosage or add a "booster" medication such as Wellbutrin or Buspar on the days you are planning to have sex.

In addition:

- Seek support from a sexuality counselor—we suggest choosing a practitioner certified by AASECT (the American Association of Sexuality Educators, Counselors and Therapists). These folks can be tremendously helpful and supportive in managing the sexual side effects of anxiety meds.
- We have read lots of research about the use of ginkgo biloba (an extract from the leaf of the Chinese ginkgo tree) as a treatment for libido issues and anorgasmia. In one study, ginkgo biloba was found to be 84 percent effective in treating sexual side effects caused by SSRIs.[9] Note: You *must* discuss this with your prescriber before taking it. There may be drug interactions or contraindications.
- SSRIs and SNRIs are notorious for desensitizing key body parts. Fortunately, there are many toys available in all shapes and sizes to help out. There are many reputable stores and e-tailers you can contact for advice and products. A few of our faves are we-vibe.com, evesgarden

.com, thepleasurechest.com, and goodvibes.com. Toys, like drugs, affect individuals differently, so don't be afraid to experiment until you find the right fit.

Going Off Your Meds

This is a really complicated subject about which entire books have been written. Some folks can go off their anxiety meds with little to no difficulty. Lots of folks have a terrible time of it. We have heard hundreds of stories from both groups. What follows is our take.

Unless you are specifically advised by a physician to do so, **never, ever, ever abruptly stop taking your SSRI/SNRI.** This is especially true if you have been taking your antidepressant for a long time. While these drugs are not technically addictive (they don't make you high and people don't crave them), they can create a physiological dependence. They target brain chemistry and therefore can create withdrawal symptoms—some of them severe—if you don't taper off.

Running out of your medication may seem like a logical time to quit, but trust us, you will regret that decision. We know more than one Anxiety Sister who ended up in a psychiatric ward because of psychosis induced by quitting SSRIs or SNRIs cold turkey. While those cases are extreme, other sudden quitters have told us about angry outbursts, flushing, nausea and vomiting, headaches, brain "zaps," blurred vision, and a whole buffet of horrendous consequences. If your prescription runs out, most pharmacists will give you a few days' worth until you can see your doctor because they know how dangerous abrupt termination can be. Seriously, don't do it.

> *Stopping my SSRI was the worst experience of my life. I didn't do it gradually—I just stopped. For the next month, it felt like the worst flu ever. I took so many days off from work, I thought I was going to get fired. The flu symptoms did go away, but then I had these weird*

*electrical sensations and spots in front of my eyes. That scared me
enough to go to a new doctor, who put me back on a low dose just to get
rid of the symptoms. It took me three more months to get off the medicine, but, honestly, I felt like crap for much longer. (Brett, age 41)*

The proper way to go off SSRIs or SNRIs is through a gradual weaning
process known as tapering, whereby you take less and less of the medication
until you can eventually stop altogether. The best way to taper is under the
guidance of a psychiatrist, psychopharmacologist, or psychiatric nurse. Truth-
fully, even medical professionals can go too quickly. This process is best under-
taken by a very seasoned expert who can take into account things like how long
you've been on the medicine, the drug's half-life (how long it stays in your
system), how your body metabolizes medication, your dosage, your age, medical conditions you may have, and other factors.

Tapering is a very individualized process. In other words, it is different for
each person. Some people can get off their meds safely in a month, while others may find themselves tapering for over a year. Please don't rush the process—
your body may need more time to adjust.

*The nausea, headaches, and brain zaps would not go away. I am still
dealing with these symptoms a year later. (Taylor, age 35)*

*After my doctor took me off Ativan I could not sleep. It took me months
to get back to a normal sleep schedule. (Olga, age 74)*

*When I came off Zoloft with my doctor's help, I had some brain zaps and
an upset stomach. But it was nothing too bad, maybe a couple of weeks.
It wasn't a big deal. (Katya, age 57)*

Even with medically supervised tapering, people often report side effects
for a period of time. Typical withdrawal side effects in the first week of

tapering can (but don't have to) include nausea or stomach upset, flushing, headaches, dizziness, and brain zaps (odd electrical sensations—not painful, but scary at first). Some Anxiety Sisters have told us that they have become angry or agitated after the SSRI or SNRI leaves their system. Others have experienced a temporary spike in anxiety or depression (we call it the six-week dip), which usually resolves itself. If it doesn't, slower tapering may be required. Occasionally, Anxiety Sisters have found that staying on a teeny-tiny dose eliminated all side effects.

> *I was able to taper off my SSRI pretty easily until I got down to the last bit. When I tried to go completely without it, I got so lethargic and fatigued. So now I take half of a half of a pill and I feel great.*
> (Josephine, age 60)

Pharmacogenomics

Many anxiety sufferers do not find the right medication (one that helps and has tolerable side effects) on the first try. In fact, many folks we have spoken with are on their third or even fourth drug, which *still* isn't working for them. A relatively new field called pharmacogenomics—the study of how genes affect an individual's response to drugs—is giving us some hope. The idea behind pharmacogenomics is that medication prescriptions can be personalized based on the patient's genetic profile. Using a simple cheek swab, scientists can analyze your DNA to determine which medications are unlikely to work well (low response, high side effects) for you. It's a bit like removing hay from the haystack in order to find the needle.

What these tests determine is how your liver metabolizes medications. They do not tell you which medications will make you feel better; they tell you which ones are more likely to have bad side effects, which can in turn cut down the number of tries it takes to figure out the right drug(s) for you.

One caveat: About 70 percent of people have livers that digest and filter normally. Therefore, genetic testing won't give those folks any new information. Still, we think it's worth discussing with your health care provider if you are having difficulty finding the right medication.

> *I struggled for years with anxiety and depression. I tried three different medications and they each had terrible side effects. Finally, my doctor suggested a genetic test. Turns out that the meds I was on were all on the red list. We chose a new med from the green list and I am feeling so much better.* (Eunice, age 70)

CBD

CBD, short for cannabidiol, is trending right now as a cure-all for everything from arthritis to anxiety. It is everywhere—from local supermarkets to coffee houses—and it is all over the internet. While we have not (yet) tried CBD oil, so many people have shared their positive experiences with us that we felt we would be remiss not to include it in this chapter.

Let's start with this: CBD does not make you high. It is a chemical compound from either the marijuana or hemp plant, but it contains only trace amounts of tetrahydrocannabinol (THC), which is the ingredient that makes weed psychoactive. Therefore, CBD is not addictive. Usually, it is taken as a tablet or tincture, but it can also be added to food, drinks, gummies, lotions, bath bombs, oils, and even products for your pet. Like we said, it's everywhere!

Many people rave about the effects of CBD for anxiety, pain management, and insomnia, and there are some studies that tout its effectiveness.[10] Unfortunately, the product used for research purposes varies greatly among studies, so it is difficult to make broad statements about CBD and anxiety at this point.

Be aware that CBD products vary widely because of the lack of FDA regulation. It is therefore extremely important to find a brand that is batch tested, made without contaminants, and independently lab tested. If you are interested in CBD as a possible treatment for anxiety, we recommend you begin by visiting the Realm of Caring Foundation's website (realmofcaring.org). As a nonprofit, they do not sell any products, but they provide excellent educational resources and the latest research on CBD as well as on marijuana. The products they suggest have been vetted for safety and purity, and they have a wonderful community you can join.

Cannabis

We know lots of folks who use pot as a way of calming their anxiety, but since recreational use in not legal in many states, we are going to focus on medical-grade marijuana, which requires a prescription from a health care provider.

Micro-dosing (using tiny amounts often enough to keep the marijuana in your system) allows you to reap the benefits of THC without side effects (read: getting so stoned you can't function). The key to this approach is to start low and go slow. Each of us is affected differently by pot, so there are no one-size-fits-all rules. **Start low and go slow**

In places where medical marijuana is legal, there are typically a lot of marijuana dispensaries. The folks who staff these dispensaries are often experts and can tell you about the different strains of pot they sell and what might be best for anxiety. Once again, we suggest you check out the Realm of Caring Foundation's website. They provide excellent information on dosing as well as access to health care professionals who specialize in the medical use of marijuana.

The research on medical marijuana is, unfortunately, a bit murky because almost all research on conventional drugs is funded and conducted by Big Pharma, which does not have the patent for medical marijuana. Thus, the studies that have been done tend to be small, and the products they use for each study vary greatly. Good pot is expensive, and investigators leading the studies often do not have the resources to buy it in large quantities. One interesting study done in 2018 found that medical marijuana users experienced a 50 percent reduction in depression symptoms and a 58 percent reduction in anxiety symptoms after two "puffs." This same study also found that over time, anxiety and depression symptoms actually *increased*, so there may be an issue with short- versus long-term usage.[11] One more caution: Some folks we've talked with have said that the use of medical marijuana elevated their heart rates and made them more anxious. A few others told us they experienced paranoia when they used pot. And then there's always the concern about psychological dependence, which is a side effect of long-term usage.[12] Anyone with a history of substance abuse is probably wise to steer clear.

Researchers are still not certain how SSRIs are affected by CBD and THC, but it is thought that the combination increases the potency of the SSRI. So if you are on certain antidepressants (e.g., Zoloft), marijuana can be contraindicated. Check with your doctor before adding marijuana to your treatment plan. Also, if you have a severe mental illness such as schizophrenia, do not use marijuana.

We wish we could give you a clear answer one way or the other, but the truth is that, while some research looks promising, the jury is still out. As is true of all medications, you have to weigh the pros and cons in order to decide if marijuana is right for you.

> *I tried a few medications and hated the way I felt on them. My doctor finally gave me a prescription for medical marijuana, and the guys at the dispensary had me try a few different strains. I've tried edibles but found smoking a small amount at a time to be best. It calms my anxiety down without leaving me feeling like a zombie. (Illyssa, age 56)*

> *I've been using CBD and it relaxes me at night so I can sleep. Since I started, I haven't been having panic attacks in the middle of the night either. (Veronica, age 41)*

Weed can really help my anxiety—if I don't smoke too much. I wait a while after each toke to see how I'm feeling. Once I get to my calm place, I stop because even one more pull will make me super-anxious.
(*Yvette, age 19*)

Psychedelics

If you thought smoking pot to treat anxiety was adventurous, wait till you hear about the most recent research on the use of psychedelic drugs such as LSD and mushrooms in a medically supervised setting. Yep—acid trips to help with anxiety and depression symptoms are on the horizon. Preliminary studies have yielded remarkable results,[13] and in response, the prestigious Johns Hopkins University has recently established its own Center for Psychedelic and Consciousness Research.

Although scientists still aren't completely sure how hallucinogens are so effective in healing anxiety and depression, they have put forth a theory that psychedelics reduce anxiety by increasing "psychological flexibility."[14] Psychological flexibility refers to our ability to manage our emotions and reactions in the moment, even if we are experiencing unpleasant sensations and thoughts. Simplistically speaking, it's how we adapt to circumstances as they arise and how able we are to shift our mindsets accordingly. Obviously, taking a psychedelic drug can be disorienting—that is actually the point of doing it. How we process that disorientation seems to factor heavily in the healing process.

According to Dr. William Richards, a psychologist at the Johns Hopkins Center, it's the memory of the drug that's healing. "You remember that something shifted in your view of yourself, your view of other people, your view of the world, your understanding of what it is to be a human being. And that's incredibly fascinating and powerful."[15]

We have not yet tried psychedelics (we confess we are pretty fascinated by the whole concept), but apparently they are neither toxic nor addictive and usually require only one or two doses to be effective. Unless you have serious heart issues or severe mental illness, the medically supervised use of psychedelics can be safe and profoundly helpful for some people.

> *It was almost a mystical experience for me—I went through periods of laughing and crying and feeling so many emotions at the same time. After, I got this sort of clarity about things. It was like I had rebooted myself and could see the world so differently. I haven't had any anxiety since I did the LSD, and it's been about four months. (Ricki, age 52)*

> *Going through an ayahuasca ceremony was exactly the spiritual and healing outlet I was looking for, although it's not for everyone and I would not have been ready for it prior to doing an intense amount of self-work in a less extreme therapeutic setting. I did get violently sick from the ayahuasca, but since the ceremony, I've felt more free to be myself than ever before, with less fear of judgment from others. Because of this, my overall anxiety is so much better. (Max, age 25)*

On a final note, we want to emphasize that medication issues are extremely complicated: Each of us has a unique body chemistry and consequently unique reactions to medication. Although stories from fellow anxiety sufferers may give us interesting insights, they are not meant to be substitutes for medical advice from a trained practitioner.

twelve

East Side Story

Time to travel again! This time we're going east—to China, India, and Japan. (Big step up from the laundry room, no?) Some of the best anxiety management techniques come from the East, and we're going to explore them. But before we do, a little background.

In the West, individualism and independence are all the rage; this means we define ourselves in terms of personal traits and achievements. Think about some of our national slogans: "Be all you can be." "Live your best life." "Rise above the rest." Very me-centered!

In the East, on the other hand, the collective is key. People tend to see themselves as interdependent and a part of a larger whole. They define themselves in terms of relationships with others. To put it simply, we are a culture of autonomy and they are a culture of connection. This distinction has a lot of implications for health, healing, and happiness.

Health in Western society is the absence of disease. Often Western medicine has been described as conceptualizing the body as a machine, like an automobile, with distinct parts. So when the body is sick, it goes in for repair and the doctor is the mechanic who will diagnose the problem and fix or replace the faulty parts. This approach sorts the body into compartments, which is why US medicine is so specialist-oriented. If your stomach is upset, you go to the gastroenterologist. If your eyes are giving you grief, you go to the ophthalmologist. If you have anxiety, you go to the psychiatrist.

In Eastern society, health is traditionally viewed as the presence of all aspects of well-being (physical, emotional, spiritual, and communal). Eastern thought pictures the body as an ecosystem, which is a network of interdependent organisms and their habitat. In traditional Eastern medicine, a holistic approach is taken, whereby all things that affect health are considered, including the surrounding environment and the community at large. Nothing is compartmentalized. Eastern medicine treats the whole person.

Eastern medicine treats the whole person

So what does this mean for anxiety sufferers? Well, in conventional Western medicine, anxiety is all about your head—nothing below the neck really matters, which is why medication and talk therapy are the principal treatments. Really, if it weren't attached, you wouldn't have to bring your body to the appointment at all (which would be great for those of us who have trouble figuring out what to wear every day). But anxiety sufferers know that emotions are not just in your head. We feel them all over. For this reason, Western medicine sometimes comes up short. Bear in mind, we've benefited greatly from our meds and talk therapy, but we are suggesting there's often more to the anxiety puzzle.

If you've read our chapter on neuroscience (chapter three), then you already know how Western medicine views anxiety: it is a brain disorder. Western treatments, therefore, focus on fixing faulty brains. Eastern medicine conceptualizes anxiety very differently: it is a disturbance of our *shen* (spirit) or an obstruction in our *qi* (energy). If your qi is not flowing smoothly, then everything else gets backed up, and that causes an imbalance in your emotional, physical, and spiritual states. (Sidebar: when we say "spiritual," we are not referring to one's religiosity but rather to a collective consciousness, which is a major cornerstone of Eastern thought.) Thus, Eastern treatments focus on relieving energy blockages and restoring balance. If you are not jiggy with the idea of qi, you can think of it as a metaphor for the chemical and electric reactions constantly occurring within the body.

If this sounds a bit woo-woo, hang in there. Energy flow may not make sense to us from our Western orientation, but these beliefs are thousands of years old and contain much wisdom. Remember, "mind-body connection" sounded like mumbo jumbo to Westerners less than forty years ago, yet it has become an important part of our understanding of how emotions affect health. Study after study has shown, for example, how chronic stress can cause physical illness, how meditation can relieve pain, and how yoga can reduce inflammation. More and more, Western research is validating Eastern practices.

We'll start with the movement-based practices because (1) you've probably already heard about them, (2) they are fairly accessible, and (3) most anxiety sufferers own yoga pants.

Yoga

Originally from India, yoga comes from the Sanskrit word for "union." The practice was conceived as a way of unifying the mind and the body as well as the individual mind with the collective spirit. Yoga consists of physical postures known as poses combined with breathing techniques. There are so many ways to practice yoga—way too many to list. The important thing is that everyone can do it. You don't have to be able to put your left leg behind your right ear in a 110-degree studio to be a yogi. Really, as long as you can breathe, you can practice yoga. (Thank goodness, because we're so uncoordinated.)

Yoga puts us in the parasympathetic (rest-and-digest) mode by reducing our heart rate, lowering our blood pressure, and slowing our breathing. As such, it is an excellent anxiety management technique. However, Westernized yoga is often an exercise class, which can promote competition and social comparison. This couldn't be further from the true spirit of Eastern yoga, which is about moving in a mindful way. The practice of yoga is a method of connecting your mind with your body and is meant to be meditative and healing. One of the guiding principles of yoga is *ahimsa*, which translates loosely to "no harm." Yoga is not about "feeling the burn" or "no pain, no gain." Don't push yourself until you hurt.

There is a wide variety of yoga practices, ranging from very athletic forms such as Bikram (hot yoga) and Ashtanga to the gentler restorative and yin. If you have physical limitations (or you just prefer sitting), there is also chair yoga. Many people practice yoga on their own, but there is something very powerful about being in a good class—all that collective energy can be transformative. One more thought: if you suffer from panic, you should avoid hot yoga, and if you suffer from PTSD, you may want to look for a trauma-sensitive yoga class.

> *I am not very good at yoga. By that I mean that I am not flexible at all. In fact, often during class I skip some of the poses that are hard for me. I can't say I even enjoy it when I am doing it. But I notice that when I stop going to class, my anxiety is much more difficult to handle. (Elizabeth, age 56)*

> *Yoga is my antianxiety medication. (Lillian, age 81)*

> *I try to practice for a few minutes every morning. Not that I am always successful, but I try. It has been so helpful in dealing with my CPTSD. I wish I had found it sooner. (Pilar, age 38)*

Tai Chi

Tai Chi began as a martial art (self-defense) in ancient China but has evolved into a popular movement practice all over the world. Often called "meditation in motion," Tai Chi is a precisely choreographed series of slow, rhythmic body motions in which each posture flows into the next without pause. Tai Chi is always done standing, and there are 108 different moves to learn. It's absolutely beautiful to watch—like seeing a ballet—and surprisingly difficult to execute.

The idea behind Tai Chi is to create flow between body parts, between mind and body, and between body and nature. For those of you familiar with the lingo, it is supposed to promote balance between the yin and the yang (opposing forces) so that your qi can circulate freely and you can experience total harmony. For those of you not familiar with the lingo, it's a really cool way to meditate without sitting still.

Tai Chi is low impact and requires no equipment, so anyone can try it. In addition, there are many health benefits associated with this practice. More than seven hundred studies have shown that Tai Chi lessens the symptoms of arthritis[1] (both the American College of Rheumatology and the Arthritis Foundation recommend Tai Chi), boosts cardiovascular health by lowering blood pressure,[2] and improves balance[3] (among the elderly, regularly doing Tai Chi reduces falls by up to 50 percent). According to Harvard Medical School, when done consistently, Tai Chi can be comparable to resistance training and brisk walking. And some research has shown a correlation between Tai Chi and lowered anxiety and depression.[4]

Because of the flowy nature of Tai Chi postures, it would be difficult for us to explain them. However, the names of the movements are so visually descriptive, we thought we'd share some of them with you:

- White Stork Spreads Wings
- Carry Tiger to Mountain
- Grasp Bird's Tail
- Parting Wild Horse's Mane

Abs's favorite move is called Needle at Sea Bottom, which is kind of like a squat during which you dive with your hands toward the floor (without falling over).

Whenever I try to meditate, I get so restless. It makes my mind race more! My friend suggested I go with her to her Tai Chi class. It was so much better. I joined the class and I am really getting the hang of the deep breathing, which I could never do before. I love that you are always moving. (Ingrid, age 21)

My naturopath actually suggested Tai Chi because I was having some inner ear issues and felt my balance was off. First, it is really hard. Second, I am so much less anxious about falling now because I feel more balanced. But the thing I did not expect was how deeply relaxing the class would be for me. (Gloria, age 77)

In addition to these movements you can do, Eastern medicine includes healing practices done *to* you. The following is a sampling of the most popular massage-type techniques.

Acupuncture

Needles all over my body? Are you crazy? Nope. Just anxious. And acupuncture is a great tool for managing anxiety. Based on ancient Chinese medical practices, acupuncture works to balance the life force or energy current (qi) that travels via specific meridians throughout the body. When these pathways are blocked, the qi doesn't flow well and the resulting imbalance causes illness and disease, including anxiety. In its typically circular fashion, anxiety can also cause blocked meridians.

Acupuncturists use teeny-tiny, eensy-weensy needles (.00325 inches, or the width of a single hair), which they insert about a quarter inch into the body. And Japanese acupuncturists use even tinier needles with even shallower insertions. Thus, Japanese acupuncture is thought of as a gentler practice than Chinese acupuncture. We've done both and have found neither to be painful.

Let's stop here and say that we are both needle-phobes. Abs has fainted during injections, and Mags was actually asked *not* to give blood again by the people at the Red Cross due to her reaction to the needle. So, if we tell you acupuncture needles aren't scary, you should believe us. (Mags has been invited back to her acupuncturist several times!)

The purpose of these needles is to unblock the pathway by (1) bringing blood flow and healing to a particular area, (2) causing the nervous system to release natural painkillers (endorphins), and (3) stimulating the brain's limbic system, which, you may remember from chapter three, is the part that controls emotions. Additionally, acupuncture reduces the body's production of cortisol, adrenaline, and other stress hormones.

If you have not yet tried this technique, you should strongly consider it, as there are no real risks (the only side effects we have ever heard about were a little dizziness and some sensitivity at insertion sites, and these are quite rare), and we have read some pretty impressive studies about the effectiveness of acupuncture in the treatment of anxiety. The only thing that we would advise is that you invest some time in finding a well-trained, highly recommended acupuncturist. Make sure whoever you choose is listed as certified by the National Certification Commission for Acupuncture and Oriental Medicine (NCCAOM) as well as by the acupuncture board of the state in which you reside. Your acupuncturist should also be licensed (look for the initials LAc after his or her name).

If the teeny-tiny needles are still a deal breaker for you (no judgment), you can try acupressure, during which the practitioner uses his or her fingers to press against the same places where a needle would otherwise be inserted. Some folks say acupressure has worked well for them, but most people we've spoken with—including practitioners themselves—and the research suggest that acupressure may not be quite as effective as acupuncture. A benefit of acupressure, however, is that you can learn to do it yourself. For example, one anxiety acupressure point is the spot between your eyebrows. If you press softly on that point with your thumb and massage in a circular motion for a few minutes, you may begin to feel calmer.

Lately I've been seeing a Chinese doctor for my anxiety. He has been spending time on this spot on my wrist which he calls my "spirit gate." He rubs that spot for a few minutes and I swear it calms me right down. It makes my heart beat slower! Sometimes, if I can't sleep, I try it on myself, and it really works. (Juliette, age 43)

I actually fall asleep on the table. I wish I could afford to do it every day. (Fabiola, age 31)

My therapist suggested I try acupuncture for my anxiety, which I did. Let me tell you, it was the most painful experience of my life. I couldn't even stay for the whole session! (Charlotte, age 29)

I still can't figure out how they stick a needle in one part of my body and I feel it in an entirely different area. I know it has something to do with the way the body is interconnected. All I can say is that it has helped a lot with my anxiety. (Gayle, age 64)

Reflexology

Foot massage? Count us in! Although with reflexology, there's much more to it. The Chinese are usually given credit for the massage practice of reflexology, but symbols resembling reflexology maps were found on the feet of Buddha statues in India even earlier, so it's really Indo-Chinese. Reflexology is based on the idea that the reflexes in the foot are mirror images of all the organs, tissues, muscles, and glands in the body.

As is the case with all Eastern medicine, energy flow (qi) and balance are a big part of reflexology—the practitioner will search for blockages and try to release them. With more than seven thousand nerve endings, the foot is an excellent access point for the entire body, although reflexology can also be performed on the hands. While reflexology was considered an alternative or unconventional therapy when it was first introduced to the West, it has in recent decades become a very popular practice, particularly in spas and wellness centers, as well as in chiropractic and physical therapy. Many mainstream doctors now recommend it, particularly to treat neuropathy (pain, numbness, or tingling) of the legs, feet, and toes.

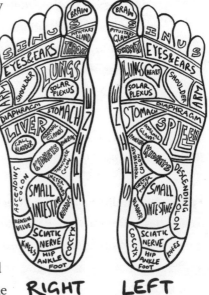

RIGHT   LEFT

There is some skepticism regarding the connection between points on the foot and parts of the body. In fact, Abs was quite the skeptic herself. So, in the name of research, she decided to try this therapy. She went to a highly skilled reflexologist at a wellness center who was able to tell her within five minutes of touching her feet that she has thyroid issues, went through premature menopause, and has chronic lower back pain. The reflexologist had no access to this information, as Abs did not fill out any health forms or talk to anyone at the center about her conditions. Needless to say, Abs is now a believer.

Reflexology is performed by applying pressure with thumbs and fingers, often in specific patterns, to certain points on the foot, which are thought to correlate with other body parts. This is why when a reflexologist presses a certain spot on your instep, you might feel it in your stomach, or when he or she pinches the tips of your toes, you might feel it in your head. One reflexologist put it this way: "Feet talk to me. They tell me what parts of the body need attention."

Several studies have shown the effectiveness of reflexology in managing numerous medical conditions, including hypertension,[5] diabetes[6] and kidney disease.[7] One that caught our eye was done in 2000 with twenty-three cancer patients, who through reflexology significantly reduced their anxiety and pain.[8]

I have severe PTSD, so I'm not about to get a massage—I just can't be
vulnerable with a total stranger. Reflexology, on the other hand, is great.
I can do it sitting up with my clothes on, and I can watch what the mas-
sage therapist is doing the whole time. And it really eases my anxiety.
(Nicolette, age 35)

Reiki

Perhaps more than any other practice we've talked about, reiki is the hardest
to buy into. How can hand movements over a fully clothed body result in real
healing? This is really one of those things you have to try in order to believe.
We have both tried it, and now we both believe.

Just as I was telling the reiki practitioner that I didn't really believe in
this kind of stuff, she held her hands together about four inches above
my right arm. "Can you feel that?" she asked. And I really did. I mean
it felt like a warm brick was pressing down on my arm. It couldn't have
been more real. (Abs, age 52)

Reiki originated in twentieth-century Japan. The idea behind it is not to fix
what is wrong but rather to unblock *ki* (the Japanese equivalent of qi) in order
to restore balance. Reiki aims to help the body heal itself through a series of
prescribed hand movements, customized for an individual's needs. One practitioner explained to us that the reiki energy in the therapist's hands connects
with the places in the body where the recipient has blockages. How do they do
this? Reiki practitioners are able, through training, to sense energy fields. We
know how it sounds—but for many, it really works.

Truth be told, research on reiki is fairly limited and the studies are quite
small. They have, however, shown that reiki activates the parasympathetic
(rest-and-digest) response in our nervous systems. Major medical centers like

Johns Hopkins and the Mayo Clinic have embraced it as part of their integrative health programs. One of the real advantages of reiki is that you can be taught by a master how to perform it on yourself.

> *As a rape survivor I had a lot of issues with sex. Reiki was so helpful in allowing me to feel safe—it was the first thing that really helped me to relax my whole body. I'm not sure how it works, to be honest. But it does. (Bianca, age 23)*

Shirodhara

If you have not yet heard of this Ayurvedic practice, you are definitely missing out on an incredibly soothing experience. Thought of by many scholars as the oldest healing science, Ayurveda began in India more than five thousand years ago. According to Ayurvedic medicine, each of us comprises a unique combination of elements (air, ether, fire, water, and earth) that creates a bodily constitution, or type, called a dosha. Depending on your own element combo, you are characterized as predominantly one of three doshas: vata (air + ether), pitta (fire + water), or kapha (earth + water). When your dosha becomes imbalanced, your energy is disrupted and this results in illness. The goal of Ayurvedic medicine is to restore balance and harmony to your dosha.

Shirodhara, from the Sanskrit words for "head" and "flow," is an Ayurvedic treatment during which a stream of warm oil is dripped and then poured onto your forehead for a total of thirty minutes. It may not sound that appealing, but believe us when we tell you, it is heavenly. And here's a bonus: your hair looks and feels like a million bucks after all that oil. Abs doesn't wash it out until the next day, and she swears it's the best deep-conditioning treatment there is.

Research reveals that shirodhara can result in the same effects as meditation: a decrease in reported anxiety as well as lowered heart rate, slower breathing, and reduced blood pressure.[9] In other words, it's a pretty good way

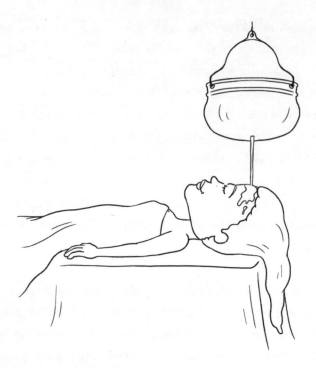

to get your body and mind to move into a relaxed state. Shirodhara has been shown to affect brain waves—it promotes alpha-wave activity, which is the resting state—so it is also able to improve sleep quality and reduce insomnia. And there are no side effects whatsoever. Win, win! Except for the price, which can be pretty steep. One way to justify having shirodhara is that it takes just one session to reap the benefits of the treatment, so, unlike with acupuncture, you're only looking at a onetime charge.

> *I tried shirodhara at a hotel spa. It was an amazing experience—so relaxing. I fell asleep in the middle of the session! What was really something was that for three days afterward, I slept like a baby, which may not sound that amazing, but I am a serious insomniac. (Haley, age 61)*

> *Nothing works as well for me as shirodhara when I am going through a lot of anxiety. I can sometimes spend days all panicky and*

crazed. Shirodhara brings me right down. It's almost immediate.
(Shoshana, age 44)

It puts me in a trance! (Erin, age 70)

Meditation

As we said in chapter eight, there is a good amount of scientific evidence that meditation works to calm the nervous system. There are, however, even deeper reasons meditation is such a powerful practice for anxiety sufferers. It would be great to have a Buddhist monk explain what we mean—luckily, we know one. Donald Altman, who is also a psychotherapist, points out that we live a splintered existence. So many different things are demanding our attention all at once, we are bombarded by stimuli literally all day long, every day. As a result, we have fifteen to twenty thoughts per minute, which, if you do the math, comes to twenty thousand thoughts per day. Anxiety sufferers, with our overactive brains, may even exceed that number. The consequence of this cacophony of thoughts is that we don't know where to place our attention. In fact, we often erroneously direct our attention to thoughts that are not only unhelpful but also untrue. No wonder we feel so fractured and distracted.

Meditation, according to Altman, is the solution to this problem because we practice observing and noticing our thoughts without getting caught up in them. Essentially, meditation teaches us to pause (take a breath) between a thought and our reaction. When we stop paying attention to all the crap, we start to notice the stuff that matters. Meditation shows us how to filter out the distractions.

Meditation teaches us to pause (take a breath) between a thought and our reaction

For Anxiety Sisters, letting things go is a tall order. Meditation helps us work on this skill. Especially in the beginning, everyone struggles with wandering thoughts and distractions. So many feel like they are doing it wrong and give up in frustration. But the thing is, that's what meditation is: noticing your mind wandering and gently, without judgment, starting again. As world-renowned meditation expert Sharon Salzberg explains it, meditation exercises our "letting-go muscles" and teaches us to begin again, without losing heart. We call this resilience.

Those of us who suffer from anxiety tend to live in our heads, which is why it is always so shocking when we experience it in our bodies. Part of the reason we feel anxiety so physically is because our bodies hold on to our emotions. The mind and body are not separate. Meditation (and all the Eastern practices we've talked about in this chapter) reminds us that they are not independent. It is not just something you do in your head.

Perhaps the most profound benefit of a meditation practice—collective energy—is also the hardest for Westerners to grasp. We in the West are very focused on the individual experience, which is why we've become very comfortable with the concept of a mind-body connection. It's still me-centered. The idea that we are connected with one another's energy is a trickier one to grasp, but it is a central tenet of Eastern thought. Meditation is about connecting with your energy through the breath and then connecting with all of humanity through your energy.

> *It's ironic that doing a solo practice can make you feel part of something bigger. I love the idea that we are all part of a larger force. That we all affect one another. Since I've been meditating regularly, I've felt so much less alone. (Courtney, age 54)*

> *I was doing a meditation that involved sending compassionate energy to other people. Through that practice, I started to understand that there is no difference between the concept of self-compassion and turning compassion outward to the world. (Aasfa, age 27)*

Reflection

Another practice with roots in the Buddhist tradition is reflection, which is a meditative form of journaling. The idea is to turn inward to explore some deeper questions about ourselves and the world we inhabit. It's also a great way to tune out the chitchat in your brain and focus your thoughts more mindfully. According to Donald Altman, reflection encourages us to question our old scripts and assumptions, making way for new perspectives. In his excellent book *Reflect*, Altman provides 108 prompts for reflective thought and journaling. Here is one of our favorites:

> To live authentically, accept your true nature. An acorn cannot grow into a palm tree no matter how hard it tries. Have others ever dictated that you become a palm or an oak or a fir? How would they know what seed lives within? Become the seed you nurture. How will you grow today? What is your heart's path? Reflect on this.[10]

> *Sometimes at night, when I am trying to go to sleep, I get what I call "busy brain." Reflective journaling really brings the noise level down so I can focus on just one thing. It's how I can get back to sleep. (Mia, age 18)*

Lessons Learned from the East

- The mind and the body are intertwined.
- In Eastern cultures, health is not just about curing diseases—it's about promoting overall wellness. As such, preventive measures are a big part of Eastern medicine. We need to learn to take care of our *whole* selves on a daily basis and not wait until we are in acute distress. Self-care is not just physical, but emotional and spiritual as well.

- Stories are powerful contributors to the healing process. While anecdotal evidence is not given the same weight as quantitative evidence in Western cultures, Eastern cultures place a lot of value in listening to others' experiences. Having shared more than three hundred stories in this book, we obviously agree.

- Agency (one of our prereqs for happiness) doesn't have to mean meeting a goal or making a big splash, as it often does in Western cultures. In Eastern cultures, agency is more subtle: it can be found by taking a breath or in the pause you take before reacting to your thoughts.

  You can have a lot of agency in your life just by being mindful

  You can have a lot of agency in your life just by being mindful.

- Acceptance (another cornerstone of being anxiously happy) means participating fully in your life *as it is*. Instead of trying to run away from or bury your feelings, you understand that what you are experiencing is temporary. The more open you are to what is, the more engaged in your life and connected to others you are. This is a very Buddhist way to say "ride the wave."

- We are all connected in a common humanity. Being part of something larger is what gives our lives meaning. Which is why we always say, "Anxiety Sisters don't go it alone!"

thirteen

Anxiety Management Gems

This chapter is about things we can do that, in addition to soothing anxiety, can (and here's what makes them gems) provide a sense of well-being, and in some cases real joy. Without further ado, we present the anxiety management gems.

Sensory Soothers

Often when you are experiencing anxiety, your senses go into overdrive. Because of the hypervigilance that accompanies anxiety, even normal sounds, smells, and lighting can overwhelm you. The following are ways to soothe your senses, which, consequently, will calm your nervous system.

WORRY STONES

Sometimes called "pocket tranquilizers," worry stones have been used since the beginning of humankind (yes, anxiety is that old). Ancient Greeks used palm stones smoothed by the sea, and komboloi, which are worry beads, similar to rosary beads used in Catholicism or mala beads used in Buddhism. Many Native American cultures considered stones sacred—especially quartz, which was thought to have the power to remove negativity. Tribespeople from all over the world have passed stone bundles down from generation to generation in order to promote healing and peace.

Polished until smooth, these gemstones are typically oval in shape with a slight indentation for the thumb. Sometimes they have messages on them (such as Peace, Breathe, Brave, or Be Here Now). They can be any color, shape, or size.

Here's the gem part: in addition to providing your hands with something to do when you are anxious (rather than, say, smoke a cigarette or bite your nails), worry stones also stimulate nerves in your thumb tip that release endorphins (your body's feel-good chemicals), which promote calm and relaxation.

The best news is that worry stones are cheap (you can get nice ones for under ten bucks), calorie-free, and portable. If you're crafty, you can even make your own. We particularly recommend worry stones for anxious flyers. And if you are a "floaty sister" (you tend to dissociate or get spacey), holding something with a bit of weight in your hand is super-grounding.

FLOAT THERAPY

Pay attention, water babies—this one's for you. Float therapy is the latest non-pharmacological treatment for all sorts of ailments, including chronic pain, sleeplessness, anxiety, and depression. Also said to improve creativity and enhance athletic performance, the practice is trending nationwide as floating "studios" and "clinics" are popping up everywhere.

Although the health benefits of floating have not been scientifically proven, recent research has been promising. In one small study of fifty anxiety sufferers, 100 percent of participants experienced lowered blood pressure, relaxed muscles, decreased brain activity, and reduced anxiety symptoms after just one session.[1] Other studies using MRIs of the brain before, during, and after floating have shown that it is akin to deep meditation. And the anecdotal evidence is overwhelming—Anxiety Sisters have been swearing by this simple yet expensive (a one-hour session can cost from fifty to a hundred dollars, depending on location) activity.

Here's how it works: Wearing your birthday suit, you enter a "pod" (a soundproof, unlit tank), where you lie, belly-up, in a foot of salt water the same temperature as the air. Then you float there for sixty minutes, in the quiet dark, and allow the salt water to work its magic. Because of the concentration of Epsom salts, your body feels completely weightless, so there is no stress on any muscle group. Additionally, magnesium, which is the main ingredient in Epsom salts, has calming properties of its own.

Proponents say that when they emerge from the tank, they feel as though they have taken the most relaxing nap of their lives. They are not only refreshed but also completely calm, and these effects can last for up to twenty-four hours.

> *I was scared to try floating because I'm claustrophobic, but I found this place that has "open" pools and dim lighting. It is so relaxing—I completely lose track of time. It's my new favorite thing!* (Cheryl, age 61)

BUBBLES

This gem is a particularly good anxiety management technique, and it's so much fun! Blowing bubbles forces you to inhale deeply and exhale powerfully—which is exactly what everyone is trying to get you to do when you are anxious or overwhelmed (or delivering a baby). We give away bubbles at every event, workshop, or party we attend—that's how much we love them.

Besides encouraging deep breathing, bubbles are colorful and relaxing to look at. And they can really be fun to do with your kids (or even other adults). There are all kinds of bubble games you can play, including contests to see who can create the biggest, longest-lasting, prettiest, heart-shaped, bubble-within-a-bubble, and more.

Another way to use bubbles to defuse anxiety is to visualize blowing your anxiety away. We have used this method with kids and teenagers, and it is really effective. In fact, we often encourage teachers to keep bubbles in their classrooms for an anxiety break.

Blowing bubbles is also a terrific distraction from obsessive thinking and worry. Believe it or not, it requires some concentration to blow a good bubble—enough to guide your mind away from anxious thoughts.

> *As a school social worker, I often use bubbles when I am working with young kids and teens. It is not only a great way to reinforce inhaling and exhaling deeply, but it also creates instant delight. They are a great stress-busting tool.* (Sharon, age 70)

WEIGHTED BLANKETS

Weighted blankets (heavy blankets filled with pellets or beads) have long been used in the autism community to help calm down kids with sensory and attention issues. Nowadays, weighted blankets have moved out of the autism community and become commonplace for folks with anxiety—particularly those with insomnia or sleep-related issues.

Clinical research is scant at this point, but there is plenty of anecdotal evidence to support the use of these blankets. Unless you're claustrophobic, the compression can feel wonderful—like you are being swaddled. People who prefer deep pressure rather than a softer touch really swear by their weighted blankets. It can be the ultimate grounding tool for some anxiety sufferers. If you're still wondering if you would like one of these blankets, ask yourself how you feel about those lead aprons dentists put on you before you get X-rays. If that amount of pressure feels soothing to you, odds are good you'll like a weighted blanket.

Weighted blankets come in various weights (usually 10, 12, 15, or 20 pounds for adults). Some professionals suggest that the blanket be no more than 10 to 15 percent of a person's body weight. Just be careful that you do research on the best blanket weight for children—these should be substantially lighter than adult blankets.

I bring my weighted blanket to chemotherapy sessions because of my anxiety. It really calms me down. (Florence, age 76)

Ever since I started using a weighted blanket, my night anxiety has really been reduced. It makes me feel safe and warm. Like I'm in a cocoon. (Violet, age 22)

AROMATHERAPY AND ESSENTIAL OILS

Aromatherapy or essential (from the word "essence") oil therapy uses extracts from plants, flowers, and seeds to promote a feeling of relaxation and well-being. When you inhale the fragrance from these oils, your amygdala is immediately calmed, and—here's the gem part—without any side effects. Some people, however, do experience skin irritation when they rub oils into their skin.

There are tons of aromatherapy products on the market, including facial masks, compresses, diffusers, inhalers, sprays, pillows, sachets, lotions, soaps, and dried flowers (attention cat lovers: dried flowers are often toxic to your furry family members, so proceed with caution). You can also take a small swatch of soft fabric, spritz it with your favorite essential oil, and carry it with you in your purse. Not only does this make an excellent addition to your Spin Kit, but it also works as a buffer against any unpleasant odors you may encounter. Win-win!

Many studies have shown the effectiveness of aromatherapy in treating anxiety. One small study done in 2003 found that 75 percent of participants reported a reduction in anxiety symptoms after using essential oils for six weeks.[2] In another small but notable study published in the journal *Phytomedicine* in 2010, lavender oil was shown to be just as effective as the pharmaceutical drug lorazepam (Ativan)—a medicine commonly prescribed in the treatment of anxiety.[3] Furthermore, lavender oil did not cause drowsiness, a common side effect of Ativan.

Although several essential oils are used for anxiety management, there are a few that we keep hearing about over and over: (1) lavender, (2) ylang-ylang,

(3) rose, (4) bergamot, and (5) chamomile. All of these oils are thought to reduce stress hormones and, in the case of lavender, increase serotonin levels.

A few things to note about aromatherapy: If you have a very sensitive sniffer
like Abs, you will need to use much less oil in order to reduce the strength of
the aroma, and some scents may simply be too much. Also, essential oils are
unregulated by the FDA, so make sure you check out the company that manu-
factures the oil. There should be no synthetic additives to the oil whatsoever,
and if it comes in a plastic bottle, do not buy it. (Reputable companies know
that oil degrades plastic; they will sell only glass containers.) You should also
make sure that whichever oil you choose will not interact with any drugs or
herbs you may be taking.

> *My son has ADHD and gets very frustrated with his schoolwork. Some-*
> *times just putting a bit of essential oil on his wrists and letting him*
> *spend a few minutes smelling it helps to refocus him and cuts down on*
> *the frustration. In fact, now I use it when I am frustrated or anxious as*
> *well.* (Noelle, age 43)

> *I wake up with night panic a lot. One way I cope with that is by using a*
> *diffuser with lavender oil. I leave it on all night and it makes it easier for*
> *me to get back to sleep.* (Aisha, age 19)

Creative Outlets

Here's a factoid you might like: research has found a strong link between anxiety and creativity. Van Gogh may have been anxious enough to cut off his ear,
but he was one hell of an artist! So there may be an advantage to anxiety after
all—strong imaginations spark beautiful music, poetry, art, sculpture, writing, and more. Engaging in creative behaviors has been shown to improve
brain function, boost immunity, and decrease both depression and anxiety.[4]

Expressing creativity floods your brain with do-pamine, which makes you feel good. There are endless ways to use your creativity. Here are a few suggestions.

Expressing creativity floods your brain with dopamine, which makes you feel good

COLORING

Lately, you may have noticed that "adult" coloring books are popping up everywhere. But this pastime is more than a trend—it is a wonderful soother for anxiety. Coloring requires the mind to become task-oriented, thus distracting it from its limbic (emotional) overdrive—in other words, it keeps your amygdala from misfiring. In addition, coloring forces the brain to be "in the moment" and therefore has a meditative effect. For this reason, coloring is also a good tool for kids and adults with ADHD and difficulty focusing.

Science backs up these claims. Several studies on the effects of coloring on anxiety have been conducted in the past decade.[5] Researchers have discovered decreases in heart rate and changes in brain waves—which is what happens during meditation—as a direct result of coloring.[6] Concentrating on staying in the lines, choosing colors, discerning patterns, and comparing shapes consume the brain's attention fully, thus making it hard for negative thoughts to take over and spiral out of control. In addition, the repetition involved in coloring produces a calming effect. There is also some evidence to suggest the bright, colorful images you create can replace negative ones in your mind, which reduces and sometimes even eliminates anxiety and obsessional thinking. Plus, you can make pretty pictures to hang on your fridge!

What makes coloring such a gem is (1) anybody can do it, and (2) it can be a social activity. You can do it with your kids, your spouse, or even a group of friends. We attended a coloring party once and it was so much fun (the wine didn't hurt).

We really enjoy coloring mandalas, which are Buddhist symbols for the universe. Coloring these concentric circles with all kinds of intricate designs is not only meditative but also addictive. There is even research showing the benefits of coloring this specific type of design.[7] Check out our resource section on our website for great coloring books, or you can find free downloads on the internet.

> *People laugh when I tell them about my coloring habit, but it is so relaxing. Believe me, I have zero talent in the art department, but I can certainly choose pretty color combinations! I do it almost every day after work—it's my wind-down time.* (Holly, age 50)

CROCHET, KNITTING, AND NEEDLEWORK

Some of you may believe that activities like crochet, needlework, and knitting are the domain of grandmothers. This, however, is not the case. According to the Craft Yarn Council, about a third of women ages twenty-five to thirty-five knit or crochet. Needlework groups for all ages and genders are popping up on college campuses, in libraries, and in community centers. Most important, knitting, needlework, and crochet can be powerful tools for anyone who suffers from anxiety.

A number of studies have shown that needlework can put you in a relaxed, meditative state. It actually lowers heart rate, blood pressure, and levels of the stress hormone cortisol.[8] Focusing your brain on your hands—on the tactile sensations and rhythmic finger movements—serves to both ground you in the present and distract you from your anxiety. (Note: the relaxation response happens once you gain a certain fluency with these crafts, as beginners have a learning curve.) Needlework is also affordable and portable, which makes it a perfect soother for your Spin Kit.

Afraid of flying? Bring your knitting needles. Get anxious in the doctor's office? Bring your crochet. Whenever you feel that obsessive worrying, grab your yarn and refocus your mind. You'll end up relaxing and breathing deeper without even telling yourself to do so.

What makes crochet and knitting gems is how indirectly social they are (the focus is on the craft, not necessarily on conversation). Knitting and crochet circles are thus especially wonderful for social anxiety sufferers. And think of all the lovely gifts you can make for the people in your life.

> *When I am really anxious I can't read or concentrate well. Sometimes music even bothers me. So, when I am flying, cross-stitch is my go-to activity. It is simple enough that I don't have to concentrate, but I still have to pay attention to what I am doing. It takes my mind off my anxiety.* (Lucinda, age 68)

JOURNALING

For us, journaling serves two purposes: (1) it helps us problem-solve, and (2) it provides us with an artistic outlet. By writing down details about a problem you are facing, you can be more expansive in your thinking—it's like a private brainstorming session! According to psychotherapist Maud Purcell, writing engages the analytical left brain, so the creative right brain is free to imagine and feel without judgment.[9]

Keeping a daily or weekly journal can also release stress by allowing you to vent and clarify how you are feeling about difficult situations and challenges. Writing about emotions tends to reduce their intensity, which in turn reduces anxiety associated with those feelings.

One more benefit of journaling is the self-awareness that inevitably arises from clarifying your emotions and expressing your views on a regular basis. Going back and rereading older entries can be so helpful, especially when you start to see certain patterns and trends in your feelings and choices.

If you are thinking about starting a journaling practice, we suggest three guidelines:

1. Do not censor or edit yourself—your journal is a safe and private place for you to say *anything*.
2. Make your journal something you enjoy spending time with. Use colored pencils, stickers, and any other decorative items, if you like

that kind of thing. If not, keep it simple. You don't have to spend a lot of money on a customized diary; you can use a plain spiral notebook or Post-it Notes, if that suits you.

3. Don't make writing in your journal a chore. If you don't want to write anything on a given day or week or month, then don't. Remember, the goal is to soothe anxiety, not create it!

Every year, I order a custom journal that has not only a calendar but also coloring pages, notes pages, graph paper, and many other places for self-expression. Being a sticker-holic, I love to decorate my pages with quotes, mantras, pep talks, and pictures of various activities I [plan to] do. I even do mini vision boards on some of the blank pages of the book. My journal has become an addiction—an activity that always distracts me and soothes me when my anxiety spikes. (Abs, age 52)

I often use my journal as a self-sounding board. I may write a "letter" to someone who has hurt me to understand what I want to say to them. I may write about my goals and how I am going to reach them. Sometimes I am just having an anxious and shitty day, and writing about it makes it feel more manageable. (Summer, age 23)

MUSIC

From the time human beings learned to make music, they understood its power to soothe and heal. South American shamans and Native American tribesmen have used chanting in healing ceremonies. Andrew Solomon, an author well known for his work on mental health issues, talks about being treated for depression at an African drumming ceremony. Around the world, many cultures and religions use music as a form of group connection and healing.

Of course, we all know the power of music in our own lives. We can put on a song and remember the best or worst night of our lives. Certain songs can make us dance wildly or weep desperately. We cannot help singing along (often to the dismay of our families) to certain favorite songs. Really, we use music in just about every aspect of our lives (weddings, religious services, funerals, parties, workouts, daily commutes, etc.).

Science has backed up the ability of music to alter our moods. Researchers at Stanford University concluded that "listening to music seems to be able to change brain functioning to the same extent as medication."[10] Music actually changes the distribution of neurotransmitters (such as serotonin). Using MRI scans, scientists can see that music lights up parts of the brain not easily engaged by other activities—even talking and listening. We also know that music can affect our heart rate, stress hormones, and blood pressure. And you don't have to be a musician to reap all these rewards: just listening to music activates those hard-to-reach parts of the brain.

It makes sense, then, that music therapy has become a really important part of treating mental health issues. Small studies have shown that music therapy can help decrease insomnia, depression, and anxiety.[11] When people are resistant or unable to engage in traditional talk therapy, music is a wonderful way to explore emotions.

A music therapist can work with an individual or groups. Therapy can involve drumming circles, music composition, discussion and writing of lyrics, movement activities, meditation with music, and many other innovative practices. Participants can even learn to use these techniques on their own.

Even if you do not have access to music therapy, you can benefit by including music more purposefully in your life. Learning to play an instrument, joining a drumming circle (often at yoga studios), singing, and downloading music you like are all extremely helpful in dealing with anxiety.

BAKING

During the COVID-19 lockdown, in addition to the run on toilet paper, it was almost impossible to locate flour, yeast, and cake mixes. Clearly, folks were stress-baking. Which makes sense because "stressed" spelled backward is "desserts"! There's lots of good science to explain this phenomenon.

First a bit of neuroscience: Remember we said that the amygdala in the brain's limbic system is activated during anxiety? When this occurs, your prefrontal cortex (your rational-decision-making center) takes a backseat. Baking, with its sequential demands (following a recipe, measuring, etc.), actually activates your prefrontal cortex, which in turn slows the amygdala down so you can stop spinning and start thinking. In addition, repetitive tasks such as stirring, sifting, and kneading can become a form of meditation. It keeps us engaged and in the present so that our anxious minds can't get out of control.

Speaking of control, baking is one of those projects where you can feel real agency and accomplishment in a relatively small amount of time. It's something that seems manageable, even when you are experiencing some anxiety.

When it comes to engaging and soothing senses, we can think of few activities better than baking. Whether it's putting your hands in dough, smelling freshly baked chocolate chip cookies, or licking icing from a spoon, all of your senses participate and keep you grounded. And if these reasons weren't enough, there's also that creative piece—experimenting with flavors, the use of shape and color, and so on. A 2018 study found that people who take on small creative projects are both happier and more relaxed.[12]

> *I get very scattered when I am feeling anxious, and baking requires me to do things in order. But the best part of baking is that I share it with my neighbors and coworkers and they get so excited. (Beverly, age 65)*

The Natural World

Plants and animals are true gems because in addition to being anxiety soothers, they are also major happiness providers. So much research has been done on how nature affects us both physically and psychologically. The following are some of our favorite ways to interact with the natural world.

BEING OUTDOORS

Easy to access and completely free, the outdoors is a powerful soother for anxiety. And you don't need to do a backwoods camping trip in a national park in order to reap nature's calming benefits. Any time outside, whether you are reading a book in a hammock or gardening in the backyard or simply sitting in the grass in a park, can reduce anxiety. So get outside—it's worth the mosquito bites!

In one recent study, participants ruminating on a problem were asked to take a walk on a busy street or in a local park. After the walk, participants who had been in the park reported feeling much less stressed and worrying less about the problem than did participants on the crowded street. Furthermore, the physiological markings for stress (e.g., cortisol levels) were significantly lower in the park walkers.[13]

Some Anxiety Sisters struggle when it comes to spending time outside. There are many anxiety sufferers who have a fear of wide-open spaces. These folks should avoid meadows and large parks and stick with more enclosed spaces, such as wooded hiking trails or small gardens. Even an open-air porch with views of nature can have an anxiety-reducing effect.

Those Anxiety Sisters struggling with agoraphobia cannot comfortably leave their homes. But they don't have to miss out on nature's soothing qualities—if they cannot go out into nature, they can bring nature inside to them. Patients recovering from surgery have been shown to heal faster if there is a plant in the room or a soothing view of nature.[14] There have even been improvements in patients who are shown pictures of trees!

In the 1980s, Japan started a public health initiative called forest bathing (*shinrin-yoku*) to get people to experience the benefits of being outside. The idea behind forest bathing is to engage all our senses while we are spending time in nature—to immerse ourselves in it. The Japanese have gone so far as to build forest-bathing parks (with doctors and guides) in response to the extensive research they have done on its myriad benefits (decreased stress hormones, lowered blood pressure, reduced glucose levels, etc.).[15]

The good news is we don't have to go all the way to Japan and meet with a certified forest-bathing guide to take advantage of this practice. You too can forest-bathe, just by going to a place with a lot of trees and spending some time noticing the sounds, sights, and smells. Exercise is not the goal here. Rather, take a slow, meditative walk or even sit and take in the surroundings. Having a picnic among the trees also counts. The idea is to bathe in the beauty of the trees and soak in the phytoncides—an organic compound produced by trees in order to protect them from harmful germs and bugs—which can boost our immune systems and may even be helpful in preventing cancer. So, whether you are forest bathing or wandering in your garden, get outside—or at least bring the outside in!

> *Walking in the woods is my anxiety medicine. Just looking up at the magnificent trees reminds me how much beauty is in the world, and, somehow, my problems seem smaller. (Dottie, age 84)*

> *I have severe agoraphobia and don't get out much. But I do have a lot of plants—even an herb garden on my windowsill. Taking care of my plants is so good for me. Sometimes I even talk to them! (June, age 56)*

PETS

If you are an animal lover, you already know that just cuddling with your pet can really calm you down when your anxiety is at a fever pitch. But there is actual scientific research that shows the benefits of having a pet if you are an anxiety sufferer. Here is a sample of some of those benefits:

- Having the companionship of an animal decreases feelings of loneliness. Abs says that talking with her cats always makes her feel like she's in good company (better company than some humans, truth be told).
- Stroking an animal lowers blood pressure and heart rate.

- The purr of a cat, particularly when the cat is on the owner's lap (or head), is very soothing and meditative and has been shown to deepen respiration in humans.
- Interaction with friendly dogs stimulates the body's production of oxytocin, a feel-good hormone known to reduce anxiety, and it reduces cortisol, a stress hormone. (The same holds true for friendly cats and, we imagine, friendly ferrets.)
- Caring for a pet promotes feelings of self-worth and establishes routines (feeding, walking, grooming, etc.), both of which have been shown to reduce anxiety and depression. Even when your anxiety is really bad, you still have to get out of bed and walk the dog or you will have new (smelly) furniture in your living room.
- Social anxiety sufferers report fewer symptoms when their dogs accompany them in social situations.[16] Also, dogs provide a vehicle for social connection at dog parks, on beaches, or on the street.
- Playing with pets offers an excellent distraction when the mind begins to spin out of control. Focusing your attention on your pet can get you out of your head and keep you grounded.

In a 2015 study done by the Centers for Disease Control (CDC), approximately 650 children, half with pet dogs and half without, were observed for eighteen months. The results showed that the kids with dogs had significantly reduced anxiety, particularly separation and social anxiety.[17] So if you're not sure if a pet can soothe your anxiety, you may want to consider the benefits for your kids.

> Since I lost my husband, I have been so lonely and anxious. I've never really been an animal person, but my friend suggested that I adopt a cat. So I did. It was the best decision of my life. This cat can sense when I'm sad and curls right up in my lap. And he's been sleeping next to me at night so I have a snuggle buddy. I can't imagine my life without him.
> (Alice, age 77)

I have severe PTSD. Occasionally, when I am triggered, I find myself unable to move—I literally become paralyzed. My emotional support dog will come over and lie right next to me. Sometimes I can only touch her with a few fingers. But she stays right by me, and slowly my breathing calms and I am able to pet her. Little by little I am able to move my body again. (Brooke, age 41)

DIYers

This group of gems requires a professional to teach you the technique, but then you take over and do them on your own. What's great about these is that they are doable anywhere at any time—even during an anxiety crisis. Not only are they empowering, but they also give you a tangible activity to rely on in high-anxiety moments.

BIOFEEDBACK

Often referred to as "Zen technology," the practice of consciously controlling your heart rate, oxygen intake, and body temperature as a technique to soothe anxiety has been around for thousands of years. Now known as biofeedback (it received this name in the 1960s), it's rooted in the Eastern techniques of yoga and meditation.

Biofeedback is a method of measuring physiological functions we are not typically aware of (such as skin temperature, muscle tension, and brain waves) and then learning how to control these functions. In a nutshell, biofeedback practitioners develop the ability to listen to their bodies so they can regulate themselves. As you might imagine, this process can be very empowering—especially for those of us who feel that our anxiety is controlling our lives.

The process of biofeedback is noninvasive and involves no medication. In fact, biofeedback sessions are often very relaxing, as therapists use deep breathing and guided imagery to help you slow your functions down. The process involves detecting small changes in your body through electrodes or finger sensors and providing you with visual images (usually on a computer screen) of these changes. Thus, the biological information is "fed back" to you. When you see this information, you can then experiment until you learn to control your biological response. If all goes as planned, eventually you won't even need the feedback—just your own ability.

You can find biofeedback kits to use on your own personal computer for around three hundred dollars, but we recommend a few visits to a good therapist instead. The human interaction is so soothing, and figuring out new technology can be very anxiety-provoking! Most studies have shown that it takes between six and twelve sessions—depending on the complexity and intensity of the anxiety disorder—to experience significant symptom relief. To find a qualified biofeedback provider in your area, contact the Association for Applied Psychophysiology and Biofeedback.

> *I am a big fan of biofeedback, as I have used it very successfully to treat my anxiety, particularly when it comes to panic. After only three sessions, I was able to learn how to slow down my heart rate and lengthen my breaths. This has been my go-to trick when I start hyperventilating. (Harper, age 28)*

> *The only thing that worked to soothe my father during his long and painful illness was biofeedback. He was not able to take any antianxiety medication due to his health conditions. However, when he would go in for his biofeedback appointments he would come out so relaxed. (Mags, age 52)*

TAPPING

You won't need any special dance shoes for this activity—just your fingers and your voice. Often called EFT (emotional freedom technique), tapping uses principles from traditional Chinese medicine to ease chronic pain, anxiety, and other forms of distress. Yep, we're going back to qi—your energy—which gets disrupted by physical and emotional pain. And when your life force (qi) gets disrupted, it needs to be recalibrated.

In EFT, you use your fingers to stimulate nine different energy meridians (located on your head, your face, your hands, your neck, and under your arms) in order to restore balance. Sounds a lot like acupuncture, no? Well, tapping is based on the same philosophy. Essentially, tapping is free acupuncture without needles!

You can learn tapping from a trained therapist—which we recommend. There's a lot to know, and having another human show you the ropes is very helpful. If that is not an option, however, you can definitely get the basics from YouTube. Here's a very simple version you can try (but still try to go to a trained EFT practitioner, who can use tapping in many different ways to help you manage your anxiety):

1. Start by thinking of a situation or object that makes you feel anxious.

2. Rate your level of anxiety from 0 to 10, with 10 being the most intense.

3. Create what's referred to as your "setup statement," which should first recognize the problem and then provide an affirmation. This is the typical format for a setup statement: "Even though I feel anxious about _____, I deeply and completely accept myself." For example, "Even though I feel anxious about going to the doctor tomorrow, I deeply and completely accept myself." Or "Even though I experience panic attacks, I deeply and completely accept myself."

4. Say your setup statement aloud a couple of times.

5. If you look at the illustration, you will see where each of the energy meridians are located. Now you are ready to begin tapping. Using four fingers (no fingernails!), gently tap against the EFT points, starting with

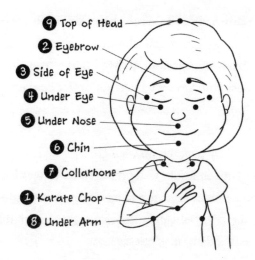

9 Top of Head
2 Eyebrow
3 Side of Eye
4 Under Eye
5 Under Nose
6 Chin
7 Collarbone
1 Karate Chop
8 Under Arm

your outer hand (a.k.a. your "karate chop"), moving next to the eyebrow, and then sequentially according to the diagram. Applying just enough pressure so that you can feel the sensation (but not so hard that you'll feel discomfort), tap five to seven times per meridian while repeating your setup statement or a shortened version of it. On particularly sensitive areas, like under your eye, you can use two fingers. You can make a loop by starting on one side of your body and ending on the other.

6. When you have completed the loop, take a nice deep breath and reevaluate your anxiety. If it's higher than a 2, repeat the sequence.

Not so sure about this one? We get it. We were skeptical as well, until we read some research on stress responses in the brain and tapping. In one study, cortisol was measured in eighty-three subjects before and after a one-hour tapping session. The average reduction in the stress hormone (one of many anxiety markers) was 24 percent, with some participants experiencing as much as a 50 percent decrease.[18]

The Stress Project, which trains veterans with PTSD how to perform EFT, reports a 63 percent reduction in anxiety symptoms after just six rounds of tapping.[19] In fact, there have been more than one hundred papers published in peer-reviewed psychology and medical journals that show EFT is an effective treatment for phobias, depression, PTSD, panic, and generalized anxiety. Since EFT is painless and doesn't have side effects, we think it's certainly worth a try.

I had to have a PET scan recently, but I'm terrified of closed-in spaces. The first time I attempted the test, I got so panicked they had to stop the machine. The second time, they had this EFT person who did a tapping session with me first. Not only was I able to get through the test, but I was pretty relaxed doing it. (Elyse, age 67)

I used tapping to help me get over my fear of squirrels. My therapist asked me to imagine that I was face-to-face with a squirrel on my deck. It made me pretty anxious. Then I tapped the pressure points while repeating, "Even though I have this fear of squirrels, I am okay in this moment." It took a few rounds, but visualizing the squirrel got a lot less scary. (Ilana, age 35)

My OCD is about germs and I spend a lot of time washing my hands. I usually allow myself a certain number of washes per day so I don't get too caught up in it. When it's really bad, though, I can spend hours scrubbing myself raw. When that happens, the best thing for me is tapping. I call my therapist and he does it with me over the phone. It takes about ten minutes and it can stop the urges altogether. (Chloe, age 21)

Wonder

Our last gem is in a category all by itself. How does wonder soothe anxiety? To understand this, you have to first know the definition of wonder, which is a deeply rooted curiosity about and profound connection with art, music, spirituality, or nature. In other words, it is that feeling of transcendence you get when you are awed and inspired.

In 2015 at the University of California, Berkeley, researchers learned that wonder had amazing physical and emotional effects on the subjects of their study. Participants who were able to "lose themselves" in something wondrous were found to have significantly lower levels of cytokines, proteins in the body that cause inflammation and related diseases.[20] High levels of cytokines are also implicated in the development of depression and anxiety, so reducing those levels is yet another way to treat these brain disorders.

The best part of cultivating your sense of wonder is the exploration itself—finding out how to lose yourself in awe is in itself a mood boost. For us, a beautiful piece of music, a walk in nature, and looking at art are three of the ways we experience wonder. Other Anxiety Sisters find wonder in religious settings, through poetry, or by communing with animals. The number of ways to experience awe is virtually infinite.

> *Even though I can't afford to travel, I still dream about it all the time. I keep a file on my computer with pictures of all the places I want to go. I have this one collection of photos of the Sistine Chapel in Italy—I really love churches and art, so I can stare at those shots forever. If I'm feeling some anxiety, I just click on the folder and away I go!* (Paige, age 65)

> *I have always been fascinated by astronomy. I am not a scientist by training, but I can lose myself for hours looking through my telescope. That's where I go when things seem overwhelming.* (Enid, age 59)

> *The older I get, the more I connect to my own sense of wonder about the world. I've seen the world change so much; I always want to know what will happen next. It keeps me eager to wake up every day.* (Siobhan, age 98)

Chocolate

Okay, we lied. We have one more gem. And it's in a category all by itself because . . . well, just because. We love chocolate for its quintessential yummi-ness, but it would be completely irresponsible of us if we didn't point out its benefits in soothing anxiety:

- Chocolate contains magnesium, which naturally soothes anxiety and relaxes muscles. If you are lacking magnesium, you are more likely to be anxious and also to crave sources of magnesium to correct the deficit.
- It is no secret that chocolate contains sugar. What you may not know, however, is that the body's release of insulin in response to moderate amounts of sugar causes the release of serotonin, the feel-good neurotransmitter antidepressants seek to increase.
- There is evidence that, for some people, eating chocolate causes their brain to produce substances akin to opiates such as heroin. Chocolate high, anyone?
- Chocolate contains cannabinoids, which stimulate the production of anandamide, also called "natural THC," the active ingredient in marijuana. Once again, chocolate high, anyone?
- Chocolate is rich in antioxidants. In fact, one regular-size chocolate bar has as many flavonoids as a glass of red wine.

Me love cookies. Especially chocolate chip. Makes me feel happy!
(Cookie Monster, age 50)

fourteen

We're All in This Together

A lone monkey is a dead monkey. Not that we're trying to make you (more) anxious, but Harry Harlow's famous line is truly relevant to both the management of anxiety and the pursuit of happiness. We have said it before many times: human beings are a social species. The need for connection is wired into our genes. In fact, the human brain is the biggest (relative to body size) in the animal world, and brain size is directly correlated with how social a species is. All of the functions related to social engagement take up a lot of real estate in the neocortex.

The need for connection is wired into our genes

Have you ever heard of mirror neurons? Basically, they are nerve cells that are activated when we observe another human, and these cells cause us to mirror their behavior. Humans are constantly "reading" other humans and then reflecting back to them what they see or experience. To see mirror neurons in action, all you have to do is smile at someone. Typically, that will cause the person to smile back. Even if you don't see a big smile, the zygomaticus major (the muscles in your face that make you smile) are automatically engaged through mirroring. And this is true across cultures.

We're not gonna beat around the bush—here's what science has to say about our need for social ties:

- Social connections allow us to live longer lives. Research has shown that people with social ties live longer than people without social ties—and here's the kicker: this is true even when the people with social ties have major health risks, including smoking, obesity, and a sedentary lifestyle.[1] In other words, you're better off being a fat couch potato with an active social life than a skinny gym rat with no friends. (This makes us feel soooo much better.)

- Recovery from trauma is significantly boosted by social connection.[2] Being with other humans makes us stronger and more resilient when it comes to dealing with the hard stuff.

- Social connection predicts happiness. A famous Harvard study, which followed people over a period of eighty years, revealed that those with social ties—even casual ones—were both the happiest and the healthiest. In fact, feeling connected to others throughout one's lifetime seemed to be the biggest predictor of happiness.[3]

• Several studies have shown that folks with social connections experience less depression and anxiety.[4] A lot less depression and anxiety.

For all these reasons, we believe in creating social connections as a *treatment* for anxiety. We consider it just as important as medication, therapy, meditation, or any other technique we have presented in this book. No lone monkeys on our watch! (Unless you're self-quarantining during the COVID-19 pandemic—but that's a whole other story.)

We should clarify that "lone" does not refer to being by yourself. It's the loneliness, not aloneness, that creates anxiety. The sense of isolation—of not belonging—is what causes all the problems. In fact, loneliness is so detrimental to our well-being, it even affects us at the cellular level, by causing inflammation and lowered immunity. We are designed to be connectors.

The problem is that our culture has become very disconnecting, which makes us even lonelier. More than 60 percent of Americans report feeling lonely, left out, and misunderstood.[5] Add to that the systemic racism and discrimination pervasive in our society as well as the stigma surrounding mental illness and you have a recipe for a mental health epidemic. Even our doctors don't routinely screen for social isolation, despite the overwhelming evidence showing its negative impact on our health.

Before you panic about not having enough friends, we have some good news: social connections don't have to be intimate. In terms of decreasing anxiety and being happier, you can create a sense of belonging with casual connections. Waving to your neighbors, thanking the pharmacist, knowing the name of your dry cleaner—all of these are legitimate social connections. Eye contact, chitchat, and smiles all help us fill the need to be part of a community.

One 2014 study found that people who made personal contact (i.e., they smiled, made eye contact, or chatted) with the person serving them coffee were 17 percent happier upon leaving the café than those customers who did not make any personal contact.[6] In another study, scientists asked one group of Chicago commuters to initiate a conversation with a stranger on the train and another group to keep to themselves. The former group reported being significantly happier than the latter group.[7] Contrary to everything we've ever been taught, talking to strangers was actually beneficial. So don't give up your small talk!

We should also mention that when human beings share experiences—even if they don't know each other—the experience is made better for both parties. One study had participants eat a piece of chocolate alone and then together but without any communication with each other. The subjects reported that the chocolate tasted better during the shared experience than it did when they ate it alone, even though the chocolate came from the same candy bar.[8] Mental note: we need to replicate this study at home!

But I'm an introvert, we hear you saying. *I don't even like people.* First things first, being an introvert has nothing to do with whether or not you like people. It doesn't even mean that you're shy. Introversion is about how you get your energy. Extroverts get energy from other people and introverts get energy from within themselves. You can need time alone—even prefer it—but still be socially connected. Whether or not you are an introvert, you can wave to a fellow dog walker or say hello to your bus driver. And with the advent of the internet, there are so many opportunities for shy folks to create casual social connections.

> *I'm a freelance writer, so I spend a lot of time on my own. When my therapist suggested I do a little socializing, I joined an online book club. I have to say, that group has been life-changing. I can honestly say, even though I've never met them, that these people are my friends.*
> (Alma, age 54)

> *I live alone and don't have many friends or family members around. I know my neighbors, the people at my grocery store, and those in*

nearby shops. On a snowy day, a neighbor might stop by to ask if I need anything from the store. Even my mailman makes sure I am doing okay. It is really comforting because I know if I need help or something is wrong, people will notice and be there for me.
(Edna, age 85)

Self-Compassion

A great way to increase your social connectedness, particularly if you suffer from social anxiety, is through the practice of self-compassion. We've talked about self-compassion in the context of riding the wave, but here we want to talk about it in terms of social connection. If you think about it, it's really hard to feel connected to others if you don't feel connected to yourself first. In other words, you have to understand and accept your own emotions before you can share them with others. Plus, when you show compassion for yourself, you mirror it for others to copy. Compassion can thus be contagious.

A very concrete way to use self-compassion to connect with others is something called the loving-kindness, or "metta," meditation, which comes from a Buddhist prayer. Metta, in Pali, means unconditional, inclusive love, which is the goal of this meditation. We start by offering ourselves this love and then extend it to others. The idea is that by saying this prayer, you can create the experience of loving and being loved.

The following is a loose translation of the loving-kindness meditation. Feel free to change the words to make them more meaningful to you. First say these words about yourself:

- May I be safe.
- May I be peaceful.
- May I be healthy.
- May I live with ease.

You can repeat them several times, if you'd like. Then choose someone you would like to offer loving-kindness. It can be a friend, a family member, or even a stranger. Just visualize that person as you say the following words:

- May you be safe.
- May you be peaceful.
- May you be healthy.
- May you live with ease.

Research has shown that even a few minutes of this loving-kindness meditation significantly increases feelings of belonging and social connection.[9] It's just such a great antidote to loneliness. If you prefer a guided loving-kindness meditation, Kristin Neff has a great one on her website (self-compassion.org).

Giving

Another way to combat loneliness is by giving to others. An interesting study of alcoholics participating in Alcoholics Anonymous (AA) found that those members who helped others throughout the program were twice as likely to still be sober a year later (and they reported less depression).[10] Researchers from Harvard conducted an experiment whereby students on a college campus were given envelopes of money (twenty dollars). One group was instructed to spend the money on themselves by the end of the day. The other group was told to spend the money on someone else. Participants in the latter group reported feeling much happier and more connected than participants in the former group.[11] In an NIH study, researchers discovered that donating to charity lights up the same region of the brain on an MRI scan as when you receive a monetary reward.[12] We could go on and on—there is that much science to back the benefits of giving.

There are lots of ways to give of yourself with varying degrees of commitment—you can donate money or possessions, you can perform random acts of kindness, or you can volunteer, which has its own particular set of rewards, including better longevity[13] and a heightened sense of purpose.

> *I read to kids at the local library once a week after school. It is such a wonderful time for all of us—I go home feeling so loved.* (Hazel, age 79)

> *I volunteer at a high school tutoring English. I have become extremely close to a few of the students. Now I am invited to school plays, graduations, and even parties for the teachers and staff. Whatever I have given, I have gotten so much more.* (Irene, age 60)

Group Activities

Obviously, doing a group activity is a great way to increase your social connectedness. For many of us with social anxiety, however, joining is not such an easy task. Don't despair. There are lots of ways to get your connection dose. Remember, just being in the presence of other humans counts.

Nowadays, there is a group for everything under the sun, and whatever interests you probably interests other people too. Some examples include birdwatching, hiking or biking, fitness classes, wine tasting, religious organizations, choir, sewing clubs, courses, and book clubs. Are you a Civil War buff? There are reenactment groups that dress up in full regalia and spend the weekend in the 1800s. Love your ferret? There's a ferret fancier's group near you. Obsessed with the Backstreet Boys? There are fan clubs all over the country. (For info, contact Abs.)

> *My local supermarket has these free cooking classes every Wednesday night. I started going by myself, but now I have a group of friends I met in the class. I really look forward to cooking night!* (Melanie, age 46)

What's great about a knitting circle is that you don't really have to say anything to be a part of the group. We all help one another out with our projects and talk about things going on in the world. Sometimes we are pretty quiet when we're concentrating. But it still feels so nice to be with other people once in a while. (Wanda, age 74)

My husband and I have been in an archaeology club for over fifty years. Some people have become friends and others stayed acquaintances, but we have loved learning together. (Hilda, age 83)

The Harmony Project is a choir and service group that is so important to me. When I am singing, performing, or volunteering with my group, I feel part of something special. (Jordan, age 28)

Support Groups

Mental health challenges affect so many aspects of our lives—from relationships to work life and everything in between. So it would make sense that one way to connect with others is by joining a support group. In fact, we founded the Anxiety Sisterhood—our free, online community—because sharing experiences and supporting one another is so valuable. Plus, there's that whole connection thing.

My biggest takeaway from being in the Anxiety Sisters community is that whatever weird symptom or phobia I have is an actual thing with a name. And I am not the only one who is feeling it! We can share experiences about what helps or how to deal with it. I am so lucky to have found this group. (Bonita, age 51)

When we were beginning our anxiety journeys, finding a support group was a challenge, but now, with the internet at your fingertips, you are always just a Google search away from an online or in-person support group for just about anything that ails you. We have included a list of places to find support with mental health challenges in the Resources section on our website.

> *I go to a twice-monthly support group for my OCD run by a local thera-pist. She is so great—so supportive, and she makes us feel so comfortable. There are ten of us and we have become fast friends. I guess talking about all your craziness can make you feel pretty close! (Neela, age 26)*

Designated Anxiety Buddy (DAB)

Those of you familiar with scuba diving know how important it is to take a buddy with you in case of emergency, as well as to lend a hand with equipment, and so on. Your Designated Anxiety Buddy (DAB) performs the same func-tions: She (or he) is there for both crises and check-ins. She is the person you can call without explanation who understands anxiety and will be there to support you whenever you need it. Your DAB does not have to be a family member or a close friend—she can be someone you know very loosely or some-one you've met online, so long as you feel comfortable and safe with her. Often, you will be your DAB's DAB, so it is a reciprocal relationship. Lots of folks in our Anxiety Sisterhood have become each other's DABs, so if you are at a loss, consider joining us.

> *I am part of a small online support group for my anxiety. We've been one another's anxiety lifelines for a couple of years now, and I must say, I couldn't ask for a more supportive and caring group of women. Once, when I was in the waiting room for a doctor's appointment, I got so anxious that I actually texted the group. Several of the women responded. It was so nice not to have to go through it alone. (Amanda, age 56)*

Four of my friends and I have an anxiety emergency group on Whats-App. If anyone reaches out, we all immediately get in touch to support that person. (Zara, age 22)

My cousin lives across the country, so we don't see each other too much, but we are each other's anxiety "partner." We're just there for each other if things get rough. We text each other 9-1-1 if we really need help right away. (Roxanne, age 47)

How to Ask for Support

Sometimes the people in your life can behave in a very un-DABlike manner. We all have encountered different degrees of unsupportive folks who do everything except make us feel understood. It is especially challenging when these people either live with us or are part of our inner circle. These individuals compound our anxiety and make it that much harder to cope.

The following are some talking points we and other Anxiety Sisters have found helpful. Please feel free to take any of these words as your own.

- I really appreciate your willingness to learn more about my disorder, which can be so confusing—even for me. I can seem fine one minute and then be unable to function the next with no logical reason. And then it's very hard to figure out how to help me get through the anxiety; honestly, I don't usually know what to do either. I understand how you are feeling because I feel that way too. This disorder baffles, frustrates, and terrifies me even more than it does you!

- Anxiety is a brain disorder. All human beings have the fight, flight, or freeze instinct, which keeps us safe in many situations. From an evolutionary perspective, our anxious instincts kept us from becoming dinner for saber-toothed tigers or rattlesnakes. In the modern day, anxiety brains, for many physiological reasons, perceive threats in places or situations that are perfectly safe. In other words, I can experience the fight, flight, or freeze instinct (and it is instinct and not rational thought) in the grocery store, at a restaurant, while driving on a sunny day, or while sleeping in the middle of the night. The part of my brain that signals danger is overactive. As a result, I can become anxious without any apparent reason at all. My trigger-happy brain misfires for no rational reason, so I cannot control when it comes and goes. Which is frustrating and scary for me (and for you too).

• Anxiety is not a choice or a decision or a character flaw. As such, I can't "just relax" or "stop thinking about it" or "snap out of it," even though there is nothing I'd rather do. The truth is, when people tell me to calm down, it only makes the anxiety worse.

• Sometimes my anxiety is so intense that I cannot function at all. It's like a crippling migraine or stomach flu in that it takes over my body and I cannot do anything until it subsides. Please know that I am not flaky, lazy, or inconsiderate when I cancel plans. One of the hardest parts of my anxiety disorder is its unpredictability—even when I *really* want to see you or be at an event, my disorder may make that impossible for me. You should know I am as disappointed and frustrated about having to cancel plans as the people in my life affected by it.

• Anxiety is very physical—I don't just feel anxious in my mind. And the physical symptoms of anxiety are excruciating. I really feel like I am dying during a panic attack. Some common symptoms are a rapid heartbeat, dizziness, shortness of breath, sweating, nausea and vomiting, and even skin rashes, but there are many other physical manifestations as well. Sometimes the symptoms are so painful and frightening that I have to visit the doctor or ER to make sure it is really anxiety.

- Likewise, I am often dealing with intense emotional symptoms. I may feel "separated" from my body (depersonalization or dissociation), have obsessive thoughts playing in a loop, and become sensitive to noise, smells, and light.

- For all these reasons, anxiety is utterly exhausting. If I am sleeping a lot or during the day, it is because I am completely wrung out from fighting the anxiety and dealing with the symptoms.

- Anxiety does not diminish intelligence, so please do not dismiss the legitimacy of my concerns or observations just because I have anxiety.

Here's how you can be supportive of me and help me through my anxiety:

- Ask me (preferably when I am not in the throes of a panic attack) how you can help. Different people need different things. Some of us like to be hugged or swaddled, while others cannot be touched. Ask me what I need (it may be different each time). I also may react to noise, light, smells, or any sensory stimulation when I am anxious, so I could use a calm and quiet space to myself. Sometimes I would just like you to sit with me and tell me it's going to be okay.

- Understand that no matter what you do, you cannot end or take away my anxiety. But knowing that you care means so much and will definitely make the situation easier to handle.

- Accept me, have patience with me, and realize how brave I am for living with anxiety. I know it is not easy to deal with my anxiety, but I do need to know that you still love me—that my brain disorder hasn't taken you away from me.

• Keep learning about anxiety. I can direct you to some good websites that will help you understand my disorder. And keep the lines of communication open—we need to talk about the hard stuff. Your support means everything to me.

Other Ways to Connect

• Take your dog to a dog park. You don't have to interact with anyone—let your pup make the introductions.
• Enroll in a course, either at a local school or online. You will automatically have an activity in common, which makes connecting much easier. There are usually forums set up for this very purpose.
• Get involved in a community garden. Two benefits for the price of one: being in nature and connecting with others.
• Check out your library's bulletin board for local goings-on. There's a gold mine of group possibilities here.
• Make it a habit to say hello to your local proprietors. It will make your errands so much more fun.
• Go to a community meeting, such as a zoning board. You don't have to say anything, but you can still feel like part of a group.
• Join an online gaming community. If you like playing cards, for example, you can be part of an internet canasta, gin, bridge, or poker group. If you enjoy Scrabble, you can play online as well. And if you are feeling less intellectual, you can play any number of silly games (Abs loves *Fishdom*) with virtual buddies.
• Cook or bake for a neighbor.
• Volunteer to coach or to be an assistant to a coach for kids' sports.
• Visit a senior center or eldercare facility. They are always looking for folks to drop in and chat, play a game of checkers, or watch a movie with

residents. These are often some of the loneliest people around, so you will be doing something truly special.

There are so many ways to engage socially that it would be impossible for us to list them all. However you choose to connect with others, be sure you do it. Healing from anxiety is not a solo project. Neither, for that matter, is living a happy life. Both really require a village. Consider it part of your treatment plan to create one.

Healing from anxiety is not a solo project

fifteen

A Happy Note

Have you ever noticed how mysterious happiness is? We're all on a quest for this elusive, ephemeral concept that most of us can't even define. It's this big cosmic puzzle we're all trying to figure out. Everyone is constantly searching for happiness and we want people who have "found" it to share their secret.

The whole thing reminds us of one of our favorite stories ever—*The Wizard of Oz*. In this tale, Dorothy, who has found herself in a strange land, just wants to go home to her Auntie Em. Believing the Wizard will have all the answers, she and some friends go schlepping all over the land of Oz. They suffer through many trials and tribulations along the way (although they do get a spa day at the end), and eventually find themselves in the Wizard's chamber. Pulling the curtain back, Dorothy discovers that the Wizard is really just a short balding guy with a microphone. Not magical. Not mysterious. She then learns that she has had the power to take herself home all along.

In this comparison, the Wizard is the magical grantor of happiness and Dorothy represents all of us going through hell trying to find it. And just like in the story, the happiness we seek is actually within us. We mean this literally: happiness is created in the part of our brain called the left prefrontal cortex. So the whole quest thing is a bit of a sham. We know where to find the happiness. We just need to get better at activating it.

Before we tell you how to create more happiness in your brain, we want to first remind you of what we said in chapter one: stuff does not make us happy. This is worth repeating because it's so deeply ingrained in our national psyche that getting and having more stuff is the Yellow Brick Road to happiness. Our national psyche, however, needs some rewiring because study after study has shown that the pursuit of stuff does not make us happier. As David Myers points out in *The American Paradox*, today's young adults have oodles more stuff than their grandparents did yet are significantly less happy. In fact, stuff-obsessed folks have more diagnosed mental health disorders than people who aren't materialistic.[1]

Why doesn't stuff make us happier? First, we tend to mis-predict what will make us happy. We imagine that, say, a certain car will make us feel excited, young, powerful, and so on. So we purchase said automobile and find out that we don't actually feel so excited, young, or powerful. We may enjoy having the new vehicle. But we mis-predict just how happy it will actually make us feel. In fact, we often experience disappointment that we didn't feel as happy as we predicted we would!

Second, we think stuff will make us happy for a long time, but in reality, stuff-based happiness is fleeting. This is because we get used to things so quickly—new stuff becomes the same old stuff in the blink of an eye. As Dan Gilbert, author of *Stumbling on Happiness*, so cleverly put it, "Part of us believes that the new car is better because it lasts longer. But in fact, that's the worst thing about the new car. It will stay around to disappoint you."

Third, even if we manage to obtain stuff that makes us happy, as soon as we see our friend's Instagram depicting a newer, better model (anyone ever purchase an iPhone?), suddenly our stuff isn't so fantastic. This is called social comparison, and thanks to social media, it has done a lot to make us *less* happy.

Americans are pretty unhappy people overall. The annual *World Happiness*

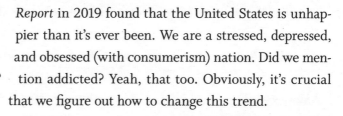

Report in 2019 found that the United States is unhappier than it's ever been. We are a stressed, depressed, and obsessed (with consumerism) nation. Did we mention addicted? Yeah, that too. Obviously, it's crucial that we figure out how to change this trend.

By the way, we're not suggesting that no material things are worth buying. Or that it's wrong to want something. We both like stuff. We just know that stuff isn't the source of our happiness and that getting more stuff probably won't make us happier. Which is not to say that we don't mis-predict from time to time. (Every time we walk into Williams-Sonoma.)

What we *are* suggesting is that you focus more of your attention on experiences. Unlike with stuff, we don't get used to experiences because they are fleeting, by definition. We have a lovely picnic with a dear friend that lasts for the afternoon—after that, it's just a memory. But the memory itself boosts happiness, as does the anticipation you feel before the experience. In fact, lots of Anxiety Sisters report that looking forward to experiences is what helps them cope with hard times.

A night out with my friends, planning my garden for this year,
a weekend camping with my partner . . . looking forward helps me.
(Sherrie, age 50)

Another way experiences make us happier is that we can share them with others, either directly or after the fact. And it's so much more fun for others to hear stories about your activities than it is for them to hear about your stuff.

We built my grandchildren a really intricate dollhouse and decorated it
as well. Along the way, we made a little "book" that told the story of us

building the dollhouse and showed pictures of all the places we went to get materials and all the work we did each step of the way. They liked the dollhouse but what they really loved was the book. (Anita, age 63)

We recognize that for those of us with brain disorders like anxiety and depression, planning experiences can feel like climbing Mount Everest—it's just too overwhelming. We get that. Experiences, however, don't need to be grand gestures like vacations, concerts, parties, or even lunch dates. They can be as simple as planning a nice walk with your dog or a phone call to reconnect with an old friend. Walking in nature is our most favorite experience and the one that boosts our moods the quickest. Really, anything you can look forward to, enjoy, and remember will fit the bill.

In the past couple of decades, researchers have decided that it is just as important to investigate human strengths as it is to look at our deficits. Thus, the positive psychology movement was born, bringing with it a wealth of studies on happiness and well-being. What we've learned from all this research is that there are several behaviors that promote happiness—actual skills we can develop in order to make our lives more fulfilling.

Use Your Superpowers

You know that game—which superpower would you choose? Some pick flying (probably not Panic Sisters), some pick invisibility (Social Anxiety Sisters?), some pick X-ray vision (not germaphobes!). It's fun to imagine what we could do given extraordinary abilities. But what if we told you that you already have superpowers?

We typically take for granted things we are good at—many of us are much better at describing and lamenting our faults and failings. Often our strengths come easily to us, so we don't recognize them as a big deal. For example, one

Anxiety Sister we know has a fantastic sense of humor, a very supportive extended family, and an unshakable faith in God. She doesn't see these things as particularly special, but when things are difficult, she can see the humor in a dark situation, call in her army of support, and use her belief to feel grounded.

Now, some of you may be thinking that you don't have any superpowers. You are wrong. We have been helping people find their strengths for the past ten years, and we have *never* come across an individual whose superpowers we couldn't locate—no matter how adamant she was that she didn't have any. All human beings are a balance of strengths and weaknesses. Anxiety Sisters are just more accustomed to focusing on the weaknesses.

> *One of my strengths is perseverance. I just don't give up, no matter what. This helps me in my anxiety struggle. For one thing, my mantra that I say to myself when I'm feeling really bad is "I will outlast this." This reminds me that I can overcome whatever my anxiety throws at me. My perseverance superpower means I can stick it out. (Abs, age 52)*

> *I get on really well with animals. Anyway, I never really thought of it as a superpower, but I see now how much pleasure I get from spending time on the farm. I actually breathe better when I'm with the horses and the goats and the chickens. (Pippa, age 38)*

> *People tend to connect easily with me. I am the one that friends (and even strangers) confide in. I can be confident that no matter where I am, I will make a friend. (Sasha, age 25)*

> *I am a fairly good cook. I never realized it was a superpower but now I do. I feed my family and friends all the time and create a really welcoming home. It's so nice to be able to bring people together. (Tammy, age 68)*

The following are ways to help you figure out your superpowers:

- Ask your closest friends (they will know because your superpowers are what drew them to you).
- Think about something that comes easily to you—something you take for granted—that isn't so easy for everyone else. Not necessarily a talent (although talents can certainly be superpowers), but more along the lines of a character trait.
- Think about a triumphant moment—what caused it? Chances are your superpower was responsible.
- What are you good at?
- What are you proud of?
- What do others admire about you?
- Fill in the blank: "I am at my best when I _____."

Once you've identified some of your superpowers, try to look for experiences that require you to use them. Studies have shown that the more an individual uses her strengths, the happier she will be. This makes sense: when we engage the best parts of ourselves, our experiences feel more meaningful. Your activities become less chorelike and more like a calling.

Because activating your superpowers gives you a greater sense of agency, try to do it as often as possible. Researchers found that folks who came up with new ways to use their strengths every day for a week increased their happiness levels for *six months* thereafter.[2] So it is a worthwhile undertaking to discover your superpowers and then make use of them as frequently as possible. For example, if humor is one of your superpowers, you may decide to send a daily email blast to give your family and friends a laugh. Or if love of learning is one of your strengths, you may choose to take a free online course just for the heck of it.

Activating your superpowers gives you a greater sense of agency

As I have always been very friendly, my therapist suggested finding a volunteer position where I could use that part of myself. So I volunteer a few days a week at the airport. I meet so many interesting people from all over the world, and I have made friends with other volunteers.
(Nika, age 19)

Vitamin G

According to Robert Emmons, gratitude is defined as an affirmation of goodness in an imperfect life.[3] We like this definition because it recognizes that things don't have to be easy in order for you to feel grateful.

Gratitude is all the rage in pop culture these days. Just scroll through your feed and you will find no fewer than ten memes instructing you to be thankful for everything you have. But here's the thing: These memes make it sound so easy to do. It's not.

Suffering, by definition, is all-consuming. When we are caught in the grip of profound anxiety or depression, for example, that is *all* we can feel. We cannot look outside ourselves when our selves are so desperate. For some of us, anxiety can feel like a fight for our lives. It's hard to stop mid–spin cycle to remember how "lucky" we are to be alive. In fact, we get annoyed by the suggestion that we should feel gratitude at these particular moments.

Of course, we can always find somebody who has it worse than we do, but that is not a particularly fruitful game. In fact, it can cause a spiral of shame, depression, and anxiety. How can we justify our own struggles when we put them up against those in dire straits?

Well-meaning people trying to help us may often use the "At least you're not . . ." strategy. They believe that not seeing the bigger picture is our problem. But we know two things: (1) this strategy does not help, and (2) people with anxiety tend to be the most empathetic people on earth. We are all too aware of the suffering out there.

This is not to say that gratitude is not an important component of the anxiously happy life. We like to think of it as a vitamin to be taken preventively. Study after study has revealed the powerful effects of expressing gratitude to increase overall well-being and mental health. Here are some ways to practice gratitude in your everyday life:

- Send a thank-you note (or email) to someone you appreciate. It can even be someone from your past.
- Go on a gratitude visit—go see someone you are grateful for and let that person know how you feel, face-to-face.
- Keep a daily or weekly journal in which you write things you are grateful for.
- Make a list of three good things from your day.
- Notice the beauty around you, like a leaf on a tree or a sunrise or your child's smile.
- Recognize and acknowledge the small things you might take for granted—like your partner taking out the trash or making your morning cup of coffee.
- Be generous with compliments.
- Ditto with the words "thank you."
- Be grateful to your body for all it can do; this is especially helpful if you are critical of your appearance.
- Decorate a jar and drop little notes of gratitude in it. Over time, your jar will runneth over!
- Close your eyes and think about the things that are gifts in your life.

When my child comes home from school very excited about something he has learned or done that day, I often send a quick email thanking the teacher. It makes me feel so good doing it. (Victoria, age 43)

When I am really anxious I make a list of five things I am grateful for in my life. It could be my evening bike ride, the dinner I ate, or how quickly I got to work that day . . . It all counts. Doing this distracts me from my anxiety. (Hiromi, age 29)

Savoring

Closely related to gratitude is savoring—the act of truly appreciating an experience or sensation in the present moment. We often think of savoring in terms of delicious food, whereby we take our time to focus on flavors and smells. But you can savor in any context. For example, you can savor your time with someone by paying close attention to how you're feeling in their presence and how connecting with them elevates you. You can savor a hot bath by breathing in the scent of the bubbles and feeling them burst gently against your skin. You can savor sunlight on your face, a happy event, wind in your hair, the touch of a loved one. It's all about slowing down the moment so you can fully appreciate it with all your senses—you are quite literally breathing in the experience.

Savoring actually amplifies the experience and allows you to enjoy it longer. It is an act of deliberate mindfulness that allows you to keep the experience alive in real time and in your memory. Plus, the more time you spend in the present, the less time you'll spend worrying about what might happen in the future. If you share your experience with others, it will further enhance the savoring effects.

When it comes to saying goodbye to my boyfriend at the end of a visit, I really savor that hug. I memorize the weight of his arms, the way he smells, the warmth of his breath. (Angel, age 18)

My friend told me to really take in my wedding day. I have a lot of anxiety and I was freaking out about it. But she reminded me that there are so few times in life when all the people we love will be together in the same room. Several times during the wedding, I just stopped and took a breath, and felt connected to everyone. (Wren, age 30)

Movement

Let's be clear about this: movement is *not* exercise. We hate exercise. We love movement. The former is another task on our Should-Do List. The latter makes us feel better. And research has shown it makes everyone feel better. Human beings are not supposed to be sedentary. Our bodies are designed for activity, and our feel-good chemicals are released when we move.

If you love running on a treadmill, by all means, do it to your heart's content. But just putting on some music and dancing around your house counts too. As does a stroll in your neighborhood, gardening, swimming, yoga, chasing your dog, and anything else that involves moving parts of your body. Even sex can be movement, depending on how you do it!

We all know that exercise is good for the body, but movement is good for the soul. In a 2017 University of Cambridge study, researchers found that even a little movement makes people happier than sitting still.[4] Other studies have shown that active folks are better able to manage their anxiety and depression.[5]

This is going to sound weird, but whenever I am feeling down, I take out my hula hoop and give it a go. I'm awful at it—but the few minutes it takes for me to get it going always leaves me feeling happier. (Robin, age 59)

When I was younger, I loved to play tennis, but I'm a bit creakier now, so I play pickleball. Our community has several courts and we play tournaments for bragging rights. It's so much fun! (Ginger, age 82)

Learn How to Say "Not Yet"

When faced with difficulty, some folks will back away. For them, the challenge is "too hard," or they believe they are not smart, strong, or talented (or any similar adjective) enough to attempt to move forward. These people view their intelligence and abilities as set traits. To them, mistakes equal failure, and hard work is a sign of being ill-equipped. Psychologist and researcher Carol Dweck refers to this as the fixed mindset.

On the other hand, there are people who believe their intelligence and skills can be improved over time—that their innate abilities can grow. These folks understand that mistakes are part of the process and ultimately, with hard work, can lead to success. They also know that very little of value comes easily and that things take time. Dweck calls this the growth mindset.

Guess which mindset leads to happiness.

Before you start berating yourself for falling into the fixed category, you should know that we all do from time to time when the going gets tough. This is called being human. But we don't have to stay in the fixed mindset—we can learn a new perspective.

We can learn a new perspective

Choosing the growth mindset means talking to yourself differently in the face of obstacles. Instead of saying "I can't," say "Not yet." The latter phrase implies you will get there—you just aren't quite there *yet*. "Not yet" allows you to make errors, ask for help, take breaks to regroup, learn new skills, and cultivate patience. "Not yet" eliminates blame and shame. "Not yet" gives you hope. "Not yet" reminds you of your own power and adds meaning to your accomplishments.

Another way to access the growth mindset is to say something like, "I can do hard things." It's a great mantra for tackling just about any challenge. We say it to each other on a daily basis. We're not kidding.

Saying "Not yet" or "I can do hard things" rewards effort more than outcomes. When we value the process itself, we bounce back better even when the results are not (yet) ideal. In other words, the experience can still be meaning-ful, even if things don't turn out exactly how we planned. Folks who choose the growth mindset understand that sometimes even happiness is not yet.

> *No matter what I did in my calculus class, I couldn't seem to get a grade above a C. I was so discouraged—I started believing I wasn't smart enough to take the class at all. Then Abs and Mags taught me about "not yet." Game changer! I stopped focusing so much on the grades and spent more time trying to understand the concepts. Even though I ended up with a C+ in the class, I felt really good about it. (Maddie, age 21)*

Psychological Immunity

You know how we have a biological immune system that helps protect us from illness by fighting germs and toxins? Well, it turns out we also have a psycho-logical immune system, which protects us from experiencing prolonged emo-tional distress. Yes, you read that right: our brains are **We are hardwired for resilience** designed to fight off stress so we can adapt better. We are hardwired for resilience.

The problem with our psychological immune sys-tem is that we keep forgetting it's there. Harvard psychologist and researcher Dan Gilbert has dubbed this bias "immune neglect," which means that we con-stantly underestimate our ability to handle hardship. We neglect to take into account our built-in resilience when we predict how bad we are going to feel about something. This is why we so often experience relief when what we have been dreading in our minds doesn't actually turn out to be so bad.

> *I was so worried about visiting my mom last summer—we hadn't seen each other in so long and our relationship has always been difficult. We had a few tense moments here and there, but, basically, we both*

behaved ourselves and the trip was overall a success. I guess I under-estimated my ability to handle her. (Clara, age 41)

A lot of our anxiety comes from the idea that we won't survive a catastrophe. In fact, even if the worst-case scenario does happen, we will likely survive it. Our psychological immune system will do its best to see to that. So here's another useful strategy for happiness: Don't forget how resilient you are! Remember that your psychological immune system is pretty powerful, so you can most definitely deal with hard—even the hardest—circumstances.

When my son died, I didn't think I could go on. It was always my biggest fear and it happened. It's been ten years and I still struggle every day. But I'm still here. Somehow, I keep going. (Orli, age 70)

Closing Thoughts

Way back in chapter one, we said that to be (anxiously) happy, you need three things: (1) acceptance, (2) agency, and (3) connection—the ingredients in the Secret Sauce. Everything we have discussed in this chapter is in itself a pathway to all three. For example, in order to identify your superpowers, you have to first accept who you are—not just your challenges but also your strengths (not easy for Anxiety Sisters). By understanding your superpowers, you become more deeply connected to yourself, which empowers you to have more agency in your life. Also, your superpowers can be a vehicle to connect to other beings.

Think about gratitude. You have to truly accept yourself and your circumstances in order to be grateful. Gratitude lets us know we are enough, just the way we are. Practicing gratitude is therefore an act of agency—it requires effort and intention. Few things are more connecting than expressing appreciation either for yourself or for others.

And it's not just the stuff we talked about in this chapter. Every technique and strategy we have mentioned throughout this book not only alleviates anxiety but also strengthens your acceptance, agency, and connection. You don't have to work on them separately—as we said before, anxious and happy are friends.

Because your brain is very flexible and adaptive (there's that neuroplasticity thing again), you can program it to activate more happiness by using any or all of the techniques we have presented in this book. It takes about sixty-six days of consistent practice to make a behavior or thought automatic.[6] If you think about it, that's not so bad—a couple of months of, for example, savoring, meditating, doing Tai Chi, practicing self-compassion, bookending, grounding, or challenging your Go-To thoughts can alter your neural pathways. You can teach yourself to create happiness so that you no longer have to spend your time hunting for it.

One more piece of business before we wrap up. Lest you are under the impression that we spend our days savoring every moment, using our superpowers to solve all our problems, and being grateful for everything in our lives, we should say, *not yet!* Our minds still wander while we meditate, we still criticize ourselves for screwing up, and we definitely find ourselves in the spin cycle from time to time. However, we understand on a fundamental level that anxiety is part and parcel of the messy human experience and that we have the tools to ride the wave.

And now you do too.

acknowledgments

Lots of folks helped us get this book out in the world: our agent extraordinaire, Stacey Glick; our brilliant editor Marian Lizzi and her wonderful assistant, Rachel Ayotte; the TarcherPerigee sales, marketing, and publicity departments, especially: Anne Kosmoski, Rachel Dugan, Sara Johnson, Marlena Brown, and Roshe Anderson. We are so lucky and grateful to have been in such smart and capable hands. We also want to give a special shout-out to Kym Surridge, the most thorough copyeditor on the planet. Even Abs's OCD was no match for Kym's eye!

Jill Siegel and Jessica Jonap not only are consummate PR professionals, but also are Anxiety Sister whisperers. Thank you for talking us off so many ledges and for guiding us through this process. We are so fortunate to have found you and even luckier to call you our friends.

Special thanks to our remarkable illustrator from across the pond, Simon Goodway; to our first readers, Ann Nikolai and Sammi Porter Flynn; to our amazing intern, Megan Lee; to Gary Studen for astute legal advice; and to Isabelle Jung Greenberg for handling all our IP needs.

Lastly, we owe a huge thank-you to our longest-standing and steadfast member of the Anxiety Sisterhood, Susan Brust, who liked every post, listened to every podcast, and read every blog. And she's not even a relative!

Abbe's Acknowledgments

To my mother, Nancy Greenberg, who took me to my first writers' conference and has encouraged me to keep writing ever since. Her response to everything else I tried was, "You should be writing." Okay, I'll say it for the record. You were right.

To my father, Mark Greenberg, who has cheered us on every step of the way, even though he doesn't really get the whole anxiety thing. I cherished your daily emails full of suggestions and praise, and I promise we will give "biking anxiety" the attention it deserves in our next book.

To my brother, Steve Greenberg, who more than made up for cutting all the tails off my stuffed animals by paying me twice what I was worth so I could afford to pursue Anxiety Sisters. I owe you so much more than this acknowledgment and I adore you for never making me feel like I owed you anything.

To Ann Birr, Nancy Kelton, Papatya Bucak, Kate Schmitt, and Kathrine Wright—five incredible writers and teachers who believed in my voice. There aren't words to express my gratitude for all that I have learned from you.

To my kids, Dani, Nicky, and Jon—thank you for putting up with my Anxiety Sisters obsession for so many years. Your support meant everything to me. I hope I made you proud.

To my grandmother and favorite human, Viola Holtz, who never tired of hearing about all things Anxiety Sisters and reminded me every day not to quit, no matter what. I hope somehow she knows that I didn't.

To Jay—boy did I hit the lotto when it comes to husbands! Your unwavering support—especially when we made mistakes—and your encouragement that we do whatever it takes to pursue our dreams made this book and my happiness possible. You never once said no to anything, no matter the inconvenience or cost. Thank you for sharing this dream with me.

To my Mags, who has been my touchstone and true sister for the past thirty-four years. Your commitment to making the world a kinder, more just place inspires me every day. I would not be who I am without you to encourage me and gently (sometimes not-so-gently) guide (shove) me back to my path. You ask nothing of me but to be my real, hyperorganized, demanding, rule-following, overly-sensitive self. Thank you for loving me no matter what and for letting me be the boss. Your friendship has been the greatest gift.

Maggie's Acknowledgments

I am so grateful to the students and staff of the Student Life Center—some of the most extraordinary people I have ever met. I thank them for becoming my second family. I owe so much to my friend and mentor Nafissa Hannat, whose wisdom and guidance shaped me as a social worker.

My deepest appreciation goes out to the faculty and staff of the Silberman School of Social Work at Hunter College, particularly Michael Fabricant, Steve Burghardt, Glynn Rudich, Elizabeth Danto, and the late Ellie Bromberg.

I wish David Bosnick was alive to see this book. He changed my life by seeing me as a writer.

I owe so much to my parents, Shirley and Julian Sarachek, who gave me the confidence to use my voice. I miss them every day. My brothers, Joe and Russell, often stepped in to take care of me, and they never made me feel like a burden. And thank you to Jonas Rosenthal for becoming my third brother and believing in Anxiety Sisters.

My husband, Paul Weiss, has spent a quarter of a century telling me I am beautiful and loving me in all my messiness. Our children, Julian and Jack, are my heart and soul. Julian gave me so much support by following Anxiety Sisters closely and giving invaluable feedback. Jack made sure I stayed funny (whenever possible).

Last but not least, Anxiety Sisters would not exist without Abs. She is my Anxiety Sister, my soul sister, my rock, the Felix to my Oscar, and a magnificent human being. She loves generously, forgives easily (even a dark soda stain on new white carpet), and is always working to grow as a person. She is also so darn smart. I am thankful to go through this journey with her.

notes

CHAPTER 1

1. Holt-Lunstad, J., Smith, T. B., Baker, M., Harris, T., & Stephenson, D. (2015). Loneliness and social isolation as risk factors for mortality: A meta-analytic review. *Perspectives on Psychological Science, 10*(2), 227–237. https://doi.org/10.1177/1745691614568352.
2. Valtorta, N. K., Kanaan, M., Gilbody, S., Ronzi, S., & Hanratty, B. (2016). Loneliness and social isolation as risk factors for coronary heart disease and stroke: Systematic review and meta-analysis of longitudinal observational studies. *Heart, 102*(13), 1009–1016. https://doi .org/10.1136/heartjnl-2015-308790.
3. Alcaraz, K. I., Eddens, K. S., Blase, J. L., Diver, W. R., Patel, A. V., Teras, L. R., Stevens, V. L., Jacobs, E. J., & Gapstur, S. M. (2019). Social isolation and mortality in US black and white men and women. *American Journal of Epidemiology, 188*(1), 102–109. https://doi.org /10.1093/aje/kwy231.

CHAPTER 2

1. Raymond, V. (2018, February 23). *Is your chest pain a heart attack or anxiety?* Right as Rain. https://rightasrain.uwmedicine.org/well/health/your-chest-pain-heart-attack-or-anxiety.

CHAPTER 3

1. Goleman, D. (2005). *Emotional intelligence: Why it can matter more than IQ.* Bantam Books.
2. Leahy, R. L. (2008, April 30). How big a problem is anxiety? *Psychology Today.* https://www .psychologytoday.com/us/blog/anxiety-files/200804/how-big-problem-is-anxiety.
3. Hadhazy, A. (2010, February 12). Think twice: How the gut's "second brain" influences mood and well-being. *Scientific American.* https://www.scientificamerican.com/article/gut -second-brain/.
4. Helander, H. F., & Fändriks, L. (2014). Surface area of the digestive tract—Revisited. *Scandinavian Journal of Gastroenterology, 49*(6), 681–689. https://doi.org/10.3109/00365521 .2014.898326.
5. Oosthoek, S. (2014, July 14). Gut feeling: How intestinal bacteria may influence our moods.

CBC News. https://www.cbc.ca/news/gut-feeling-how-intestinal-bacteria-may-influence-our-moods-1.2701037.

6. Bercik, P., Denou, E., Collins, J., Jackson, W., Lu, J., Jury, J., Deng, Y., Blennerhassett, P., Macri, J., McCoy, K. D., Verdu, E. F., & Collins, S. M. (2011). The intestinal microbiota affect central levels of brain-derived neurotropic factor and behavior in mice. *Gastroenterology, 141*(2), 599–609. https://doi.org/10.1053/j.gastro.2011.04.052.

CHAPTER 4

1. *Anxiety disorders.* (2019, January 30). Office on Women's Health. https://www.womenshealth.gov/mental-health/mental-health-conditions/anxiety-disorders/.

2. *Specific phobia.* (2017, November). National Institute of Mental Health. https://www.nimh.nih.gov/health/statistics/specific-phobia.shtml.

3. Villafuerte, S., & Burmeister, M. (2003). Untangling genetic networks of panic, phobia, fear and anxiety. *Genome Biology, 4*(8), 224. https://doi.org/10.1186/gb-2003-4-8-224.

4. Concordia University. (2014, April 8). Surprising truth about obsessive-compulsive thinking. *ScienceDaily.* http://www.sciencedaily.com/releases/2014/04/140408122137.htm.

5. Love, S. (2019, March 7). The many obsessions that can haunt a person with OCD. *Vice.* https://www.vice.com/en_us/article/nex4qm/the-many-obsessions-that-can-haunt-a-person-with-ocd.

6. Mathews, C. A., Kaur, N., & Stein, M. B. (2008). Childhood trauma and obsessive-compulsive symptoms. *Depression & Anxiety, 25*(9), 742–751. https://doi.org/10.1002/da.20316.

CHAPTER 5

1. Davies, M. N., Verdi, S., Burri, A., Trzaskowski, M., Lee, M., Hettema, J. M., Jansen, R., Boomsma, D. I., & Spector, T. D. (2015). Generalised anxiety disorder—A twin study of genetic architecture, genome-wide association and differential gene expression. *PloS One, 10*(8), e0134865. https://doi.org/10.1371/journal.pone.0134865.

2. Gottschalk, M. G., & Domschke, K. (2016). Novel developments in genetic and epigenetic mechanisms of anxiety. *Current Opinion in Psychiatry, (29)*1, 32–38. https://doi.org/10.1097/YCO.0000000000000219.

3. Dincheva, I., Drysdale, A. T., Hartley, C. A., Johnson, D. C., Jing, D., King, E. C., Ra, S., Gray, J. M., Yang, R., DeGruccio, A. M., Huang, C., Cravatt, B. F., Glatt, C. E., Hill, M. N., Casey, B. J., & Lee, F. S. (2015). FAAH genetic variation enhances fronto-amygdala function in mouse and human. *Nature Communications, 6*, 6395. https://doi.org/10.1038/ncomms7395.

4. Levey, D. F., Gelernter, J., Polimanti, R., Zhou, H., Cheng, Z., Aslan, M., Quaden, R., Concato, J., Radhakrishnan, K., Bryois, J., Sullivan, P. F., the Million Veteran Program, & Stein,

M. B. (2020). Reproducible genetic risk loci for anxiety: Results from ~200,000 participants in the million veteran program. *American Journal of Psychiatry, 177*(3), 223–232. https://doi.org/10.1176/appi.ajp.2019.19030256.

5. Rodriguez, T. (2015, March 1). Descendants of Holocaust survivors have altered stress hormones. *Scientific American Mind.* https://doi.org/10.1038/scientificamericanmind0315-10a.

6. Halloran, M. J. (2019). African American health and posttraumatic slave syndrome: A terror management theory account. *Journal of Black Studies, 50*(1), 45–65. https://doi.org/10.1177/0021934718803737.

7. Nishizawa, S., Benkelfat, C., Young, S. N., Leyton, M., Mzengeza, S., de Montigny, C., Blier, P., & Diksic, M. (1997). Differences between males and females in rates of serotonin synthesis in human brain. *Proceedings of the National Academy of Sciences, 94*(10), 5308–5313. https://doi.org/10.1073/pnas.94.10.5308.

8. *5 myths about polycystic ovary syndrome (PCOS).* (2020, March 18). Penn Medicine. https://www.pennmedicine.org/updates/blogs/fertility-blog/2020/march/five-myths-about-pcos.

9. Cooney, L. G., Lee, I., Sammel, M. D., & Dokras, A. (2017). High prevalence of moderate and severe depressive and anxiety symptoms in polycystic ovary syndrome: A systematic review and meta-analysis. *Human Reproduction, 32*(5), 1075–1091. https://doi.org/10.1093/humrep/dex044.

10. Postpartum Support International. (n.d.). Anxiety during pregnancy and postpartum. https://www.postpartum.net/learn-more/anxiety-during-pregnancy-postpartum/.

11. Gautam, M., Agrawal, M., Gautam, M., Sharma, P., Gautam, A. S., & Gautam, S. (2012). Role of antioxidants in generalised anxiety disorder and depression. *Indian Journal of Psychiatry, 54*(3), 244–247. https://doi.org/10.4103/0019-5545.102424.

12. Kessler, R. C., Chiu, W. T., Demler, O., & Walters, E. E. (2005). Prevalence, severity, and comorbidity of 12-month DSM-IV disorders in the National Comorbidity Survey Replication. *Archives of General Psychiatry, 62*(6), 617–627. https://doi.org/10.1001/archpsyc.62.6.617–627.

13. Cohen, H. (2016, May 17). *Depression versus anxiety.* PsychCentral. https://psychcentral.com/lib/depression-versus-anxiety/.

CHAPTER 6

1. Todd, A. R., Forstmann, M., Burgmer, P., Brooks, A. W., & Galinsky, A. D. (2015). Anxious and egocentric: How specific emotions influence perspective taking. *Journal of Experimental Psychology: General, 144*(2), 374–391. https://doi.org/10.1037/xge0000048.

2. Teigen, K. H. (1994). Yerkes-Dodson: A law for all seasons. *Theory & Psychology, 4*(4), 525–547. https://doi.org/10.1177/0959354394044004.

3. Risk and prognostic factors for 300.22 agoraphobia without history of panic disorder. (2013). *Diagnostic and Statistical Manual of Mental Disorders, Fifth Edition,* 220.

CHAPTER 7

1. Dahm, K. A., Meyer, E. C., Neff, K. D., Kimbrel, N. A., Gulliver, S. B., & Morissette, S. B. (2015). Mindfulness, self-compassion, posttraumatic stress disorder symptoms, and functional disability in U.S. Iraq and Afghanistan war veterans. *Journal of Traumatic Stress, 28*(5), 460–464. https://doi.org/10.1002/jts.22045.

2. Neff, K. D., Hseih, Y., & Dejitterat, K. (2005). Self-compassion, achievement goals, and coping with academic failure. *Self and Identity, 4*(3), 263–287. https://doi.org/10.1080/13576500 444000317.

3. Sbarra, D. A., Smith, H. L., & Mehl, M. R. (2012). When leaving your ex, love yourself: Observational ratings of self-compassion predict the course of emotional recovery following marital separation. *Psychological Science, 23*(3), 261–269. https://doi.org/10.1177/0956797 611429466.

4. Brion, J. M., Leary, M. R., & Drabkin, A. S. (2014). Self-compassion and reactions to serious illness: The case of HIV. *Journal of Health Psychology, 19*(2), 218–229. https://doi.org/10.1177 /1359105312467391.

5. Carvalho, S. A., Gillanders, D., Palmeira, L., Pinto-Gouveia, J., & Castilho, P. (2018). Mindfulness, self-compassion, and depressive symptoms in chronic pain: The role of pain acceptance. *Journal of Clinical Psychology, 74*(12), 2094–2106. https://doi.org/10.1002/jclp.22689.

6. Zessin, U., Dickhäuser, O., & Garbade, S. (2015). The relationship between self-compassion and well-being: A meta-analysis. *Applied Psychology: Health and Well-Being, 7*(3), 360–364 https://doi.org/10.1111/aphw.12051.

7. Sirois, F. M., Molnar, D. S., & Hirsch, J. K. (2015). Self-compassion, stress, and coping in the context of chronic illness. *Self and Identity, 14*(3), 334–347. https://doi.org/10.1080 /15298868.2014.996249.

8. Neff, K. D., & Pommier, E. (2013). The relationship between self-compassion and other-focused concern among college undergraduates, community adults, and practicing meditators. *Self and Identity, 12*(2), 160–176. https://doi.org/10.1080/15298868.2011.649546.

9. Vazeou-Nieuwenhuis, A., & Schumann, K. (2018). Self-compassionate and apologetic? How and why having compassion toward the self relates to a willingness to apologize. *Personality and Individual Differences, 124*, 71–76. https://doi.org/10.1016/j.paid.2017.12.002.

10. Neff, K. D. (2003). Development and validation of a scale to measure self-compassion. *Self and Identity, 2*(3), 223–250. https://doi.org/10.1080/15298860309027.

CHAPTER 8

1. Reiner, K., Tibi, L., & Lipsitz, J. D. (2013). Do mindfulness-based interventions reduce pain intensity? A critical review of the literature. *Pain medicine, 14*(2), 230–242. https://doi.org /10.1111/pme.12006.

2. Goyal, M., Singh, S., Sibinga, E. M. S., Gould, N. F., Rowland-Seymour, A., Sharma, R.,

Berger, Z., Sleicher, D., Maron, D. D., Shihab, H. M., Ranasinghe, P. D., Linn, S., Saha, S., Bass, E. B., & Haythornthwaite, J. A. (2014). Meditation programs for psychological stress and well-being: A systematic review and meta-analysis. *JAMA Internal Medicine, 174*(3), 357–368. https://doi.org/10.1001/jamainternmed.2013.13018.

3. Sundquist, J., Palmér, K., Johansson, L. M., & Sundquist, K. (2017). The effect of mindfulness group therapy on a broad range of psychiatric symptoms: A randomised controlled trial in primary health care. *European Psychiatry, 43,* 19–27. https://doi.org/10.1016/j.eurpsy.2017.01.328.

4. Kral, T. R. A., Schuyler, B. S., Mumford, J. A., Rosenkranz, M. A., Lutz, A., & Davidson, R. J. (2018). Impact of short- and long-term mindfulness meditation training on amygdala reactivity to emotional stimuli. *NeuroImage, 181,* 301–313. https://doi.org/10.1016/j.neuroimage.2018.07.013; Taren, A. A., Gianaros, P. J., Greco, C. M., Lindsay, E. K., Fairgrieve, A., Brown, K. W., Rosen, R. K., Ferris, J. L., Julson, E., Marsland, A. L., Bursley, J. K., Ramsburg, J., & Creswell, J. D. (2015). Mindfulness meditation training alters stress-related amygdala resting state functional connectivity: A randomized controlled trial. *Social Cognitive and Affective Neuroscience, 10*(12), 1758–1768. https://doi.org/10.1093/scan/nsv066.

5. Wegner, D. M., Schneider, D. J., Carter, S. R., & White, T. L. (1987). Paradoxical effects of thought suppression. *Journal of Personality and Social Psychology, 53*(1), 5–13. https://doi.org/10.1037/0022-3514.53.1.5.

6. Baird, B., Smallwood, J., Mrazek, M. D., Kam, J. W. Y., Franklin, M. S., & Schooler, J. W. (2012). Inspired by distraction: Mind wandering facilitates creative incubation. *Psychological Science, 23*(10), 1117–1122. https://doi.org/10.1177/0956797612446024; Leszczynski, M., Chaieb, L., Reber, T. P., Derner, M., Axmacher, N., & Fell, J. (2017). Mind wandering simultaneously prolongs reactions and promotes creative incubation. *Scientific Reports, 7*(1). https://doi.org/10.1038/s41598-017-10616-3.

7. Hoffart, M. B., & Keene, E. P. (1998). Body-mind-spirit: The benefits of visualization. *American Journal of Nursing, 98*(12), 44–47.

CHAPTER 11

1. National Institute on Drug Abuse. (2021, February 3). *Benzodiazepines and opioids.* https://www.drugabuse.gov/drug-topics/opioids/benzodiazepines-opioids.

2. Maust, D. T., Lin, L. A., & Blow, F. C. (2019). Benzodiazepine use and misuse among adults in the United States. *Psychiatric Services, 70*(2), 97–106. https://doi.org/10.1176/appi.ps.201800321.

3. De Gage, S. B., Moride, Y., Ducruet, T., Kurth, T., Verdoux, H., Tournier, M., Pariente, A., & Bégaud, B. (2014). Benzodiazepine use and risk of Alzheimer's disease: Case-control study. *BMJ, 349,* g5205. https://doi.org/10.1136/bmj.g5205.

4. Wilson, R. S., Krueger, K. R., Arnold, S. E., Schneider, J. A., Kelly, J. F., Barnes, L. L., Tang, Y., & Bennett, D. A. (2007). Loneliness and risk of Alzheimer disease. *Archives of General Psychiatry, 64*(2), 234–240. https://doi.org/10.1001/archpsyc.64.2.234.

5. Miller, M. C. (2018, October 12). Ease off antidepressants, don't just stop. https://www.orlandosentinel.com/news/os-xpm-2009-01-06-0901020040-story.html.

6. Blumenthal, S. R., Castro, V. M., Clements, C. C., Rosenfield, H. R., Murphy, S. N., Fava, M., Weilburg, J. B., Erb, J. L., Churchill, S. E., Kohane, I. S., Smoller, J. W., & Perlis, R. H. (2014). An electronic health records study of long-term weight gain following antidepressant use. *JAMA Psychiatry, 71*(8), 889–896. https://doi.org/10.1001/jamapsychiatry.2014.414.

7. Tomiyama, A. J., Hunger, J. M., Nguyen-Cuu, J., & Wells, C. (2016). Misclassification of cardiometabolic health when using body mass index categories in NHANES 2005–2012. *International Journal of Obesity, 40*(5), 883–886. https://doi.org/10.1038/ijo.2016.17.

8. Higgins, A., Nash, M., & Lynch, A. M. (2010). Antidepressant-associated sexual dysfunction: Impact, effects, and treatment. *Drug, Healthcare and Patient Safety, 2*, 141–150. https://doi.org/10.2147/DHPS.S7634.

9. Cohen, A. J., & Bartlik, B. (1998). Ginkgo biloba for antidepressant-induced sexual dysfunction. *Journal of Sex & Marital Therapy, 24*(2), 139–143. https://doi.org/10.1080/00926239808404927.

10. Blessing, E. M., Steenkamp, M. M., Manzanares, J., & Marmar, C. R. (2015). Cannabidiol as a potential treatment for anxiety disorders. *Neurotherapeutics, 12*(4), 825–836. https://doi.org/10.1007/s13311-015-0387-1; Shannon, S., Lewis, N., Lee, H., & Hughes, S. (2019). Cannabidiol in anxiety and sleep: A large case series. *Permanente Journal, 23*, 18–041. https://doi.org/10.7812/TPP/18-041.

11. Cuttler, C., Spradlin, A., & McLaughlin, R. J. (2018). A naturalistic examination of the perceived effects of cannabis on negative affect. *Journal of Affective Disorders, 235*, 198–205. https://doi.org/10.1016/j.jad.2018.04.054.

12. Volkow, N. D., Baler, R. D., Compton, W. M., & Weiss, S. R. B. (2014). Adverse health effects of marijuana use. *New England Journal of Medicine, 370*(23), 2219–2227. https://doi.org/10.1056/NEJMra1402309.

13. Muttoni, S., Ardissino, M., & John, C. (2019). Classical psychedelics for the treatment of depression and anxiety: A systematic review. *Journal of Affective Disorders, 258*, 11–24. https://doi.org/10.1016/j.jad.2019.07.076.

14. Davis, A. K., Barrett, F. S., & Griffiths, R. R. (2020). Psychological flexibility mediates the relations between acute psychedelic effects and subjective decreases in depression and anxiety. *Journal of Contextual Behavioral Science, 15*, 39–45. https://doi.org/10.1016/j.jcbs.2019.11.004.

15. Hobson, J., & McMahon, S. (2019, October 9). How psychedelic substances can help treat anxiety, depression and other mental illnesses. *WBUR Here and Now*. https://www.wbur.org /hereandnow/2019/10/09/psychedelics-mental-illness-lsd-psilocybin.

CHAPTER 12

1. Song, R., Lee, E. O., Lam, P., & Bae, S. C. (2003). Effects of Tai Chi exercise on pain, balance, muscle strength, and perceived difficulties in physical functioning in older women with osteoarthritis: A randomized clinical trial. *Journal of Rheumatology, 30*(9), 2039–2044.

2. Yeh, G. Y., Wang, C., Wayne, P. M., & Phillips, R. S. (2008). The effect of Tai Chi exercise on blood pressure: A systematic review. *Preventive Cardiology, 11*(2), 82–89. https://doi.org /10.1111/j.1751-7141.2008.07565.x.

3. Lomas-Vega, R., Obrero-Gaitán, E., Molina-Ortega, F. J., & Del-Pino-Casado, R. (2017). Tai Chi for risk of falls. A meta-analysis. *Journal of the American Geriatrics Society, 65*(9), 2037–2043. https://doi.org/10.1111/jgs.15008.

4. Wang, F., Lee, E. K. O., Wu, T., Benson, H., Fricchione, G., Wang, W., & Yeung, A. S. (2014). The effects of Tai Chi on depression, anxiety, and psychological well-being: A systematic review and meta-analysis. *International Journal of Behavioral Medicine, 21*(4), 605–617. https://doi.org/10.1007/s12529-013-9351-9.

5. Park, H. S., & Cho, G. Y. (2004). Effects of foot reflexology on essential hypertension patients. *Journal of Korean Academy of Nursing, 34*(5), 739–750. https://doi.org/10.4040/jkan .2004.34.5.739.

6. Devi, S. R., & Venkatesan, B. (2018). Effectiveness of foot reflexology on diabetic peripheral neuropathic pain among patients with diabetes. *International Journal of Advances in Nursing Management, 6*(2), 91–92. https://doi.org/10.5958/2454-2652.2018.00019.7.

7. Habibzadeh, H., Wosoi Dalavan, O., Alilu, L., Wardle, J., Khalkhali, H., & Nozad, A. (2020). Effects of foot massage on severity of fatigue and quality of life in hemodialysis patients: A randomized controlled trial. *International Journal of Community Based Nursing and Midwifery, 8*(2), 92–102. https://doi.org/10.30476/IJCBNM.2020.81662.0.

8. Stephenson, N. L., Weinrich, S. P., & Tavakoli, A. S. (2000). The effects of foot reflexology on anxiety and pain in patients with breast and lung cancer. *Oncology Nursing Forum, 27*(1), 67–72.

9. Uebaba, K., Xu, F. H., Tagawa, M., Asakura, R., Itou, T., Tatsue, T., Taguchi, Y., Ogawa, H., Shimabayashi, M., & Hisajima, T. (2005). Using a healing robot for the scientific study of Shirodhara. *IEEE Engineering in Medicine and Biology Magazine, 24*(2), 69–78. https://doi .org/10.1109/memb.2005.1411351.

10. Altman, D. (2019). *Reflect: Awaken to the wisdom of the here and now.* PESI Publishing & Media.

CHAPTER 13

1. Feinstein, J. S., Khalsa, S. S., Yeh, H. W., Wohlrab, C., Simmons, W. K., Stein, M. B., & Paulus, M. P. (2018). Examining the short-term anxiolytic and antidepressant effect of Floatation-REST. *PloS One, 13*(2), e0190292. https://doi.org/10.1371/journal.pone.0190292.

2. Edge, J. (2003). A pilot study addressing the effect of aromatherapy massage on mood, anxiety and relaxation in adult mental health. *Complementary Therapies in Nursing and Midwifery, 9*(2), 90–97. https://doi.org/10.1016/s1353-6117(02)00104-x.

3. Woelk, H., & Schläfke, S. (2010). A multi-center, double-blind, randomised study of the lavender oil preparation Silexan in comparison to lorazepam for generalized anxiety disorder. *Phytomedicine, 17*(2), 94–99. https://doi.org/10.1016/j.phymed.2009.10.006.

4. Cohut, M. (2018, February 16). What are the health benefits of being creative? *Medical News Today.* https://www.medicalnewstoday.com/articles/320947.

5. Ashlock, L. E., Miller-Perrin, C., & Krumrei-Mancuso, E. (2018). The effectiveness of structured coloring activities for anxiety reduction. *Art Therapy, 35*(4), 195–201. https://doi.org/10.1080/07421656.2018.1540823; Flett, J. A. M., Lie, C., Riordan, B. C., Thompson, L. M., Conner, T. S., & Hayne, H. (2017). Sharpen your pencils: Preliminary evidence that adult coloring reduces depressive symptoms and anxiety. *Creativity Research Journal, 29*(4), 409–416. https://doi.org/10.1080/10400419.2017.1376505.

6. Carter, J. S. (2015, September 4). *The science behind adult colouring books.* ABC. http://www.abc.net.au/radionational/programs/booksandarts/why-are-australian-adults-drawn-to-colouring-in-books/6750808.

7. Van der Vennet, R., & Serice, S. (2012). Can coloring mandalas reduce anxiety? A replication study. *Art Therapy, 29*(2), 87–92. https://doi.org/10.1080/07421656.2012.680047; Mehmood Noor, S., Saleem, T., Azmat, J., & Arouj, K. (2017). Mandala-coloring as a therapeutic intervention for anxiety reduction in university students. *Pakistan Armed Forces Medical Journal, 67*(6), 904–907. https://mail.pafmj.org/index.php/PAFMJ/article/view/1040.

8. Brody, J. E. (2016, January 25). The health benefits of knitting. *New York Times.* https://well.blogs.nytimes.com/2016/01/25/the-health-benefits-of-knitting/.

9. *Journaling: Relief for anxiety and depression, with Maud Purcell.* (2019, August 14). Journaling.com. https://www.journaling.com/articles/journaling-relief-for-anxiety-and-depression-with-maud-purcell/.

10. Saarman, E. (2006, May 31). Feeling the beat: Symposium explores the therapeutic effects of rhythmic music. *Stanford News.* https://news.stanford.edu/news/2006/may31/brainwave-053106.html.

11. Jasemi, M., Aazami, S., & Zabihi, R. E. (2016). The effects of music therapy on anxiety and depression of cancer patients. *Indian Journal of Palliative Care, 22*(4), 455–458. https://doi.org/10.4103/0973-1075.191823.

12. Conner, T. S., DeYoung, C. G., & Silvia, P. J. (2018). Everyday creative activity as a path to

flourishing. *Journal of Positive Psychology, 13*(2), 181–189. https://doi.org/10.1080/17439760
.2016.1257049.

13. Kobayashi, H., Song, C., Ikei, H., Park, B. J., Kagawa, T., & Miyazaki, Y. (2019). Combined
effect of walking and forest environment on salivary cortisol concentration. *Frontiers in
Public Health, 7*, 376. https://doi.org/10.3389/fpubh.2019.00376.

14. Park, S. H., & Mattson, R. H. (2009). Ornamental indoor plants in hospital rooms en-
hanced health outcomes of patients recovering from surgery. *Journal of Alternative and
Complementary Medicine, 15*(9), 975–980. https://doi.org/10.1089/acm.2009.0075.

15. Yu, C. P., Lin, C. M., Tsai, M. J., Tsai, Y. C., & Chen, C. Y. (2017). Effects of short forest
bathing program on autonomic nervous system activity and mood states in middle-aged and
elderly individuals. *International Journal of Environmental Research and Public Health, 14*(8),
897. https://doi.org/10.3390/ijerph14080897; Ohtsuka, Y., Yabunaka, N., & Takayama, S.
(1998). Shinrin-yoku (forest-air bathing and walking) effectively decreases blood glucose
levels in diabetic patients. *International Journal of Biometeorology, 41*(3), 125–127. https://doi
.org/10.1007/s004840050064.

16. Polheber, J. P., & Matchock, R. L. (2014). The presence of a dog attenuates cortisol and
heart rate in the Trier Social Stress Test compared to human friends. *Journal of Behavioral
Medicine, 37*(5), 860–867. https://doi.org/10.1007/s10865-013-9546-1.

17. Gadomski, A. M., Scribani, M. B., Krupa, N., Jenkins, P., Nagykaldi, Z., & Olson, A. L.
(2015). Pet dogs and children's health: Opportunities for chronic disease prevention? *Preventing Chronic Disease, 12*(11). https://doi.org/10.5888/pcd12.150204.

18. Church, D., Yount, G., & Brooks, A. J. (2012). The effect of emotional freedom techniques
on stress biochemistry: A randomized controlled trial. *Journal of Nervous and Mental Disease, 200*(10), 891–896. https://doi.org/10.1097/NMD.0b013e31826b9fc1.

19. Church, D., Hawk, C., Brooks, A. J., Toukolehto, O., Wren, M., Dinter, I., & Stein, P. (2013).
Psychological trauma symptom improvement in veterans using emotional freedom techniques:
A randomized controlled trial. *Journal of Nervous and Mental Disease, 201*(2), 153–160. https://
doi.org/10.1097/NMD.0b013e31827f6351.

20. Stellar, J. E., John-Henderson, N., Anderson, C. L., Gordon, A. M., McNeil, G. D., & Kelt-
ner, D. (2015). Positive affect and markers of inflammation: Discrete positive emotions
predict lower levels of inflammatory cytokines. *Emotion, 15*(2), 129–133. https://doi.org/10
.1037/emo0000033.

CHAPTER 14

1. Holt-Lunstad, J., Smith, T. B., & Layton, J. B. (2010). Social relationships and mortality risk:
A meta-analytic review. *PLoS Medicine, 7*(7): e1000316. https://doi.org/10.1371/journal.pmed
.1000316.

2. Ozbay, F., Johnson, D. C., Dimoulas, E., Morgan, C. A. III, Charney, D., & Southwick, S. (2007). Social support and resilience to stress: From neurobiology to clinical practice. *Psychiatry (Edgmont), 4*(5), 35–40.

3. From https://www.adultdevelopmentstudy.org/grantandglueckstudy: "The Study of Adult Development is a longitudinal study that has been following two groups of men over the last 80 years to identify the psychosocial predictors of healthy aging. [There are] two groups of participants: The Grant Study that is composed of 268 Harvard graduates from the classes of 1939–1944 and the Glueck Study group that is made up of 456 men who grew up in the inner-city neighborhoods of Boston." Robert Waldinger, one of the study's principal investigators, summarized the findings of this eight-decade project by saying, "The clearest message that we get from this 75-year study is this: Good relationships keep us happier and healthier. Period."

4. Seppala, E. (2014, May 8). *Connectedness & health: The science of social connection.* Stanford Medicine. http://ccare.stanford.edu/uncategorized/connectedness-health-the-science -of-social-connection-infographic/.

5. Demarinis, S. (2020). Loneliness at epidemic levels in America. *Explore, 16*(5), 278–279. https://doi.org/10.1016/j.explore.2020.06.008.

6. Sandstrom, G. M., & Dunn, E. W. (2014). Is efficiency overrated? Minimal social interactions lead to belonging and positive affect. *Social Psychological and Personality Science, 5*(4), 437–442. https://doi.org/10.1177/1948550613502990.

7. Epley, N., & Schroeder, J. (2014). Mistakenly seeking solitude. *Journal of Experimental Psychology. General, 143*(5), 1980–1999. https://doi.org/10.1037/a0037323.

8. Boothby, E. J., Clark, M. S., & Bargh, J. A. (2014). Shared experiences are amplified. *Psychological Science, 25*(12), 2209–2216. https://doi.org/10.1177/0956797614551162.

9. Hutcherson, C. A., Seppala, E. M., & Gross, J. J. (2008). Loving-kindness meditation increases social connectedness. *Emotion, 8*(5), 720–724. https://doi.org/10.1037/a0013237.

10. Pagano, M. E., Friend, K. B., Tonigan, J. S., & Stout, R. L. (2004). Helping other alcoholics in Alcoholics Anonymous and drinking outcomes: Findings from project MATCH. *Journal of Studies on Alcohol, 65*(6), 766–773. https://doi.org/10.15288/jsa.2004.65.766.

11. Dunn, E. W., Aknin, L. B., & Norton, M. I. (2008). Spending money on others promotes happiness. *Science, 319*(5870), 1687–1688. https://doi.org/10.1126/science.1150952.

12. Harbaugh, W. T., Mayr, U., & Burghart, D. R. (2007). Neural responses to taxation and voluntary giving reveal motives for charitable donations. *Science, 316*(5831), 1622–1625. https://doi.org/10.1126/science.1140738.

13. Okun, M. A., Yeung, E. W., & Brown, S. (2013). Volunteering by older adults and risk of mortality: A meta-analysis. *Psychology and Aging, 28*(2), 564–577. https://doi.org/10.1037 /a0031519.

CHAPTER 15

1. Dittmar, H., Bond, R., Hurst, M., & Kasser, T. (2014). The relationship between materialism and personal well-being: A meta-analysis. *Journal of Personality and Social Psychology, 107*(5), 879–924. https://doi.org/10.1037/a0037409.

2. Gander, F., Proyer, R. T., Ruch, W., & Wyss, T. (2013). Strength-based positive interventions: Further evidence for their potential in enhancing well-being and alleviating depression. *Journal of Happiness Studies, 14*(4), 1241–1259. https://doi.org/10.1007/s10902-012 -9380-0.

3. Emmons, R. (2010, November 16). Why gratitude is good. *Greater Good Magazine.* https:// greatergood.berkeley.edu/article/item/why_gratitude_is_good.

4. Lathia, N., Sandstrom, G. M., Mascolo, C., & Rentfrow, P. J. (2017). Happier people live more active lives: Using smartphones to link happiness and physical activity. *PLoS One, 12*(1), e0160589. https://doi.org/10.1371/journal.pone.0160589.

5. Mayo Clinic. (2017, September 27). Depression and anxiety: Exercise eases symptoms. https://www.mayoclinic.org/diseases-conditions/depression/in-depth/depression-and -exercise/art-20046495; Guszkowska, M. (2004). Effects of exercise on anxiety, depression and mood. *Psychiatria Polska, 38*(4), 611–620.

6. Lally, P., van Jaarsveld, C. H. M., Potts, H. W., & Wardle, J. (2010). How are habits formed: Modelling habit formation in the real world. *European Journal of Social Psychology, 40*(6), 998–1009. https://doi.org/10.1002/ejsp.674.

index

about the authors

Abbe Greenberg, MCIS, and Maggie Sarachek, MSW, are trained counselors, mental health advocates, researchers, educators, writers, and longtime anxiety sufferers. In 2017, they launched their online community, which now includes more than two hundred thousand people in two-hundred-plus countries and territories. Together the Anxiety Sisters write an award-winning blog and host a monthly podcast (*The Spin Cycle*). Having learned to live happily with anxiety, they spend their time coaching anxiety sufferers and conducting workshops and retreats.

Photo credit: Bonnie Weiss